THE
ESQUILINE
TREASURE

FOR
W.J.D., M.C. AND A.P.P.

THE ESQUILINE TREASURE

KATHLEEN J. SHELTON

Published for
The Trustees of the British Museum by
British Museum Publications Limited

© 1981, The Trustees of the British Museum
ISBN 0 7141 1356 5
Published by British Museum Publications Ltd
46 Bloomsbury Street, London WC1B 3QQ

British Library Cataloguing in Publication Data
Shelton, Kathleen J.
The Esquiline Treasure.
1. Silverwork, Roman — Exhibitions
2. Rome (City) — Antiquities
I. Title   II. British Museum
739.2′3′737   NK7107.3
ISBN 0-7141-1356-5

Text set in Monotype Times and printed in Great Britain by
The Eastern Press Ltd, London and Reading
Plates printed at the University Press, Oxford, by
Eric Buckley, Printer to the University

Contents

Acknowledgments

The efforts of many people have aided my research and writing. I should like to thank Joanna Close-Brooks of the Scottish National Museum of Antiquities, Catherine Metzger of the Louvre, Max Martin of the Römermuseum, Augst, and Herbert Cahn, editor of the publication of the Kaiseraugst Treasure, for making museum collections and archives easily available. I am especially grateful to members of the British Museum staff who have been unfailingly helpful, and, in particular, I should like to thank Richard Camber and David Buckton for innumerable favours over the past several years. Virginia Brown and Erica Cruikshank Dodd have advised me on matters relating to the Esquiline silver. The preparation of the manuscript has benefited from the critical reading of Richard Brilliant, Alfred Frazer, Arnaldo Momigliano, Florentine Mütherich, Morton Smith and Neil Stratford. Each has helped me to see the material from a new perspective, although the responsibility for the finished product is mine alone. I am grateful to Diane Ignashev for patient typing, Alice Christ for careful proofreading, Jane Desforges for work on the bibliography, and Carey Miller for translating my humble, if accurate, drawings into handsome text figures. Aspects of my work have been generously supported by the American Council of Learned Societies, the British Museum, Columbia University, and the Dumbarton Oaks Center for Byzantine Studies. It is a pleasure to acknowledge these debts.

I am also grateful to the following museums and institutions for their kind permission to reproduce photographs:

British Library: figs. 2, 3, 4, 7, 10, 15, 27; Hirmer Verlag München: pl. 19 (Parabiago Patera); Musée du Petit Palais: pl. 21; Musei Vaticani, archivio fotografico: fig. 16; National Museum of Antiquities of Scotland: pls. 18, 23 (Traprain Law fluted bowl); Soprintendenza Archeologica delle Province di Napoli e Caserta: pl. 32; Victoria and Albert Museum: pl. 20.

All other photographs are reproduced by courtesy of the British Museum. The Corbridge lanx (pl. 19) is on loan to the British Museum from the Duke of Northumberland.

KATHLEEN J. SHELTON
University of Chicago
October 1979

List of Figures

List of Plates

Introduction

In 1793 workers digging a well at the foot of the Esquiline hill in Rome accidentally uncovered a large collection of silver vessels. No inventory of the find survives, and a lengthy essay on the treasure, written by Ennio Quirino Visconti within a year of the discovery, discussed in detail only those vessels thought to be of major importance.[1] The nature and quantity of the other, supposedly minor, pieces must be inferred from a few vague references in Visconti's text. This situation was not essentially altered until 1930, when the first inventory of pieces corresponding to the present definition of the Esquiline Treasure was published as a preface to an essay on the dating and ownership of the collection.[2] By this date some pieces documented in earlier accounts had been lost; the treasure had been divided among three museums in London, Naples, and Paris; and these museum holdings, in turn, represented the final destination for objects which had passed through numerous private collections during the eighteenth and nineteenth centuries. As pieces had been lost, so too the possibility exists that the original find had been augmented during its travels. The body of sixty-one objects currently identified as the Esquiline Treasure is, in fact, a modern convention.

If the present contents of the treasure are in part the result of two centuries of scholarship, the narrow fixed dates of AD 379 to 383 associated with the collection represent an eighteenth-century hypothesis which has come to be accepted as fact. A treasure is normally examined for objects of different origins and different dates, since silver heirlooms and odd pieces may be kept over generations for their personal or intrinsic value. The close dating of the large Esquiline find, however, would seem to contradict this often-demonstrated rule; it also implies a homogeneity or tight interdependence among all the objects of the treasure. In practice, the date is discussed only in reference to the most lavish pieces. Nevertheless, the implication remains, and it impedes an understanding of the different groupings of objects within the treasure based on various criteria such as technique, style, iconography, and function.

The origins of the singularly specific dates are closely tied to the focus of early investigations: the search for the owners of the treasure. Coins, so often associated with silver treasures, were apparently absent or unrecorded in the Esquiline find. Dating was therefore dependent on the reading of inscriptions and the decipherment of monograms found within the treasure which appeared to yield two names: Turcius Secundus and Proiecta Turcii, husband and wife. These names were linked to inscriptions known to late eighteenth- and early nineteenth-century antiquarians. Secundus was identified with one of several members of the *gens* Turcia prominent in Rome in the fourth and fifth centuries AD; Proiecta was matched with one Proiecta celebrated in a securely dated epitaph written by Pope Damasus (366–84). As might be anticipated, the latitude of several generations allowed by some for the identification of the husband gives the hypothesis some flexibility in any attempt to redate the treasure. But it is Proiecta who is the source of the tightly fixed dates accepted by scholars in a period lacking large numbers of art objects associated with clear dates and known patrons. Unfortunately, if the Proiecta of the treasure cannot be matched with the Proiecta of the epitaph, dating becomes an open question.

So securely have the dates AD 379 to 383 been attached to the treasure that modern scholarship would appear to have lost sight of their origin in the identification of one of the owners of the collection. The two patrons, as husband and wife, are the source of yet another 'fact' regarding the treasure: the majority of the lavish pieces are understood as bridal presents to the couple which celebrate specific scenes of the Roman marriage ritual. This hypothesis, like many others, has discouraged scholars from investigating alternative solutions suggested both by the re-examination of well-known materials and by the abundant archaeological finds in major and minor arts which occurred after the problems posed by the Esquiline pieces were regarded as successfully solved.

This situation was created in large measure by the extraordinary quality and complexity of Visconti's discussion of the treasure published in 1793. Most later scholarship on the collection reads as a less flexible exegesis of his text. Within a decade of its discovery, the Esquiline Treasure was established as the largest find of antique silver then known in the western world. It had a secure find site in the city of Rome and a firm date. The owners of the treasure were known and linked to the highest ranks of the Roman imperial bureaucracy and to the papacy of the early Christian church. The iconography and function of many pieces provided details of antique rituals of daily life—a perennial source of public and academic fascination. Added to this constellation of accepted theories was the opinion, implied by Visconti and consistently reiterated, that Proiecta and Secundus had had the good taste to imitate the art of earlier eras. From the first years of its evaluation, the Esquiline Treasure was implicitly understood as demonstrating a revival of earlier, more classical forms.

The concept of a renaissance movement in both East and West dating to the second half of the fourth century and originating, in the West, in the senatorial aristocracy found an exemplar in the Esquiline Treasure. Linked to such objects as the sarcophagus of Junius Bassus and the ivories of the Nicomachi and Symmachi, the Esquiline Treasure became firmly established not only as a thoroughly documented find in its own right but also as part of a larger artistic movement with rich parallels in the political and literary events of fourth-century Rome.

The theory of a fourth-century renaissance movement does not depend solely on evidence furnished by the Esquiline Treasure, but the general acceptance of the revival theory has served in part to remove the treasure from the realm of scholarly debate. To question the basic assumptions held regarding the Esquiline Treasure may imply a questioning of the larger context in which the treasure is most commonly understood in modern scholarship. The theory of the fourth-century revival, however, is far more broadly based, and the aims of the present investigation more narrowly defined.

Many, if not all, of the assumptions of the early researchers do not bear close scrutiny. A reading of the available literature immediately reveals considerable confusion regarding the simple contents of the treasure: the objects, whether extant, lost, or spurious, have never been catalogued as a whole with serious discussions of the individual pieces. In addition to giving an accurate count and a complete catalogue, it is now possible to offer new answers to old questions, to derive a more flexible date, to discuss matters of iconography more broadly, and to suggest new identities for the owners of the treasure. It also seems appropriate and necessary to ask new questions and to suggest answers to them, to establish the find site and possible archaeological contexts of the treasure, to trace the modern history of the collection, to analyse the component parts or groups within the treasure, and to discuss the relations of the treasure to other numerous, contemporary silver finds of relatively recent discovery. It is, perhaps, a revisionist effort. The study of the Esquiline Treasure reveals the slow but apparently inexorable process whereby one scholar's hypothesis becomes the established fact of the second and the basis for new research on the part of the third. What follows is an attempt to present what can be known and what might be hypothesised concerning the Esquiline Treasure.

NOTES

1. Visconti's essay was addressed as a letter to Monsignore Giulio Maria della Somaglia and dated 7 August 1793. The essay was published as a small pamphlet of twenty-two pages in Rome in the same year and was reviewed by G. F. Galeani Napione in the December issue of the Turinese journal *Biblioteca dell'anno M.DCC.XC.III.* (255–71). It was somewhat awkwardly divided into three sections plus its original postscript and reprinted in four consecutive issues of the Roman journal *Antologia romana*, XX (1794) (no. 37, 289–93; no. 38, 297–302; no. 39, 305–9; no. 40, 313–15). In 1827 two separate editions of the essay were printed. The more lavish was published as a single volume in Rome by P. P. Montagnani-Mirabili (*Lettera di Ennio Quirino Visconti intorno ad una antica supelletile d'argento scoperta in Roma nell'anno 1793*). This edition contained twenty-five plates engraved specially for the publication, Montagnani-Mirabili's dedication of the volume to the Duc de Blacas, his preface and his notes, in addition to Visconti's original 1793 text. Appended were extracts of Seroux d'Agincourt's *L'Histoire de l'art par les monuments depuis sa décadence au IVᵉ siècle jusqu'à son renouvellement au XVIᵉ* (6 vols., Paris, 1810–23, III, 8ff) and an essay, again in letter form, from Galeani Napione to Visconti, dated 20 October 1794, in which Galeani Napione expanded on themes mentioned in his earlier review and considered new materials discovered between December 1793 and October 1794 ('*Lettera con alcune congetture intorno all'Asterio, possessore della suppellettile d'argento trovata in Roma*'). Montagnani-Mirabili states in his preface that by 1827 the Visconti essay had become very difficult to obtain, hence his publishing effort ('*Prefazioni ai lettori*', vi).

The other edition of 1827 was published in Milan in a collection of Visconti's shorter essays edited by G. Labus (E. Q. Visconti, '*Lettera su di una antica argenteria nuovamente scoperta in Roma*', *Opere varie italiane e francesi*, 4 vols., Milan, 1827–31, I, 210–35). Two plates were engraved for this edition by one M. Palagi (D. Raoul-Rochette, '*Oeuvres diverses italiennes et françaises d'Ennius Quirinus Visconti, recueillies et publiées par le docteur J. Labus*', *Journal des savants*, 1830, 614), but the engravings are clearly copied from Seroux d'Agincourt (*L'Histoire*, IV, pl. IX). Labus, like Montagnani-Mirabili, added editorial notes; far more importantly, the text of the essay published by Labus had been annotated after 1793 by Visconti himself. In the preface to the collection, Labus states that he received a hand-corrected copy of the manuscript from Visconti's brother, Fillipo Aurelio, for the publication ('*Prefazione*', *Opere varie*, I, x–xi).

The essay in the Labus collection is slightly condensed. Because the Montagnani-Mirabili publication is the more complete, most references will be made to that edition. Significant differences between the two texts resulting from Visconti's corrections will be noted. For convenience, the editions will be cited as Visconti:M-M and Visconti:L.

2. S. Poglayen-Neuwall, '*Uber die ursprünglichen Besitzer des spätantiken Silberfundes vom Esquilin und seine Datierung*', *Mitteilungen des Deutschen Archäologischen Instituts, Römische Abteilung*, XLV (1930), 125f.

The Find Site

The Esquiline Treasure was discovered in the summer of 1793. Despite the statement of Seroux d'Agincourt that '*les diverses parties en furent trouvées presque toutes en ma présence*',[1] it would appear that the accidental find occurred without scholarly witness. Seroux d'Agincourt's comments on the treasure contain concrete details not found in other authors, his accompanying engravings represent aspects of individual objects verified by observation yet omitted in most representations of the treasure, but his text betrays a dependence on Visconti and an ignorance of the chronology of the separate finds that came to be known as a single treasure.[2] Visconti himself admitted that some time had passed between the discovery, his first observation of the pieces, and his descriptive essay.[3] No other authors claim or appear to have early, first-hand knowledge of the find, and, therefore, the limited testimony of Seroux d'Agincourt and Visconti forms the basis for our knowledge of the nature and location of the discovery.

Visconti stated that the treasure was found at the base of the Esquiline hill, just beyond the Subura, near the convent of the Minims: '*presso il monistero delle religiose Minime sull'Esquilino . . . presso le radici del colle poco oltre la Suburra*'. To locate the site more precisely, Visconti added that the objects were found in '*un avanzo di camere antiche di buona fabrica, murate, ed ingombre dalla ruina de' superiori edifizj*'.[4] No streets are named. The convent is identified only by the religious order of its nuns. No other information is given which would locate the site in relation to standing structures, and no further indication is forthcoming regarding the ancient rooms or the later buildings, now collapsed, which once rose above them. In an antiquarian essay on Roman women published in 1803, Karl August Böttiger referred to objects from the treasure and claimed that the silver had been found fifteen feet below ground in a vaulted room. The source of Böttiger's information remains unknown. None of the details can be verified, but the idea that the treasure had been found in a vault or vaulted chamber enjoyed some currency.[5]

Both the depth of the find and the nature of the site as described by Böttiger seem possible, but his text carried the far more elementary assumptions that there had been but one discovery and that it had occurred in a single room. Visconti had stated that the site was a ruin of ancient rooms, '*camere antiche*'. The number was unspecified but definitely plural. It seems a small discrepancy, but, in fact, the number of rooms involved in the discoveries of 1793 might indicate something of the nature or cause of the original burial. Although Visconti is silent where Böttiger is detailed, he does refer to pieces of the treasure as '*adunati insieme*' and '*conservati insieme*', possibly indicating an indirect knowledge of the nature of the find.[6] Visconti's essay, however, was completed after the largest, but only the first, of two finds had been made at the site: his discussion accounts for the majority but not the whole of the treasure. It is clear that Visconti saw many pieces assembled as a group a short time after they had been recovered, and it is possible that this grouping presented to Visconti accurately reflected the first discovery of 1793.

Visconti's brief comments can therefore be taken to indicate that most of the silver was found preserved in a single room of the ruin. While the nature of the burial is therefore somewhat clarified, its cause remains open to debate. Visconti understood the alternatives: the silver vessels could have been purposely collected and buried together as a hoard, or they might have been accidentally buried as the result of a natural disaster. Visconti preferred the first suggestion but admitted the possibility of the second. The concept of the purposeful burial, however, carried with it overtones of human drama which proved to be far more attractive. Visconti, who commonly referred to the find as a silver service, called it a '*tesoro*' when discussing the burial. He hypothesised an owner assembling his silver in haste, burying the collection, and being prevented from recovering his possessions. The scene had a definite location and time: it was the Rome of the fifth-century barbarian invasions.[7] So persuasive was the description that the question of an accidental burial was never raised again. The silver became a hoard, and the fact was duly reflected in its conventional name, the Esquiline Treasure.

Soon the treasure was described as being found in a vault, and its burial became quite methodical. According to Böttiger, nearly all the pieces of the treasure had been packed inside one of its large caskets, a feat which is physically impossible.[8] The uniformity and ease with which later scholars adopted Visconti's hypothetical scene not only denied the alternative posed by Visconti himself but also ignored the emendations made by the author to the original essay. In a postscript to his essay published in 1793, Visconti noted that continuing work at the site had uncovered several important pieces to be added to the group discussed in the body of the text. These new finds were made near the site of the first discovery, but Visconti thought it quite possible that they represented a separate burial.[9] He added in a hand-corrected copy of the manuscript that additional fragments had been found after the publication of his essay with its postscript.[10] Seroux d'Agincourt, who did not discriminate between the two large finds, knew of the fragments and the date of their discovery relative to the publication of Visconti's description. In an effort to account for all pieces of the original burial, Seroux d'Agincourt published an engraving of an open-work bowl found near the site in 1632 (see fig. 15).[11] This last was ignored in later literature, but also ignored were the sequence of the discoveries, their separate find sites, and the possible deduction that the finds might have resulted either from a single collection of silver found at different points within the '*avanzo di camere*

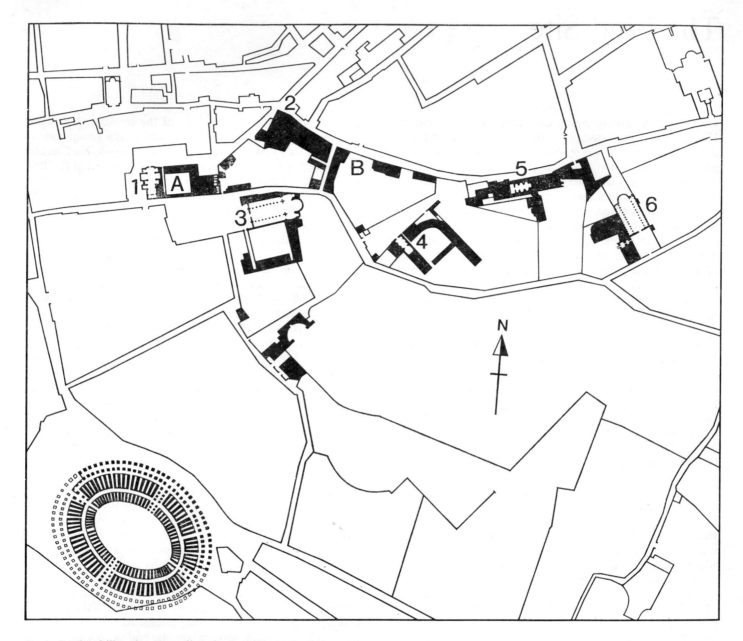

fig. 1 Oppian hill and surroundings in the eighteenth century:

1. S. Francesco di Paolo:
   A. church and monastery, B. convent.
2. Piazza della Subura.
3. S. Pietro in Vincoli.
4. Sta Maria della Purificazione.
5. Sta Lucia in Selcis.
6. S. Martino ai Monti.

The Strada della Subura ran approximately from the Piazza (no. 2) to S. Martino (no. 6).

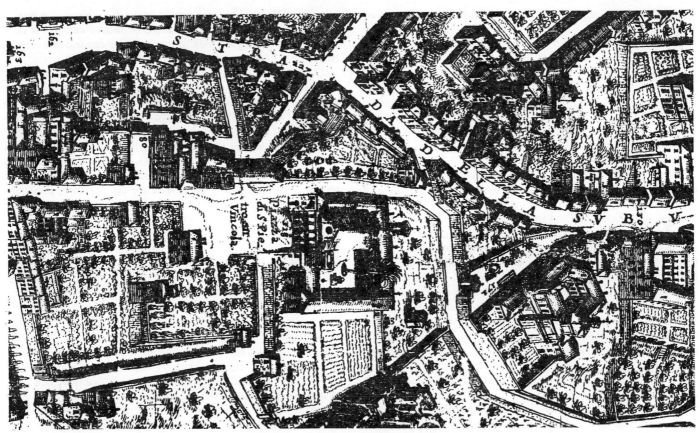

fig. 2 Oppian hill, detail from the Falda map of Rome, 1676. S. Francesco di Paolo is no. 80.

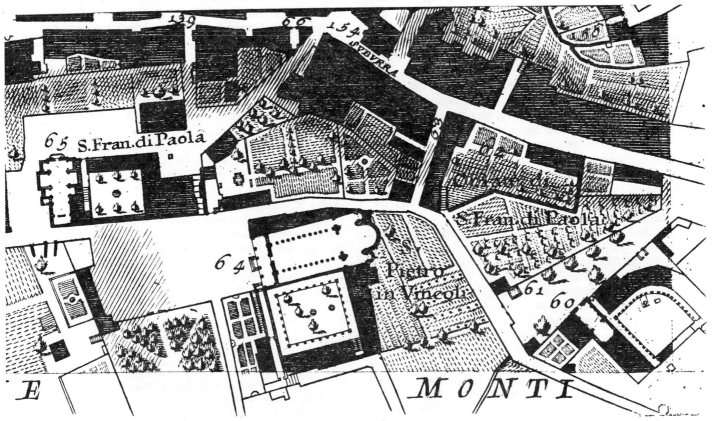

fig. 3 Oppian hill, detail from the Nolli map of Rome, 1748. The church of S. Francesco di Paolo is no. 65; the convent is no. 62.

antiche' or from separate collections buried in close proximity.

It remains to locate the ruin more precisely (see fig. 1). As mentioned, the early authors specified a site at the foot of the Esquiline hill, just beyond the Subura, near a convent of Minims. Apparently the silver was found on ground owned by the nuns, for the objects were declared the property of the convent after the discovery had been properly reported to the government.[12] After repeating the location as given by Visconti, Seroux d'Agincourt added that the treasure had been found *'dans l'enceinte du monastère des Sts. Silvestre et Martin'*.[13] This statement unfortunately seems both to answer and to raise questions. The church of SS. Silvestro e Martino (more commonly known as S. Martino ai Monti) is located on a slope of the Oppian spur of the Esquiline hill, raised on an artificial platform (fig. 1,6). Ten metres below the floor of the present church and to the west is an early third-century Roman building, with neighbouring structures dating to the late third and early fourth centuries. The original Roman structure was a six-bay hall with an annexe, an enclosed courtyard, a vaulted cellar, and an upper storey. It may have served as the substructure for a Carolingian convent; it definitely served that function for a thirteenth-century monastery which rose over the Roman buildings and extended to the south. Parts of the thirteenth-century structure, apparently in dangerous disrepair, were torn down in 1870.[14] It seems possible to locate Visconti's *'ruina de' superiori edifizj'* in the crumbling thirteenth-century monastery below which lay extensive and well-preserved Roman buildings.

Two facts argue against this solution. The Roman structure was actively used through the ninth century and may have been used even after its inclusion in a monastic complex. In addition, by the mid-seventeenth century the Roman structure had been recovered, thoroughly excavated, studied, and published under the direction of the Prior Giovanni Antonio Filippini.[15] The likelihood is small that a collection of silver of fourth-century manufacture, evidently buried in the fourth or fifth century, was buried or lost in a building in active use. The late eighteenth-century date of the discovery of the treasure also rules out a find site in a building excavated a century and a half earlier. Ironically, Seroux d'Agincourt was attracted to the site in part by the 1632 find of the silver open-work bowl, a find which was part of the very excavations which argue against S. Martino ai Monti as the place of the later discoveries.

If the thirteenth-century monastery of S. Martino cannot be matched with Visconti's ruin, the church grounds leave ample room for exploration. Every author after Seroux d'Agincourt agreed and repeated his location, although many softened his statement, placing the site simply 'near' S. Martino.[16] But there are no nuns of the order of Minims to be found on the premises; S. Martino has been served by Carmelite friars since the fourteenth century.[17] Adjoining the property of S. Martino to the north and west, further down the Oppian slope, is Sta Lucia in Selcis with its lands and two associated convents (fig. 1,5). The proximity of Sta Lucia to S. Martino and the presence of nuns instead of friars appear to have led one scholar to choose Sta Lucia as the find site.[18] Like S. Martino, Sta Lucia has a well-preserved Roman building in its grounds; what was a public or semi-public basilica of the third or fourth century is now a convent housing Benedictine nuns. The second convent of Sta Lucia, however, is run by the Augustinian order.[19]

Despite Visconti's clear statement that the silver was found near a convent of Minims and despite the relative proximity of such a convent, scholars continued to follow Seroux d'Agincourt. Knowledge of the history of the religious order, however, allows an identification of the find site. Further to the west of S. Martino, beyond the lands of Sta Maria della Purificazione (fig. 1,4), on the steep northern slope of the Oppian spur, is a constellation of buildings and thoroughfares named after S. Francesco di Paolo, the founder of the mendicant order of Minims (fig. 1,1). Up the stairs of the Via S. Francesco di Paolo from the Strada Leonina is the Piazza S. Francesco di Paolo. The church of S. Francesco and its adjoining monastery form the southern façade of the piazza (fig. 1,1A); a convent of cloistered nuns lies to the east (fig. 1,1B). The complex was built in the course of the seventeenth century and appears, clearly labelled, in the 1676 Falda map of Rome (fig. 2).[20] The buildings and grounds meet the requirements of Visconti's site: they lie at the foot of the Esquiline hill, just beyond the Subura (fig. 1,2), and, unlike the other religious foundations in the area of the Esquiline, they are run by the order of Minims.

While the grounds of S. Francesco di Paolo have not been systematically excavated, Visconti's ruin scarcely poses a problem in the city of Rome. The Roman structures of Sta Lucia and S. Martino and those associated with the early basilicas of the Esquiline plateau give an indication of the wealth of Roman streets and structures in the immediate area. Directly south of S. Francesco di Paolo, further up the Oppian slope, the church of S. Pietro in Vincoli has been excavated (fig. 1,3): beneath the early Christian basilica lie multiple Roman buildings ranging in date from the first to the fourth century.[21] Equivalent structures can be assumed to lie beneath the seventeenth-century complex of S. Francesco. It seems probable that the eighteenth-century labourers whose job it was to dig a well for the convent worked in unmarked, open ground. Their efforts penetrated two superimposed levels of occupation and disclosed a collection of silver objects in the lower level, which was well preserved although filled with debris. The 1748 Nolli map of Rome depicts and labels the convent of S. Francesco di Paolo and shows it situated on the edge of an open field or garden (fig. 3).[22] Only forty-five years separate the Nolli plan and the discovery of the silver; what was open land in 1748 was possibly little altered by 1793. The well, and therefore the find site of the Esquiline Treasure, must, then, be located in the grounds of the convent of S. Francesco di Paolo on the slope of the Esquiline hill.

NOTES

1. Seroux d'Agincourt, *L'Histoire*, II, 37.
2. The exact dates of Seroux d'Agincourt's *L'Histoire* are subject to debate. The title pages of all six volumes carry the date 1823, and the work is frequently cited as being published in ten fascicles from 1810 to 1823. There are many indications, however, that the text and plates were available long before those dates. The authors of the *Corpus Basilicarum Christianarum*

Romae, citing Seroux d'Agincourt's preface and unpublished manuscripts, date the work 'prior to 1789' (R. Krautheimer *et al.*, *Corpus Basilicarum*, 5 vols., Vatican City, 1937–, II, 5; III, 89, n.1).

Seroux d'Agincourt's comments on and engravings of the Esquiline Treasure, which were published in volumes II, III and IV of *L'Histoire*, cannot predate 1793. Seroux d'Agincourt referred to Monsignore della Somaglia, to whom Visconti addressed his essay, as cardinal and papal vicar. Della Somaglia was named both cardinal and papal vicar in 1795; he was named papal legate in 1800 (G. Moroni, '*Somaglia*', *Dizionario di erudizione storico-ecclesiastica di S. Pietro sino ai nostri giorni*, 103 vols., Venice, 1840–61, LXVII, 175ff). Seroux d'Agincourt's reference, and with it his text, can therefore be dated after 1795 but before 1800, by which date della Somaglia had become cardinal and legate and would have been so addressed.

3. Visconti: M–M, 1.
4. Ibid., 1, n.a.
5. K. A. Böttiger, *Sabina oder Morgenscenen im Putzzimmer einer reichen Römerin*, Leipzig (1803), 59. An example of Böttiger's influence can be found in a discussion of the treasure published by the British Museum: C. T. Newton, *Guide to the Blacas Collection of Antiquities, British Museum*, London (1867), 24, 27.
6. Visconti: M–M, 17f, n.a.
7. Ibid., 13, 17f.
8. Böttiger, *Sabina*, 59, 78f.
9. Visconti: M–M, 20ff. Note his statement: '*Queste ricche antichità non dovrebbono scompagnarsi dalle già descritto alle quali e gli usi dell'antico signore, e il nascondiglio di tanti secoli le avean congiunte*' (22). The contents of the first find included Cat. nos. 1–2, 4–12, 16–17, 30–41, and a small lamp now missing. The second find consisted of nos. 3, 18, and a dish and candelabrum now missing. The pieces which can be securely identified with the two discoveries of 1793 will be designated throughout the text with an asterisk (e.g. *no. 10).
10. Labus, '*Prefazione*', x–xi; Visconti: L, 215, n.1.
11. Seroux d'Agincourt, *L'Histoire*, II, 37f, n.b.; III, 10.
12. Böttiger, *Sabina*, 59.
13. Seroux d'Agincourt, *L'Histoire*, II, 37f, n.b.
14. Krautheimer *et al.*, 'S. Martino ai Monti', *Corpus Basilicarum*, III, 97ff.
15. Ibid., 91, 123f. G. A. Filippini, *Ristretto di tutto quello che appartiene all'antichità e veneratione della chiesa de'SS. Silvestro e Martino de'Monti*, Rome (1639).
16. O. M. Dalton, *Catalogue of Early Christian Antiquities and Objects from the Christian East, British Museum*, London (1901), 61; Poglayen-Neuwall, '*Besitzer*', 124; M. T. Tozzi, '*Il tesoro di Projecta*', *Rivista di archeologia cristiana*, IX (1932), 286; H. Buschhausen, *Die spätrömischen Metallscrinia und frühchristlichen Reliquiare*, Katalog, Wiener Byzantinistische Studien, IX, Vienna (1971), 210.
17. Krautheimer *et al.*, 'S. Martino ai Monti', 91.
18. Poglayen-Neuwall, '*Besitzer*', 126.
19. For the architectural history of the church and its convents, see Krautheimer *et al.*, '*Sta. Lucia in Selcis*', *Corpus Basilicarum*, II, 186ff.
20. The church of S. Francesco di Paolo was built in the mid-seventeenth century by the architect Giovanni Pietro Morandi; a later façade dates to the eighteenth century. The monastery, the present Istituto Centrale del Restauro, is a seventeenth-century building considered contemporary with the Morandi church. I thank Joseph Connors for his help in these matters. The church is numbered 80 on the 1676 Falda plan (fig. 2); the monastery, convent and grounds are also represented but not numbered. G. B. Falda, *Nuova pianta et alzata della città di Roma*, Rome (1676).
21. Krautheimer *et al.*, '*S. Pietro in Vincoli*', *Corpus Basilicarum*, III, 189ff.
22. On the large Nolli map, the church of S. Francesco di Paolo is numbered 65; the convent, 62 (fig. 3). G. B. Nolli, *La nuova topografia di Roma*, Rome (1748). A commentary on the map is found in *Roma: Il tempo di Benedetto XIV, la pianta di Giambattista Nolli del 1748*, Vatican City (1932). On the smaller Nolli map of the same date, only the church is numbered, 116; the other buildings and grounds are located, unnumbered, to the east of the church. G. B. Nolli, *La topografia di Roma . . . d'alla maggiore in questa minor tavola*, Rome (1748).

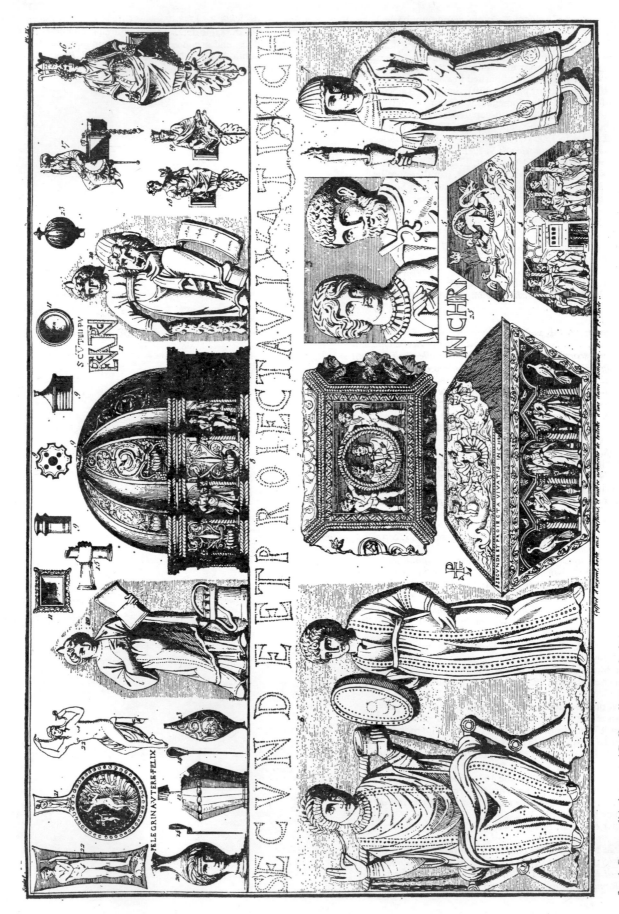

fig. 4 Seroux d'Agincourt, 'Coffret d'argent, boête aux parfums, et autres ustenciles de toilette d'une dame Romaine'. *L'Histoire*, IV, pl. IX.

The State and Contents of the Treasure

Immediately after its discovery, the treasure attracted little notice. In his essay, Visconti commented that the size of the collection and the amount of silver involved were its chief attractions: the intrinsic value of the silver was great, and finds of such size were extremely rare. Such remained the conception of the treasure into the first decade of the nineteenth century.[1] It was Visconti's essay that began to focus attention on aspects of aesthetic and historical interest relating to the individual pieces. But the essay was not without its critics. As with most antique silver, the authenticity of the collection was challenged. The charges were answered, and the questions of modern manufacture were silenced, but the critics had another complaint: Visconti was charged with profiteering, with aiding the owners of the treasure by writing the essay, attracting interest to the pieces, and thus driving up the price. The target of these accusations was Visconti, not the treasure, and the authors were chauvinistic antiquarians from 'la patrie de Winckelmann'.[2]

While the motivation of these critics may seem petty, their suspicions were not without cause. With the exception of one piece, Visconti discussed the objects in the treasure as if there were no evidence of breakage or corrosion. Analysis of the pieces, however, reveals that almost all show the effects of their centuries of burial. Of those discussed by Visconti, one-fifth were very badly damaged; one-third were damaged and subsequently restored. Since Visconti admitted he had been called in to examine the pieces some time after they had been found, restorations to the recovered items might account for his failure to discuss damaged states. There is, however, a second, nearly contemporary witness to the contrary.

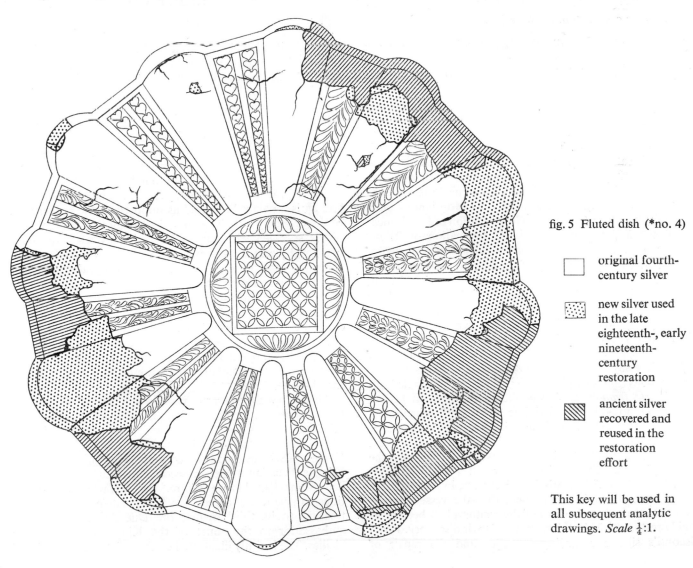

fig. 5 Fluted dish (*no. 4)

☐ original fourth-century silver

▨ new silver used in the late eighteenth-, early nineteenth-century restoration

▧ ancient silver recovered and reused in the restoration effort

This key will be used in all subsequent analytic drawings. *Scale* $\frac{1}{4}$:1.

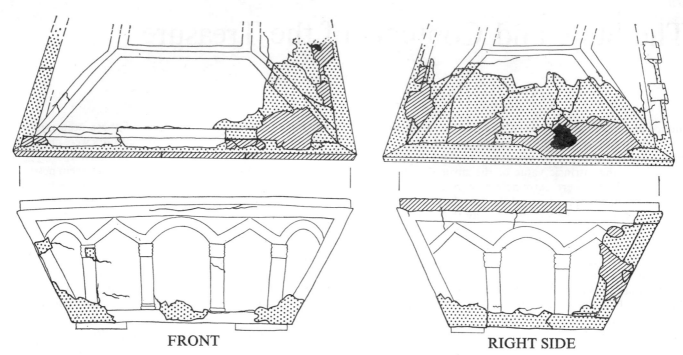

FRONT   RIGHT SIDE

fig. 6 Proiecta casket (*no. 1). *Scale* $\frac{1}{6}$:1.

Visconti and Seroux d'Agincourt examined the treasure within seven years of one another, and, of the two, Seroux d'Agincourt was definitely the second to view and discuss the pieces. Where Visconti is silent on the subject of damages, Seroux d'Agincourt discusses them and illustrates the relevant objects in fragmentary condition (fig. 4). Thus hypothetical restorations made immediately after the find cannot account for Visconti's silence. The discrepancy between the two accounts is satisfactorily explained only by the larger context of Visconti's essay. Visconti, son of an illustrious anti-quarian and himself head of the Capitoline Museum, was asked to discuss the treasure by one Monsignore della Somaglia, then Secretary of the Congregation of Indulgences and Relics and Secretary of the Congregation of Rites.[3] Della Somaglia made the request as the *de facto* trustee of the treasure, for the convent of the Minims was one of his charges.[4] Visconti responded with an essay in which all damage and potential restorations were ignored. By 1800 at the latest, della Somaglia had sold the treasure.[5]

Whether or not the objects had been restored at the time of the first sale cannot be determined. The treasure had definitely been restored by 1827, when a second edition of Visconti's essay carried engravings of the objects as they appear today; the one piece which Visconti had singled out as '*in parte frammentata*' was shown restored, in perfect condition (*no. 4, see fig. 5).[6] One of Visconti's nineteenth-century editors even took issue with Seroux d'Agincourt's description of a panel of the Proiecta casket as broken, saying that Seroux d'Agincourt must not have seen the missing pieces which were found later and carefully replaced (*no. 1, see fig. 6).[7] The missing pieces are, in fact, modern restorations. It would seem, then, that the vessels, which were not repaired at the turn of the century, had been thoroughly restored within thirty years of their discovery. From Visconti's silence regarding damages and the repair of

damages, it might be inferred that restorations were being planned by the parties who held the treasure and who had commissioned Visconti's essay.

It is quite feasible to discuss the restorations as a single effort within a limited time. All restorations did take place within a thirty-year period, but, more important, all restorations share a common vocabulary of techniques, materials, and styles. Although old fragments were occasionally incorporated in repairs, the restorations are characterised by a pale, white silver which seldom matches the darker antique silver of the individual objects. The nineteenth-century gilding is a pale yellow gold as opposed to the redder tone of the original work. The new silver is spotless, whereas the old is speckled with surface corrosion even on the best-preserved pieces. Where expanses of new silver were used in a repair, 'antiquing' was attempted with rather obvious false cracks and random patches of solder on the surfaces. The false cracks are superficial, while the joins between old and new silver are reinforced with silver strips soldered to the under-surfaces of objects. There are misunderstandings of motifs and figures specific to single works, but the restorations of decorative details can be generally characterised as sharper and more angular than the antique motifs which they imitate.

Although a single hand or workshop can be detected for the restorations, the date, location, and identity of the commissioning agent remain unknown. It is a choice between Monsignore della Somaglia, working on behalf of the Minims of S. Francesco di Paolo, and the Baron von Schellers-heim, a Prussian amateur residing in Florence, to whom della Somaglia sold the treasure.[8] By 1827, when the restorations can be documented, von Schellersheim had sold the treasure to its third owner, the Duc de Blacas, French ambassador to the court of the Kingdom of the Two Sicilies. The lavishly illustrated edition of Visconti published

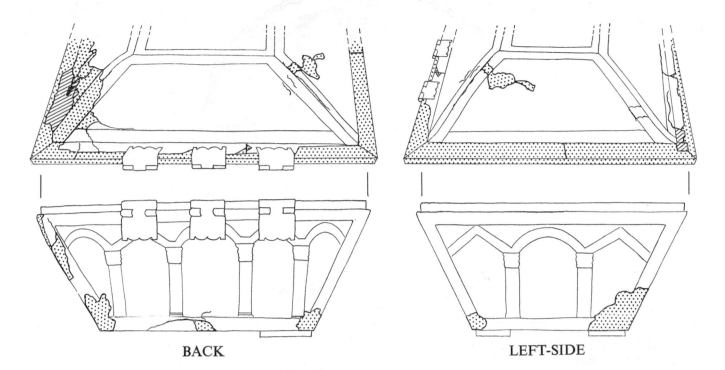

BACK   LEFT-SIDE

in 1827 was dedicated to the Duke and, in a sense, to his recent purchase.[9] In 1830, with the fall of the government of Charles X, the Duke left Naples and followed the French monarch into exile. In 1844, five years after the death of the Duke, his heir, and presumably his collection, took up residence in Paris.[10] The restored pieces, along with hundreds of other objects from the Blacas collection, were sold to the British Museum in November 1866 by the Duke's son.[11] It is in the acquisitions register for 29 December 1866 that the first clear statements regarding breakage and restoration of individual pieces are found. An unnamed clerk reported an object 'much broken and mended' with 'considerable injury on right hand side' (*no. 1, fig. 6, pl. 5); another with 'portions of side wanting and repaired' (no. 13, pl. 25); and another with 'hole in side' (no. 14, pl. 28). Some of this spirit was reflected in O. M. Dalton's brief discussions of the pieces in a 1901 catalogue of the early Christian material in the British Museum. Dalton, however, was less critical in his comments on the major pieces of the treasure, and, while he discussed breakage, he did not discuss repair.[12]

If the restorations have received scant attention, the contents of the treasure have been assumed rather than discussed. Visconti named and described only twenty-five objects; Seroux d'Agincourt discussed twenty-one of those mentioned by Visconti. One of the four pieces omitted by Seroux d'Agincourt was the dish which Visconti had described as broken (*no. 4, fig. 5). It was, in fact, the most extensively damaged object from the treasure, and its poor state may have been the reason for its omission from Seroux d'Agincourt's commentary and illustrations. The others—a plate, a candelabrum, and a small lamp—appear to have been lost or sold in the interval between the two publications.

Visconti alluded to additional objects from the find with such phrases as 'cinque vasi di bella forma', 'diversi cucchiari', 'le anse', and 'falere equestri'. With the engravings for the Montagnani-Mirabili edition of 1827, the 'cinque vasi' were matched with five distinct vessels (nos. 15, 19, 20 and *nos. 16, 17); the 'diversi cucchiari' numbered eight individually rendered spoons (nos. 21–3, 25–9); and the 'falere equestri' were illustrated by one example, their number unspecified. At some time before this publication, a silver dish from the treasure of Mâcon had been added to the Esquiline material, and Montagnani-Mirabili matched an engraving of the Mâcon dish with Visconti's description of an Esquiline plate which had been missing since the turn of the century (no. 13; fig. 7, pl. 25).[13] The handles mentioned in Visconti's text went without illustration or further comment, but the editor noted that an additional engraving reproduced 'una scodella di buona forma sfuggita alle ricerche del Autore' (no. 14). Also illustrated were eleven pieces of jewellery and random charms (nos. 42–9, 51, 54, 60), numbered as part of the treasure although not mentioned by Visconti.[14]

Visconti had wanted his text to be accompanied by illustrations.[15] The Montagnani-Mirabili edition, published nine years after his death, contained twenty-five plates with a total of forty-seven illustrated objects. The reprinted Visconti text was not altered; it still specified only twenty-five. Three objects had been lost since 1793; a dish from another treasure had been substituted for one of the missing pieces; several of Visconti's vague references, such as 'vasi' and 'cucchiari', had been translated into specific objects; other categories such as 'falere' and 'anse' still went unnumbered; and whole new categories such as jewellery had been added. It would appear that in 1827 the Duc de Blacas purchased a treasure substantially larger than that which had been found in 1793.

Some of the additions were probably quite correct. Visconti had, for example, discussed elaborate horse trappings, and the Duke purchased and later sold six almost identical pieces in various states of repair (*nos. 36–41).

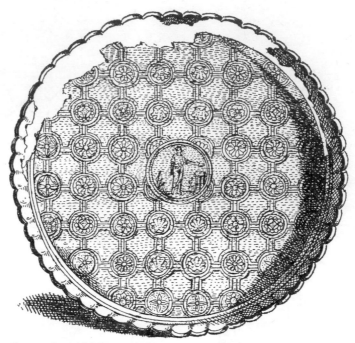

fig. 7 Comte de Caylus, dish from the treasure of Mâcon. (Like all Caylus engravings, the image is reversed.) *Recueil*, VII, pl. LXVIII, 1.

More troublesome is the identification of a dish and bowl (nos. 14, 15), two amphorae (nos, 19, 20), the spoons (nos. 21–3, 25–9), and the jewellery (nos. 42–9, 51, 54, 60) which Montagnani-Mirabili illustrates but for which the Visconti text supplies no detail and, in some cases, no evidence. Continuing the tradition, the Duke's heir sold to the British Museum a treasure of fifty-nine pieces which had entered the Blacas collection numbering fifty. The total gain was actually ten, as the Blacas family had lost one piece in the intervening years.[16] By 1866, the date of the sale to the British Museum, the treasure was actually understood to contain sixty-one pieces, for two of Visconti's original twenty-five had been sold either by della Somaglia or by von Schellersheim to two other private collectors. A silver patera (*no. 3) was in the Dutuit collection in Paris, having passed through the collection of the Gossellin family, and a bronze ewer (*no. 18), which had been in the collection of Cardinal Stefano Borgia in Velletri, was in the Museo Bourbonico (Museo Nazionale) in Naples.[17]

Since 1866, only two scholars have worked with an accurate count of the treasure. None has discriminated between the silver of the original find and that of the later, nineteenth-century additions, but there have been disagreements even as to the contents of the conventional grouping. Dalton, while omitting any reference to objects lost or held outside the British Museum, discussed the fifty-nine objects entered in the accessions register. Poglayen-Neuwall counted the sixty-one pieces held by various museums and made note of the objects no longer extant. Others, however, were less thorough. Newton, writing a British Museum guide in 1867, omitted fourteen pieces acquired in the previous year and added nine from the museum's permanent collections. In a publication of 1971, Buschhausen listed a total of fifty-one objects, overlooking many but including the three lost before 1800.[18] Other authors misread guides to the Dutuit collection and added three bronze plaques to the treasure. The plaques had simply been recorded as having been found together during an excavation on the Esquiline. As though

there had been but one excavation ever undertaken on the Esquiline hill, some scholars associated the plaques with the silver patera held by the brothers Dutuit.[19]

The misunderstanding which led to the addition of the plaques to the treasure is easily undone, for the plaques are relatively recent additions with little literature attached. It is far more difficult to date and trace the nineteenth-century accretions, although it is equally necessary to identify and disregard them in an effort to define the original contents of the treasure. The research outlined above would indicate that two of the dishes (nos. 13, 14), one bowl (no. 15), two of the vessels (nos. 19, 20), all of the spoons (nos. 21–9), and all of the jewellery, charms, and assorted fragments (nos. 42–61) are best understood as additions to the find. There is no verbal or visual record for ten of these pieces before the British Museum purchase of 1866 and the Dalton catalogue of 1901. Twenty-four have been understood as part of the treasure only since the 1827 publication of the Montagnani-Mirabili edition of Visconti with its many engravings; these additions were probably pieces from the collection of the Baron von Schellersheim passed on to the Duc de Blacas.

There is little doubt that most of these objects are ancient. The spoons conform to late antique types; the fibulae might be seen to vary in age, but none is later than the fourth century AD; and the rest of the pieces can be comfortably matched with various Roman finds.[20] It is also possible that some of these pieces were found with the treasure in 1793. Visconti did, after all, refer to the presence of spoons and handles, but the categories are broad and the objects extremely common. Unlike the matched sets of horse trappings, which are very elaborate and rarely found, the spoons and handles do not constitute unique, easily identifiable collections. As for the rest of the pieces, there is no compelling reason to associate them with the find; existing evidence does not allow them to be identified as part of the original treasure.

Twenty-seven pieces remain. They are Visconti's twenty-five minus the lamp, the candelabrum, and the two plates lost between 1793 and 1866, plus the six horse trappings most probably indicated by Visconti's reference to '*falere equestri*'. The collection is still a rich one, for the thirty-four objects added to the treasure over the years were small, largely undecorated objects and fragments. The treasure of twenty-seven pieces contains two ornate caskets (*nos. 1, 2), an elaborate patera (*no. 3), tableware with both repoussé and engraved decoration (*nos. 4–12, 16–18), three sets of paired horse trappings (*nos. 36–41), and six furniture ornaments (*nos. 30–5), four of which take the form of silver statuettes. Even within the group of sixty-one objects, it is these pieces which have always attracted the most attention because of their lavish decoration, their iconography, and their inscriptions. These twenty-seven objects can be securely identified with the find of 1793, and they therefore form the basis of any investigation of style, date, and ownership. For the purposes of accurate research, they are the Esquiline Treasure.

NOTES

1. Visconti: M–M, 1f, 18. Böttiger, *Sabina*, 59, and Küttner, quoted by Böttiger in the French edition of his *Sabina* published in 1813. *Sabine, ou matinée d'une dame romaine*, Paris (1813), 45, n. 3.
2. The critics, their prejudices, and their complaints are discussed by Raoul-Rochette, who presents a balanced view of both the strengths and weaknesses of Visconti's scholarship ('*Oeuvres diverses*', 612f, 615f). See also W. Froehner, *Collection Auguste Dutuit*, Paris (1897), 81. Chief among the critics was H. C. E. Köhler who attacks Visconti, quoting A. L. Millin: '*tout le monde recherchoit les avis de Mr. Visconti; celui qui possédoit un monument curieux croyoit avec raison en augmenter sinon le prix, au moins sa célébrité, en le faisant décrire*'. '*Uber die neue Ausgabe der Werke und Schriften des Visconti*', *Amalthea*, I (1820), 302f.
3. Visconti addresses della Somaglia also as Patriarch of Antioch and Secretary of the Congregation of Bishops and Regular Clergy (Visconti: L, 210). Della Somaglia's titles are retained in the Labus edition of Visconti's essay and omitted from that of Montagnani-Mirabili, no doubt as a result of the rededication of that edition to the Duc de Blacas. Della Somaglia went on to become cardinal, papal legate, Secretary of the Holy Office and Secretary of State to Pope Leo XII. Moroni, '*Somaglia*', 175ff.
4. Visconti: M–M, 1; Seroux d'Agincourt, *L'Histoire*, II, 37, n.b.
5. Seroux d'Agincourt laments the sale in his text which can be dated between 1795 and 1800 (*L'Histoire*, II, 37, n.b.); Böttiger notes the sale as a past event in 1803 (*Sabina*, 60).
6. Visconti: M–M, 13, pl. XVII.
7. Seroux d'Agincourt, *L'Histoire*, III, 8; Montagnani-Mirabili, notes to Seroux d'Agincourt extract, 24, n. 1: '*Qui gl'Autori delle descrizioni non avevano veduti i frammenti trovati posteriormente, i quali con ogni diligenza sono stati posti al proprio luogo*'.
8. Seroux d'Agincourt, *L'Histoire*, II, 37, n.b.; Böttiger, *Sabina*, 60, n. 1.
9. Montagnani-Mirabili, dedication, iii–v.
10. The travels of the treasure during the political upheavals of the first half of the nineteenth century can only be hypothesised. The family collection was begun in Naples during the Duke's tenure as ambassador, at which time he was also active in antiquarian circles in Rome where he founded the Institute of Archaeological Correspondence in 1829. After 1830, Charles X settled in Prague. The Duke may have been in Prague with Charles, but sources simply indicate exile in a German-speaking country. Charles and, later, Blacas died at Gorízia on the Adriatic coast near the present-day Italian–Yugoslav border.

The Duke's eldest son and heir did not return to France until 1844. (J. de Witt, '*Notice sur le Duc de Blacas*', in T. Mommsen, *Histoire de la monnaie romaine*, trans. Duc de Blacas, 4 vols., Paris, 1865–75, IV, ix–li. I am grateful to Francis H. Dowley for this reference.) The collection did not necessarily accompany the family during the fourteen years of exile.
11. For an indication of the family's holdings, see Newton, *Blacas Collection*, 3ff; *A Guide to the Exhibition Galleries of the British Museum*, rev. ed., London (1897), xxxix; H. B. Walters, *Catalogue of the Engraved Gems and Cameos, Greek, Etruscan and Roman in the British Museum*, London (1926), xi.
12. British Museum, Antiquities Register for 1866, BM M & LA nos. 66, 12–29, 1 to 66, 12–29, 59 (inclusive); Dalton, *Catalogue*, nos. 227–41, 304–45.
13. Visconti speaks of a '*piatto d'argento alquanto cupo ornato con degli arabeschi senza rilievo ma soltanto battuti o grafiti*' (Visconti: M–M, 21). The dish conventionally associated with this description is surrounded by a deep rim and covered with a chased and engraved design (no. 13, pl. 25). However appropriate the match of object and description made by Montagnani-Mirabili, this object is securely documented as part of the third-century treasure of Mâcon (France), found in 1764. An engraving of the dish (fig. 7) and a discussion of the treasure were published in 1767 by the Comte de Caylus (*Recueil d'antiquités égyptiennes, étrusques, grecques, romaines et gauloises*, 7 vols., Paris, 1752–67, VII, 239ff, pls. LXVIII, LXIX. Note pl. LXVIII, 1). I thank François Baratte for this reference.

 The Mâcon treasure, which included plates, vases, solid silver statuettes, statuette bases, jewellery, and some 30,000 gold and silver coins, was dispersed soon after its discovery despite protests from French antiquarians. In 1824 eight pieces from Mâcon entered the British Museum with the Payne Knight bequest; a ninth piece was purchased by the museum in 1919 from Lord Home (H. B. Walters, *Catalogue of the Silver Plate, Greek, Etruscan and Roman in the British Museum*, London, 1921, 8ff). The dish which entered the British Museum as part of the Esquiline Treasure is the tenth object from the treasure of Mâcon in the museum. The engraving in the Montagnani-Mirabili edition of Visconti is the earliest record of its inclusion in the Esquiline group. Its location and ownership in the years between 1764 and 1827 are unknown. For discussion of the date of the Mâcon dish, see Baratte, '*Le plat d'argent du Château d'Albâtre à Soissons*', *Revue du Louvre*, XXVII (1977), 125–30.
14. Visconti: M–M, 12, 13, n.1, 17; pls. XV–XVI, XVIII, XXIV–XXV.
15. Montagnani-Mirabili, '*Prefazioni*', vi.
16. Lost was a rectangular dish identical to *nos. 9–12. Visconti had reported five; the editions of 1827 did not correct his statement; but the Duke sold only four (British Museum, Antiquities Register, BM M & LA nos. 66, 12–29, 15–18). Pieces added to the Blacas collection between 1827 and 1866 are nos. 24, 50, 52, 53, 55–9, and 61.
17. Visconti saw the patera at the home of the geographer P. F. J. Gossellin in January 1807 (Visconti: L, 233, n. 1). It was sold at auction in 1864 to the brothers Dutuit (*Catalogue de la vente Gosselin*, Paris, 1864, 117) and passed, on the death of Auguste Dutuit in 1902, to the city of Paris. It is currently held by the Musée du Petit Palais, Paris (*La collection Dutuit*, Paris [1903], n.p.). The bronze ewer entered the Museo Bourbonico at the beginning of the nineteenth century (Poglayen-Neuwall, '*Besitzer*', 126). The dates of the early transactions are such that either della Somaglia or von Schellersheim could have been the agent of the sales.
18. Dalton, *Catalogue*, 36–8, 61–77; Poglayen-Neuwall, '*Besitzer*', 125f; Newton, *Blacas Collection*, 24ff; Buschhausen, *Metallscrinia*, 210.
19. Froehner, *Dutuit*, 131ff; Tozzi, '*Tesoro*', 279; Leclercq, *Dictionnaire d'archéologie chrétienne et de liturgie*, 15 vols. in 29, Paris (1907–51), s.v. '*Projecta*'; E. Barbier, '*La signification du cortège représenté sur le couvercle du coffret de "Projecta"*', *Cahiers archéologiques*, XII (1962), 7.
20. For general comparisons, see D. E. Strong, *Greek and Roman Gold and Silver Plate*, London (1966), 123–209, and R. A. Higgins, *Greek and Roman Jewellery*, London (1961), 178–92.

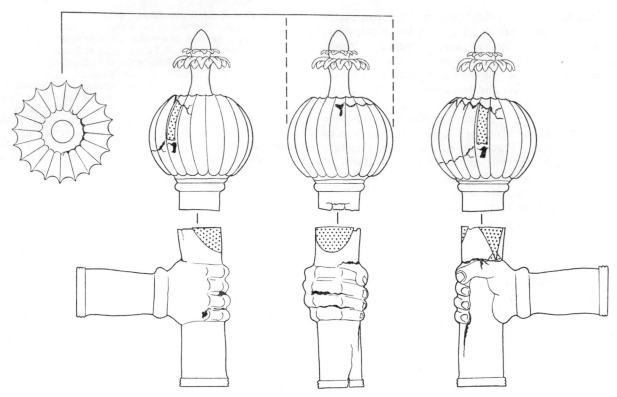

fig. 8 Right arm ornament (*no. 34). *Scale* ¼:1

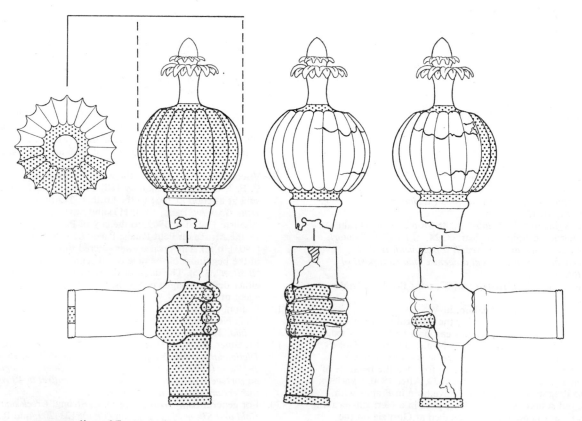

fig. 9 Left arm ornament (*no. 35). *Scale* ¼:1

Theories of Iconography and Function

The objects properly understood as the original find vary in function, and the different categories of use have been the subject of theories primarily concerning the owners of the treasure. The diversity itself can be cited as evidence of the nature of the burial. Those who understand the treasure as an accidental burial may interpret the variety of objects as the reflection of random goods preserved by chance; those who prefer the concept of a conscious burial or hoard may also cite the variety of objects but note that they are, with one exception (*no. 18), all silver. In the absence of other objects of non-precious metals, terracotta, and the like, the second theory may seem more appropriate. The absence of such materials, however, does not seem a fair consideration in the case of the Esquiline find. Had such materials been found in the discoveries of 1793, it is quite probable that they would have been ignored by parties concerned more with the market value of the silver than with its archaeological context.

The collection has never been understood as a truly random grouping: the observation was made by Visconti that it represented the household goods of a single family.[1] There is evidence in the form of inscriptions which would support this view, but the collection speaks for itself. It originally consisted of the candelabrum and lamp now missing, six fittings for larger pieces of furniture, ten serving dishes of various sizes, a flask and two ewers, a patera, two chests, and decorations for the family horses. And from the beginning, the identity of the family to whom the collection belonged was the primary focus of attention and investigation.

Working from the premise that the treasure was a domestic collection—whatever the cause of its burial—early scholars apparently felt that the analysis of the function of individual pieces would yield information concerning the ancient owners. Certainly the early scholars followed this line of reasoning, and, in their efforts to identify the owners, they placed heavy emphasis on a small number of pieces. The horse trappings and tableware were largely ignored or examined primarily for the inscriptions on their surfaces. Discussion centred on the two caskets and the furniture fittings, for these objects were thought to be evocative of their owners and their owners' social position. To a certain degree, this emphasis is understandable: it is often difficult and unnecessary to explain the function of a dish, bowl, or ewer beyond the obvious. Even artefacts far removed from contemporary culture, such as the horse trappings, have an obvious function; it is only the precious material of which they are made that gives cause for comment. But the caskets and ornaments must have seemed more exotic, and their explanation, therefore, all the more revealing. These pieces were discussed in terms of their functions and the iconography of their decorations, which were assumed to reflect their use. This assumption, regarding a necessary interrela-

tion of function and iconography, led to some confusion and to one major misunderstanding concerning wedding iconography. In large measure, however, the information derived was of continuing value. A brief review of the early theories of iconography and function clearly reveals the origins of much that is still believed concerning the owners of the treasure.

In essence, the caskets were understood to refer to a woman and the furniture fittings to a man, a division which corresponds to the *res privatae* and *res publicae* of the treasure. The evidence of the collection as a whole suggested that the family was wealthy; the details of the furniture fittings indicated that the man of the family held high public office. It should be noted that the early scholars consistently, if unconsciously, spoke of one family and, within that family, of one woman and one man. This is somewhat surprising, for these learned gentlemen knew well that few Roman families could be described so simply. If there were specific reasons for their simple description, the reasons went unrecorded. However, the model which the scholars assumed for the family affected all subsequent discussions of ownership and significant personal iconography associated with pieces in the treasure. Most important, perhaps, all subsequent discussions of the treasure began with the assumption that there had been but two owners of the entire collection.

The division of goods between male and female owners seems roughly accurate, and the observation that the furniture fittings referred to public office can be shown to be correct. All six ornaments (*nos. 30–5) can be understood as fittings for a chair or chairs, and it is the iconography of the fittings and therefore the chairs which they decorated that speaks of rank. One set of ornaments (*nos. 34–5, figs. 8–9, pls. 44–5) takes the form of a silver forearm and hand grasping a cylinder topped with a gilded sphere which is, in turn, topped with a gilded floral finial. There are two such ornaments, a right and left hand, each 33 cm (13 in) high. The size and colouring of the pieces indicate the context in which they should be understood. Visconti, who did not fully comprehend the design, nevertheless compared the spheres with their finials to the ornaments on papal thrones.[2] At a primary level of iconographic analysis, the large hands with their exaggerated grip and the stout staffs which they clasp convey an impression of great physical power. One might hypothesise that the owner of a chair adorned with such ornaments would enjoy an analogous measure of power in the Rome of the late empire. Comparative material is difficult to find, for the Esquiline ornaments are virtually unique. One similar piece, a bronze hand and staff broken above the grip, was published by Caylus in 1764 (fig. 10).[3] The bronze was approximately two-thirds the size of the silver ornaments and, like them, hollow for the reception of dowels meeting at right angles. Caylus thought it part of a

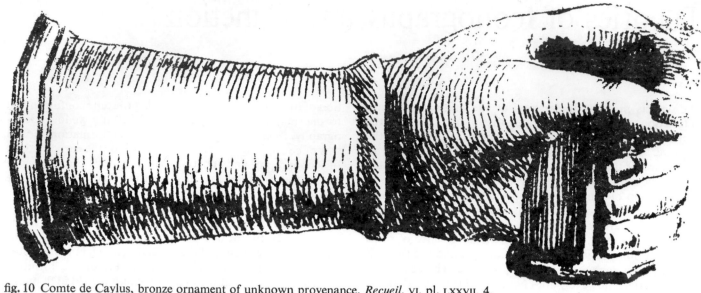

fig. 10 Comte de Caylus, bronze ornament of unknown provenance. *Recueil*, VI, pl. LXXVII, 4.

military insignia, but he admitted that the piece defied easy classification. Unfortunately, no provenance was given and its present whereabouts are unknown. A search through Roman representations of enthroned magistrates does not provide an exact parallel for the pieces, but that does not alter their gesture or the public character of their display.

The imagery of the other four fittings (*nos. 30–3, pls. 35–43) derives from the richly documented constellation of images associated with the empire and with the officials who governed it. The four silver ornaments consist of rectangular sockets on which are seated gilded female figures representing Mediterranean capitals of the late antique world. The personifications of Rome, Constantinople, Alexandria, and Antioch are identified by type and attribute. Details of their fittings indicate that the four were divided into two pairs: Rome and Constantinople, an anticipated couple, form a right- and left-hand pair as do Alexandria and Antioch. The four are most commonly identified as capping the ends of a *sedes gestatoria*, an attractive but not necessarily justified conclusion. The chair, with its ensemble of Tyche figures, carried a distinct message associated in the early literature with the vehicles appropriate to the holders of high public office.[4]

Individual Tyche figures are well documented in the ancient world in works of both large and small scale. The representations of Antioch enjoyed particular popularity in many media as copies of a Hellenistic original of the third century BC. Groups of Tyches, however, are far less common. Although assemblies of city goddesses can be cited in a few early Roman monuments, the representation of multiple Tyches appears to be a phenomenon associated with the late antique period and the many monuments which celebrate the equivalency of Rome and Constantinople and the greatness of the empire as represented by its metropolitan centres. Among these are the numerous official insignia of the *Notitia Dignitatum*, the Calendar of 354, the column base of Arcadius, the silver plate of the consul Ardabur Aspar, numerous consular diptychs, and imperial coins from

the late third until the early sixth century.[5] The extant monuments would indicate that the representation of multiple city goddesses was an aspect of late antique imagery associated with the emperor and the imperial bureaucracy. The Esquiline Tyche figures are an equivalent grouping, executed in precious metal, made to be attached to some type of chair, and, in that context, public in their function.

Tyches, along with Victories, Seasons, and conquered barbarians, are found to decorate the curule chairs of various consuls represented on ivory diptychs.[6] But the exact group of four Tyches, and the two arm ornaments, found in the Esquiline Treasure cannot be matched with the known insignia of specific offices. Their mere existence, therefore, does not prove that an owner of the treasure was a public official; their imagery, however, strongly suggests this. It is a secure hypothesis that such fittings were not the property of the common man. Their public character, their imperial iconography, and their precious material appear to signal the holders of civil or military office.

To turn from these ornaments to the caskets is to turn to objects firmly in the private sector. The information which can be derived from these pieces refers to daily rituals and to family. Visconti discussed the Proiecta casket (*no. 1, pls. 1–11) as an example of those objects specific to the *mundus muliebris*. This casket and its associated pieces, the Muse casket with its five containers (*no. 2, pls. 12–17), were understood to be parts of the toilet service of an aristocratic Roman woman. Böttiger elaborated on that concept in his publication of 1803 which detailed, somewhat satirically, the morning regimen of a Roman matron as she bathed, dressed, and applied her perfumes and cosmetics. The Proiecta casket was variously described as carrying her clothing and her towels; the Muse casket held her necessary unguents. The figural decoration of the body of the Proiecta casket represented the very activity in which the caskets would be used: '*i bassirilievi . . . son tutti allusivi allo studio d'ornarsi*'. Continuing in this line of thought, the small flask (*no. 16, pl. 30) was interpreted as a container for perfumed oils, a shallow dish (now missing) became a vessel for washing one's hands, and the patera (*no. 3, pl. 21) a ladle used in the bath.[7] While the assignment of these last objects to the bath may be debated, the function of the caskets was appropriately discussed. The relief ornament of the Proiecta casket body does represent a train of servants attending the toilet of a Roman matron (pls. 8–9). The servants carry basins and ewers, but, most interestingly, they also carry caskets analogous to the two in the treasure (note esp. pl. 9).

The early authors were mildly perplexed by the resemblance of the Muse casket to a container for literary scrolls, but the flask and canisters which it contained were obviously suited to its use as a *scrinium unguentorum*. The choice of Muse iconography, carrying with it connotations of the arts and learning, created part of the confusion. The antiquarians noted, however, that women had no use for portable libraries as they read only love letters which they carried next to their hearts.[8] The Muse imagery of the casket is best understood at a very general level as referring to the arts and simultaneously serving as decoration. The perspective of many generations of scholarship allows the observation that by the late Roman period many iconographic motifs, such as the Muses, the Seasons, the hunt, the Bacchic *thiasos*, and the marine *thiasos*, had passed into a broad repertory of popular themes. These themes can be interpreted at multiple levels from the specific reference to an activity, a personality, or a cult at one end of the spectrum to little more than decoration at the other. They are perhaps best seen as simple allusions: the Muses to the arts, the Seasons to the passing of time, the hunt to the celebration of manly virtues.[9]

Other aspects of the iconography of the caskets can be understood in this light. She who was accompanied to the bath by the Muses was also likened to Venus at her toilet: above the procession of servants on the Proiecta casket, specifically above the representation of the Roman woman fixing her hair, is the figure of Venus doing the same, as servants from the sea and the sky attend her (pls. 2, 4, 8, 11). The toilet of Venus is the visual simile of the toilet of the Roman matron; what might once have been seen as a pagan reference to the goddess and her cult of love and fertility is here a flattering analogy.

The female owner of the casket is thus seen to be complimented with rhetorical flourishes equivalent in degree but different in content from those which surround her male counterpart. The apparent equality of address, however, does not survive further analysis. In terms of ownership and social roles, it can be deduced that a male owner held public office and a female took baths. To the antiquarian mind, the two activities were of equivalent interest, with the ritual of the bath perhaps having the greater attraction as so little of it was then known. The antiquarians felt that a second ritual, previously known only from literary sources, was represented in the reliefs of the Proiecta casket. The scene in question, an event from the Roman marriage ceremony known as the *donum deductio*, was identified on the back panel of the casket lid (pl. 6).[10] The presence of both the toilet procession and the wedding ritual had the effect of relegating the furniture fittings, and with them their male owner(s), to a place of secondary importance within the treasure. One year after the collection entered the British Museum, it went on display with the label 'Silver Toilet Service of a Roman Bride'.[11]

While representations of other scenes from the Roman wedding ceremony were known in the visual arts, the *donum deductio* of the Proiecta casket was unique, and its inclusion was therefore thought to be of great significance by the early authors. The imagery of the entire casket came to be interpreted as aspects of or allusions to a wedding. The double portrait within a wreath which decorates the top surface of the casket served to reinforce this idea (pl. 4). The double portrait in which the woman holds a scroll conforms to a Roman portrait type in which a married couple and their marriage contract are depicted. Most extant examples of the type occur in a funerary context, but the portrait reference *per se* is to the marriage union. No distinction was made in the early scholarly literature between marriage as a state and the wedding as a ritual activity. As a result, the portrait couple came to be known, not as husband and wife, but as bridegroom and bride. One author even identified the two portrait figures as engaged in the *dextrarum iunctio*, or clasping of right hands, which formed part of the Roman marriage ceremony.[12] This identification ignores the details of the casket representation in which the male gestures in speech with his right hand and the female holds the scroll with both hands, but it accords with the general tendency to translate all imagery into aspects of wedding iconography.

The toilet scene on the body of the casket was variously interpreted as the wedding-night toilet of the bride, a combination of the bride's toilet on the front panel and the preparations for the *pompa nuptialis* on the side and back panels, and the display or presentation of wedding gifts held by servants before a seated bride. The casket itself was discussed as a wedding present to the couple, and the entire treasure as a trousseau.[13] There is little or no reason to hypothesise the *pompa nuptialis*, as the participants in the sacrifice, the offerings, and the implements of the ritual known from ancient sources are not represented. The interpretation of the display of gifts before the bride is weakened by the obvious action of the woman who examines her reflection in a mirror and adjusts her hair with a pin during the proceedings (pls. 8, 11). The explanation of the scene as a wedding-night toilet accords with the general concept of the lavish toilet procession depicted; it accounts for the presence of torches carried by two servants on the left end panel (pl. 9); and it agrees with the wedding imagery of the *donum deductio*. Recent research, however, suggests that the scene of the *donum deductio* is misidentified and that the interpretations of wedding rituals should be re-examined.

Scholars were correct in observing that the representation is unique. There are no other known illustrations of the *donum deductio*, but there are detailed literary references. The original identification was based on the representation of an outdoor procession of women and children entering an elaborate building, '*il palagio del novello marito*', found on the back panel of the Proiecta casket lid (pl. 6).[14] The *donum deductio* was one of the last events in the Roman wedding ceremony as the bride and six attendants, accompanied by a boisterous crowd, walked in procession from the house of her father to the house of her husband. It signified a change of legal status, and its enactment was necessary to ensure a valid ceremony. As part of the wedding rite, it was attended in the costume appropriate to the earlier events—the signing of the contract and the sacrifice and feast in the bride's home. The bride's costume involved a white wool *tunica recta* fastened with a girdle tied in the *cingulum herculeum*, saffron-coloured sandals, a saffron-coloured veil worn over the head, and a wreath variously described as made of marjoram, verbena, orange blossom, or myrtle. Her hair was braided and bound with wool bands in the same fashion as the hair of the Vestal Virgins. In the *donum deductio*, the bride was preceded by flute players, followed by five torch bearers, and accompanied by three young boys. Three young women also attended her and preceded her into her new home, one carrying a spindle and another a distaff. The larger wedding party followed this group, singing and tossing walnuts along the route. The procession ended with the groom carrying the bride over the threshold of an elaborately decorated doorway.[15] There are more details to complete the ceremony, but the procession with its participants and activities is the relevant comparison for the relief panel from the Proiecta casket.

The casket panel shows six figures, two adult women, two girls, and two young men, who carry caskets, a candelabrum, a ewer, and a patera. The number and relative ages of the figures do not accord with the texts, nor do the costumes or implements which they carry. There are no flute players, torch bearers, or walnuts. There is no groom nor anyone distinguished by action or costume as the bride. And the building towards which the six figures walk is a 'very curious representation of a palace'.[16] With its columnar entrance and ten domes, the building is more easily interpreted as a public bath than as domestic architecture. This suggestion was published in 1962 by Barbier who noted discrepancies of costumes, actors, and action between the textual references to the *donum deductio* and the scene on the casket panel.[17]

Over the years, scholars had noted 'errors' in the representation of the marriage ceremony, but, believing the identification to be essentially correct, they argued that the errors were either careless mistakes or deliberate changes necessitated by artistic style and custom. Barbier interpreted the procession represented on the casket as one to a public bath, thereby accounting for the architectural setting and the implements carried by the figures. This reference to the bath can be associated with the more elaborate toilet procession depicted on the casket body, the visual analogy of the toilet of Venus, and the use which the casket actually served. In addition, Barbier furnished examples of other similar bath processions such as those at Piazza Armerina (pl. 7) and Silistra (Bulgaria) which parallel those on the casket in costume, action, and attributes. Since 1962, it would appear that most scholars have ignored or rejected this persuasive thesis without comment.[18] Barbier's interpretation does not explain the presence of two torches and a candelabrum in the bath processions of the casket, but such details are better seen as footnotes to his larger theory.

In both old and new interpretations, the actual function of the Proiecta casket remains the same. The new theory, however, eliminates any notions of unusual wedding imagery, thought noteworthy and purposeful for its very rarity.

Certainly, there was never a logical necessity to understand the entire treasure as a collection of wedding presents; the new theory removes any temptation. An inscription on the lid of the Proiecta casket suggests that this one piece may indeed have been a wedding gift. The two processions represented on the casket, complete with torches and candelabrum, may therefore have been allusions to the bride's toilet known to have taken place the evening before a Roman wedding.[19] No longer linked with the unprecedented representation of a *donum deductio*, it seems a reasonable solution within an established iconography of bath processions.

The Proiecta casket, like the Muse casket, formed part of a toilet service which probably belonged to the woman represented on the casket body. The double portrait on the casket lid allows an identification of her, not necessarily as a bride but as a married woman. And her husband might be seen as an owner of the furniture fittings with the iconography of public office. Those scholars who insisted on the identification of the two as the groom and his young bride and the translation of the entire treasure into a trousseau did so with the support of inscriptions which came to figure in the scholarship on the treasure. Certainly, the suggestion of the *donum deductio* dates to Visconti's essay of 1793. Visconti's interpretation was incorrect but extremely popular, and when the epigraphic data was later introduced, the rare wedding iconography was assumed. The acceptance of the iconographic hypothesis led to the easy acceptance of the epigraphic evidence. The former was incorrect, and the latter open to debate, but each securely buttressed the other.

NOTES

1. Visconti: M–M, 3.
2. Each ornament consists of two parts—the sphere with its finial, and the hand and cylinder (see fig. 9). When Visconti and Seroux d'Agincourt discussed the pieces, they were understood as four separate objects rather than two. Both 1827 editions of Visconti carry editorial notes to the effect that the four were then understood to form two ornaments. Visconti: M–M, 9, 13, n.b., pl. XII; Labus 'Prefazione', xi, pl. XVIII, 15; Seroux d'Agincourt, *L'Histoire*, III, 9.
3. Caylus, *Recueil*, VI, 254f, pl. LXXVII, 4.
4. Visconti: M–M, 13ff; Seroux d'Agincourt, *L'Histoire*, II, 39; H. Sanclementi, *Musei Sanclementiani: Numismata selecta*, 4 vols., Rome (1808–9), III, 203; Dalton, *Catalogue*, 74.
5. For further discussion and previous literature see K. J. Shelton, 'Imperial Tyches', *Gesta*, XVIII (1979), 27–38.
6. Shelton, 'Tyches', 34f; Delbrueck, *Die Consulardiptychen und verwandte Denkmäler*, Berlin (1929), nos. 9, 17, 21, 22.
7. Visconti: M–M, 3f, 7f, 21f; Böttiger, *Sabina, passim*; Newton, *Blacas Collection*, 25.
8. Böttiger, *Sabina*, 70ff. See also Visconti: M–M, 7f; Seroux d'Agincourt, *L'Histoire*, III, 9.
9. Compare, for example, the different uses of hunting imagery ranging from the specific, individualised hunts of the Piazza Armerina (G. Gentili, *Mosaici di Piazza Armerina: Le scene di caccia*, Milan, 1962) to the numerous decorative uses of the theme, such as that of the Louvre oenochoe (Inv. MNE 610, F. Baratte, 'Vaiselle d'argent au bas-empire: Remarques à propos d'une vase du Musée du Louvre', *Mélanges de l'Ecole française de Rome*, LXXXVII, 1975, 1104–29) and the Berlin amphora (A. Minto, 'Spalliera in bronzo decorata ad intarsio de R. Museo Archeologico di Firenze', *Critica d'arte*, I, 1935–6, 127–35). See J. Aymard, *Essai sur les chasses romaines*, Paris (1951). G. M. A. Hanfmann discusses aspects of the generalised

iconography of the Seasons in *The Season Sarcophagus in Dumbarton Oaks*, 2 vols., Cambridge, Mass. (1951), esp. I, 201ff. For Muses, see M. Wegner, *Die Musensarkophage*, Berlin (1966).

10. *Donum deductio* is the phrase used by most scholars of the Esquiline Treasure to refer to that part of the Roman marriage ceremony more accurately termed *deductio in donum mariti* (A. Berger, *Encyclopedic Dictionary of Roman Law*, Transactions of the American Philosophical Society, N.S. XLIII, pt 2, Philadelphia, 1953, s.v. '*deductio in donum mariti*').

11. Newton, *Blacas Collection*, 4.

12. Buschhausen, *Metallscrinia*, 212. For a discussion of the *dextrarum iunctio* see E. H. Kantorowicz, 'On the Golden Marriage Belt and the Marriage Rings of the Dumbarton Oaks Collection', *Dumbarton Oaks Papers*, XIV (1960), 1–16.

13. Visconti: M–M, 6f; Böttiger, *Sabina*, 66ff; Sanclementi, *Numismata*, III, 203; Newton, *Blacas Collection*, 25; Dalton, *Catalogue*, 63; O. Pelka, *Ehedenkmäler*, Strasburg (1901), 122; Poglayen-Neuwall, '*Besitzer*', 125; Tozzi, '*Tesoro*', 299f; Buschhausen, *Metallscrinia*, 212.

14. Visconti: M–M, 5.

15. P. E. Corbett, *The Roman Law of Marriage*, Oxford (1930), 74, 92ff; J. Carcopino, *Daily Life in Ancient Rome*, ed. H. T. Rowell, trans. E. O. Lorrimer, New Haven (1940), 81ff; J. P. V. D. Balsdon, *Roman Women*, London (1962), 181ff; *The Roman Questions of Plutarch*, ed. and trans. H. J. Rose, Oxford (1924), reprint ed., New York (1974), 119f, 132f, 157f.

16. Newton, *Blacas Collection*, 24.

17. Barbier, '*Cortège*'.

18. A notable exception is Geza de Francovich who is vocal in his rejection: '*la tesi del Barbier . . . è, a mio aviso, completamente errata*'. In an appendix to an essay on pictorial representations of architecture de Francovich asserts that the original interpretation of the *donum deductio* is correct. He argues that rituals of the early empire would have changed (beyond recognition) by the date of the Proiecta casket; that Barbier cannot account for the candelabrum; and that Proiecta, a wealthy woman, would have had her own private bath and would not therefore walk in public procession to an imperial bath. The possibility of an iconographic formula denoting 'procession to a bath', the existence and use of which was independent of the specifics of wealth and station of an individual patron, is not considered.

De Francovich admits the parallel of Piazza Armerina and the Silistra tomb, adding the *hypogeum* of Trebius Justus in Rome and a tomb from Kazanlak (Bulgaria). He interprets all five monuments, however, not as bath processions but as displays of worldly goods and activities from daily life. A bath procession, as an event of daily life, is not ruled out according to this logic. The architectural representation on the casket panel is virtually ignored in the appendix, although it is labelled as a fantasy in the body of the essay. The essay itself shows that de Francovich believes pictorial representations of architecture to have relationships, however tenuous, to existing buildings; he is highly critical of the over-interpretation of pictorial sources. To see the building depicted on the casket, with its portico, main dome and smaller flanking domes, as a reflection of the urban baths of the empire, however, does not seem an over-interpretation. (G. de Francovich, '*Il soggeto della scena rappresentata nel lato posteriore del coperchio della cassetta di Projecta nel British Museum di Londra*', *Il palatium di Teodorico a Ravenna e la cosidetta 'architettura di potenza'*, Rome, 1970, 81ff.)

Toynbee accepts Barbier's thesis (review of M. Gough, *The Origins of Christian Art*, London, 1973, in *Antiquity*, XLVIII, 1974, 71) as do Grabar and Stern who supported Barbier's research (Barbier, '*Cortège*', 13, n. 6; de Francovich, '*Il soggeto*', 81).

19. Carcopino, *Daily Life*, 77; for the casket inscription, see below, p. 32–3, fig. 12.

The Inscriptions within the Treasure

Inscriptions of various types have figured in the history of the treasure. The twenty-seven pieces of the original find carry twelve Latin inscriptions; six additional inscriptions—three in Latin, three in Greek—are found on the thirty-four pieces which entered the treasure after 1793. The mixture of languages, or rather the presence of Greek inscriptions in a Roman treasure, has been cited to support various theories of eastern influence, but these objects and their inscriptions can no longer be understood as representative of the find.[1] The Latin inscriptions of the original treasure, combined with a lengthy Latin epitaph in marble, have been the source of a different type of information concerning the treasure. These inscriptions have allowed scholars to identify the man and woman represented on the Proiecta casket and therefore to name owners and to date the treasure, incorrectly.

From Visconti's essay to the articles of the 1930s, theories of ownership were debated and refined until Poglayen–Neuwall's identification of the husband was thought secure and associated with data recovered concerning the wife. The results are reflected in the names and dates now automatically associated with the treasure: Turcius Secundus and Proiecta Turcii, AD 379 to 383.[2] This information was derived from the epigraphic evidence, which, attractive as it is, is nevertheless difficult to accept. Objections can be raised to the interpretations of the inscriptions within the treasure and to the inclusion of inscriptions outside the treasure in the gathering of data and the formulation of theories.

Before turning to inscriptions outside the find, it is possible to learn a great deal about the owners from those within. There are two inscriptions which record weight—a type of notation found frequently on works of precious metals.[3] In addition, the treasure contains ten inscriptions with personal references. Two take the form of exhortations to individuals, presumably the original recipients or owners; eight are identical monograms which can be partially deciphered with care. Nine of the ten, the eight monograms and one of the two inscriptions, are engraved, nielloed and gilded, and incorporated into the design and decoration of the objects on which they appear (*nos. 5–12, fig. 13, pls. 26–7; *no. 17, fig. 11, pl. 31). The relatively large scale of these inscriptions, their prominent positions, and the multi-coloured techniques of their manufacture suggest a date in the fourth or fifth century, as do the general shapes and surface treatments of the silver vessels they decorate. In each case, the integration of object and inscription is such that they are properly understood to be contemporary with one another, designed to serve as visual complements. These nine pieces can be grouped with others of comparable design, ornamentation, and execution, which date to the late empire and indicate a taste for inscriptions and monograms as aspects of decoration in the silver of that period.

The inscription in the group of nine occurs on a large ewer (*no. 17, fig. 11, pl. 31) where, in precise serif capitals, a female owner is encouraged to enjoy the use of the vessel: PELEGRINA VTERE FELEX (felix).[4] The occasion for the gift of a silver ewer to Pelegrina cannot be known, but a second donative inscription in the treasure allows a hypothesis for the occasion of its inscription and presentation. It appears on the larger of the two toilet caskets (*no. 1, fig. 12, pl. 4) and exhorts its owners to live in Christ:

SECVNDE ET PROIECTA VIVATIS IN CHRISTO.

The inscription is certainly the most famous in the treasure, and it is the obvious source of the conventional name of the piece, the Proiecta casket.

The casket is the tenth of the ten inscribed pieces, and, while it does not have the absolute match of vessel form and epigraphic design seen in the other nine, details of its execution indicate that the casket and its inscription are best understood as contemporary with one another. The inscription is large in scale and prominently placed on the horizontal rim which runs along the front face of the casket lid. More important, its content agrees with an aspect of the casket iconography. Despite the bias of the conventional casket name, the inscription names two people, addresses them as a couple, and refers to their future life (together). Within Roman society, betrothal and marriage and the exchanges of goods and gifts associated with these activities provide the occasions for which the sentiment of such an inscription would seem most appropriate.[5] The combination of the inscription, which resembles a wedding benediction, and the marriage iconography of the double portrait represented on the casket lid suggests that the lavishly decorated piece was made and inscribed for presentation to the couple and that therefore the casket and its inscription are contemporary.[6] The early authors saw evidence for a wedding in the donum deductio and in the double portrait; they understood the inscription primarily as providing the names of the participants.[7] It is actually the inscription which begins the process, suggesting a wedding and the possible function of the casket as a present for the occasion; the donum deductio is a misinterpretation, and the iconography of the portrait is simply that of a married couple.

The inscription does provide names. It also indicates the religious affiliation of those involved. When the casket was found, the rim on which the inscription is engraved was badly damaged; Visconti could read only SECVNDE ET PROIECTA VIVATIS . . . NCH . . . In an effort to incorporate the consonant cluster and to render sense of the inscription, Visconti suggested several possible readings.[8] The rim has since been completely restored, and several important fragments of the inscription are now incorporated in the restoration. One fragment and its relationship to the damaged inscription were known to Visconti within months of the publication of his essay. Someone designated by him as 'il Prelato', possibly della Somaglia, found the pieces while

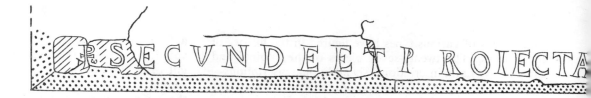

sifting through assorted fragments from the find. The s from SECVNDE, which Visconti had evidently assumed from the beginning, was found preceded by a Chi-Rho monogram. Annotating his essay at a later date, Visconti commented that, with the discovery of the monogram at the beginning of the inscription, the ending IN CHRISTO was obvious. He discarded his earlier solutions with the comment that previously he could not have suggested a Christian inscription 'sotto imagini cotanto profane'.[9] At an even later date, a fragment containing an I and part of the N preserved on the casket rim and another fragment inscribed RI were found to fit on either side of the NCH known since 1793. The ending IN CHRISTO was then explicit.[10]

The damaged inscription of Secundus and Proiecta was immediately accepted as naming the husband and wife (bridegroom and bride) portrayed on the lid when the casket was found in 1793. The Roman matron on the back panel of the lid (pl. 10) and the matron on the front panel of the casket body (pl. 11) were identified as one and the same, and she was identified, in turn, as Proiecta. The recovery of the missing fragments of the inscription, however, met with different, mixed reactions. Many, like Visconti, understood that the owners were Christians. This conclusion was first published in the 19 April 1794 edition of a Roman ecclesiastical journal and became one of the established facts of the treasure.[11] A few dissenters echoed Visconti's reservation concerning a Christian inscription in a profane context, but, unlike Visconti, they doubted the authenticity of the treasure on the grounds of its unsuitability for Christian owners and therefore thought it a modern fiction and forgery.[12] To most others, the Christian inscription in the presence of pagan and secular scenes was illustrative of the dynamic syncretism of the early Church. Their descriptions of the casket dwelt specifically on the location of the inscription beneath the representation of a nude Venus (pl. 4)—a combination referred to as possibly voluntary, the result of confusion, and implicitly understood as daring. It was clearly startling to the early scholars.[13]

It was Visconti who appears to have dealt most easily with the problem. It was a first for him, more accustomed to 'personificazioni meramente poetiche' and other figures 'di ambigua significazione' such as the personifications of the sun, the moon, the seasons, cities, and rivers. A representation of Venus was different. Visconti proposed various practical solutions—the artisan was not Christian; the Christian owner did not notice the pagan decoration; but ultimately he suggested that the Venus was simply a symbol

of beauty, a visual allusion not unlike the pagan deities mentioned in Christian poetry.[14] Visconti's note was little heeded by many who saw Christianity and the deities of the Roman state religion interacting in the fourth century as though the two cultures had been mutually exclusive until that date. Agreement existed that the inscription of the Proiecta casket documented a Christian married couple, but few subsequent scholars of the Esquiline material shared Visconti's comfortable resolution of pagan imagery and Christian ownership.

A reasonable argument can be made for the contemporary dating of many pieces of the original find,[15] and, as a result, the casket inscription may be seen to name a Christian couple with ties to public office as suggested by the furniture fittings. The office holder may be Secundus himself; if not, the treasure furnishes evidence of the family of the office

fig. 13. Monogram from circular and rectangular plates (*nos. 5–12) Scale 2:1

holder in the form of the eight matching monograms. Each of the monograms found on the small serving-dishes (*nos. 5–12, fig. 13; see pls. 26–7) is actually composed of two separate monograms which can be read to contain two names. Visconti saw the two monograms as direct parallels to the casket inscription with a name for each spouse; he deciphered the first monogram as PROIECTA and the second as TVRCI.[16] His reading was accepted and remains unchallenged, despite the fact that later he himself had doubts about the first monogram. Admittedly, there are no established guidelines for the decipherment of Latin monograms. They are conceded to be 'des jeux de calligraphie' for which it is 'inutile de rechercher des règles précises'.[17] Certain commonly used ligatures have been observed and can be seen to occur in the Esquiline monograms, but even conventional ligatures do not dictate letter order. The second monogram is composed of two such ligatures:

$\overline{R}I$ and $\lor$

fig. 11 Dedicatory inscription from Pelegrina ewer (*no. 17). *Scale* $\frac{1}{2}$:1

fig. 12 Dedicatory inscription from Proiecta casket (*no. 1). *Scale* $\frac{1}{2}$:1

These supply the letters T, R, V, and I to which can be added the free-standing C or G which is captured within the design. The substitution of G for C and C for G is frequently observed in Latin inscriptions with context dictating the correct reading.[18] Visconti's reading of TVRCI seems straightforward, and context in this case is supplied by prosopographical data which confirm that the *gens* name Turcius is well attested in Rome from the third until the end of the fifth century AD.[19] As such, the monogram might be more correctly read as TVRCII, the genitive singular or nominative plural of the *nomen*.

Visconti's association of the husband named in the Proiecta casket inscription with the second monogram is based on the frequent occurrence of the *cognomen* Secundus within the *gens* Turcia.[20] Epigraphic evidence would support this association of the casket and the eight plates, for the capitals which constitute the monograms match those of the Proiecta casket inscription in overall form, although their execution is more precise. The capitals are oblong with uniformly thick verticals and horizontals which flare at the ends; they are outlined with incised lines which occasionally appear as linear serifs. The general execution, the proportions, and the consistent letter types indicate that the casket inscription and the eight monograms were designed by the same person, if executed by two hands of varying skill. It therefore seems reasonable to conclude that the Secundus of the inscription is a member of the *gens* Turcia of the monograms and that the casket and the plates were inscribed in the same workshop. Since the casket inscription appears contemporary with the casket, and the monograms contemporary with and designed for the plates, it is probable that these nine pieces were both inscribed and manufactured in the same workshop over a limited period of time. The patrons of the shop would therefore have included the donor of the toilet casket and the donor or owner of the plates which celebrate another member of the family of the Turcii.

The Proiecta of the casket inscription was obviously a relative of Secundus by marriage, but, while she may have entered into his family (if married with *manus*), as a Roman woman she would have retained her own name. There are recorded examples of women who appended the names of their husbands' families to their own; following these examples, the wife of Turcius Secundus would have been styled Proiecta Turcia. The casket was inscribed and probably presented to Proiecta and Secundus as a married couple, but the monogram plates identify someone who was (*filius*/*filia*) Turcii.[21] In common Roman usage Visconti's reading

PROIECTA TVRCI[I] would denote a Proiecta who was directly descended through the male line of the *gens* Turcia. Certainly it is possible that Secundus married within his *gens*. It is not possible, however, to read the first monogram as Proiecta, and the fine points of Roman marriage law do not therefore seem relevant.

By analogy with the second monogram, the first might be expected to be straightforward and relatively easy to read. Such is not the case, but it seems appropriate to deduce and apply certain guidelines learned from the second monogram. There are two main ligatures:

and a free-standing C or G. The letters which can be derived are V, I, A, C or G, P and/or R, E and/or F and L. Visconti observed in later notations that '*il primo monogramma sembra contenere un "M" o un "V" che poco si accordano col nome di Projetta*'.[22] The ligature does not appear to present either an M or an N with the clarity seen in the representation of the other letters. The O and T necessary to the reading PROIECTA are not included. Somewhat unexpectedly the monogram can be read as PELEGRINA, and the ewer (*no. 17) on which this name appears is related in technique and style, if not in script, to the round monogram dishes. The analogy of the second monogram, however, suggests that the first ligature contains the beginning of the name and the second ligature plus the free-standing consonant form its end. The resultant termination CIA is extremely common for feminine Latin names, but it seems impossible to choose a 'correct' reading from the various combinations generated from the first ligature.[23] There are no criteria which might determine the selection.

The first monogram is that of a feminine name. It probably ends in the syllable CIA and it apparently belongs to a female member of the *gens* Turcia. The epigraphic evidence relative to the *gens* furnishes the names of one daughter, Eunomia, and three wives, Proiecta, Avita, and Aemilia Paterna Eunomia. The names cannot be matched with the first monogram, and no other wives or female children are recorded for the known males in the line.[24]

The treasure contains inscriptions for a Pelegrina, a Proiecta, a Turcius Secundus, and an unknown female member of his family on objects which are closely related to one another and to the other pieces of the original find. Previous scholars understood that the identification of the couple and the association of the prominent family of the

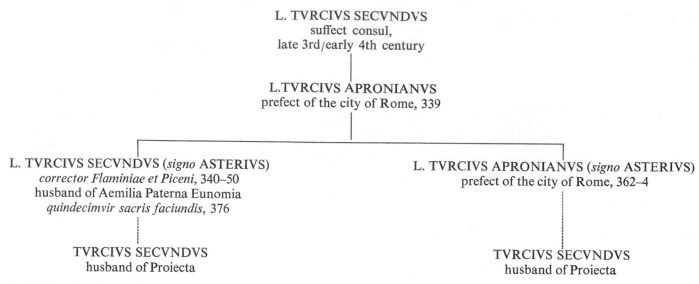

fig. 14 Stemma of the Turcii with hypothesised relationships for Turcius Secundus.

Turcii provided the most promising avenues for further research. Within the confines of the treasure, Proiecta is understood only as the wife of Turcius Secundus. While the identification of her family would aid in an effort to date the treasure, the inscriptions within the find furnish no additional information or direction. In contrast, the family of Turcius Secundus is well documented, and the scholars took the opportunity to debate the qualifications and merits of the various members to be the owner of the treasure (see fig. 14). Almost every known member of the *gens* Turcia was nominated, despite evidence to the contrary in several cases. The function and iconography of the six furniture fittings were cited in support of each, for all had held high public office. No scholar considered more than one nominee, however, since it was assumed that the whole treasure was the possession of a single man—the Secundus of the casket inscription.

Two members of the family drew the most attention, for as father and son they had both held the office of prefect of the city of Rome during the fourth century. Visconti was the first to suggest that one of the two was the likely owner of the treasure, and several scholars agreed with his hypothesis. Lucius Turcius Apronianus, prefect in 339, and Lucius Turcius Apronianus (*signo* Asterius), prefect from 362 to 364, were seriously championed despite the fact that neither bore the *cognomen* Secundus.[25] A Lucius Turcius Secundus was the father of the elder prefect and grandfather of the younger. His exact dates are not known, but inscriptions record him as suffect consul at some time in the late third or early fourth century. Considering his name and office, it is surprising that no attempt was made to claim him as owner. There are obstacles; the most obvious is the clear reference to the existence of Constantinople, not founded until 324, in the Esquiline group of Tyche statuettes.

A second grandson, Lucius Turcius Secundus (*signo* Asterius), brother to the younger city prefect, held any number of public offices during the mid-fourth century. This member of the family has been generally accepted as the owner of the treasure since Poglayen–Neuwall's essay of 1930.[26] Lucius Turcius Secundus was, at various times,

quaestor, praetor, comes Augustorum during the joint rule of Constantine's heirs (337–40), and *corrector Piceni et Flaminiae* between the years 339 and 350. An inscription also documents his marriage to one Aemilia Paterna Eunomia.[27] Proiecta, the scholars observe, must have been his second wife, and they note that the advanced age of L. Turcius Secundus is obvious in his portrait on the lid of the Proiecta casket.[28] Both portrait faces on the casket lid (pl. 4) are, in fact, bland and ageless, and the unexpectedly early death of a spouse could account for a second wife without necessitating a husband of advanced age. Another inscription, however, argues against a second marriage to Proiecta. It documents the priesthood of L. Turcius Secundus as *quindecimvir sacris faciundis* in the year 376.[29] It is extremely doubtful that this public man, a member of one of the major colleges of priests in the Roman state religion, could be the same Turcius Secundus of the casket inscription who is exhorted with his wife to live in Christ.

The editors of the *Prosopography of the Later Roman Empire*, responding perhaps to the evidence of conversion to Christianity within the pagan family of the Turcii, have hypothesised the existence of another Turcius Secundus, son of L. Turcius Secundus, to be the husband of Proiecta. He might also be proposed as the son of L. Turcius Apronianus, prefect from 362 to 364 (fig. 14). It should be noted that conversion within this family need not necessarily be pushed later in time, but the choice of a later generation accords with the observed phenomenon of the general conversion to Christianity of the Roman nobility, both men and women, by the end of the fourth or the beginning of the fifth century.[30] The clear indication of the Christianity of the owners of the casket prompted Galeani Napione to write to Visconti in 1794 to suggest Fl. Turcius Rufius Apronianus Asterius, consul in 494, as the owner of the treasure. This member of the *gens* Turcia, who was the editor of the verses of both Virgil and Sedulius, seemed to him the perfect parallel for the combination of the pagan and Christian seen in the casket decoration.[31] The omission of the *cognomen* bothered Galeani Napione, and his suggestion was ultimately rejected.

Unfortunately, the motivation for his efforts was ignored as well, and scholars came to accept the pagan L. Turcius Secundus as the owner of the treasure.

It would appear, then, that the inscriptions found on objects within the Esquiline Treasure record a male owner, a previously unknown member of the *gens* Turcia, and document him as one of the first of that family to convert to Christianity. His wife, also a Christian, and possibly as many as two other female members of his *gens* are also named. The exact relationships of the four to one another cannot be established, beyond the obvious pairing of husband and wife.[32] The interrelations of the objects associated with these individuals, however, suggest that the silver pieces and therefore their owners are roughly contemporary in date. Various members of a fourth-century Roman household are thus attested through the survival of their domestic possessions.

NOTES

1. It is an unnecessary assumption that Greek inscriptions must (always) signal eastern craftsmen. Of the objects added to the treasure after 1793, nos. 29, 59, and 60 bear Greek inscriptions; nos. 21, 22, and 23 bear Latin inscriptions.
2. See, for example, W. F. Volbach, *Early Christian Art*, London (1961), nos. 116–19; also, J. P. C. Kent and K. S. Painter (eds.), *Wealth of the Roman World, AD 300–700*, London (1977), nos. 88–98.
3. The two weight notations are found on the Proiecta casket and on one of the four round monogram dishes (*nos. 1 and 5, figs. 17 and 19). For weight notations in general, see Strong, *Silver Plate*, 20.
4. Visconti and Böttiger 'correct' the inscription to read PEREGRINA. Visconti: M–M, 12; Böttiger, *Sabina*, 92.
5. Corbett, *Marriage*, 145ff; Berger, *Roman Law*, s.v. '*donatio ante nuptias*', '*dos*', '*matrimonium*', '*sponsalia*'. It is difficult to ascertain if wedding anniversaries were occasions for the presentations of gifts.
6. It is possible that only the purchase, not the manufacture, of the vessel and its inscription are contemporary. It might also be argued that the casket with its combination of toilet scenes and marriage medallion had been in the possession of the donor, or the donor's family, for some time before its inscription and presentation to Secundus and Proiecta. Relations between casket and monogram plates indicate that both inscription and monograms, casket and plates, date to the same late, limited time period. See pp. 33; 41ff, esp. 49f. The casket could have first been in the possession of the donor's family, but, if so, it must have passed from shop to donor (to engraver), to Secundus and Proiecta in a relatively short time. The hypothesis of contemporary dates for casket and inscription, based on the match of marriage portrait iconography and wedding inscription, is the simpler solution and therefore preferable.
7. For example, Visconti: M–M, 4ff, who refers to the woman of the portrait medallion as '*una giovine sposa*'.
8. Visconti: M–M, 5f: SECVNDE ET PROIECTA VIVATIS AB EPITYNCHANO, CVM ANCHARIO, CVM SYNCHORVSA.
9. Visconti: L, 215, n. 1.
10. The precise date of the recovery of these last fragments is unknown. No comment was made when Visconti's essay was reprinted in the March and April issues of *Antologia romana* in 1794. An early reference to all three fragments is found in Galeani Napione's letter dated 20 October 1794. Galeani Napione, 'Lettera', 33.
11. The date and brief description of the journal is provided by Seroux d'Agincourt who unfortunately does not cite it by name. *L'Histoire*, II, 37, n.b.
12. See Froehner, *Dutuit*, 81, for discussion.
13. A. du Sommerard, *Les arts au moyen age*, 5 vols., Paris (1838–46), II, 139, n. 1.; F. X. Kraus, *Roma sotterranea: Die römische Katakomben*, Freiburg im Breisgau (1879), 232; V. Schultze, *Archäologie der altchristlichen Kunst*, Munich (1895), 278; Dalton, *Catalogue*, 64.
14. Visconti: L, 215, n. 1.
15. See below, pp. 41ff, 54f.
16. Visconti: M–M, 10.
17. R. Cagnat, *Cours d'épigraphie latine*, Paris (1914), 27.
18. Ibid., 16, 24ff; Visconti: M–M, 11f.
19. Visconti: M–M, 10f; A. H. M. Jones *et al.* (eds.), *The Prosopography of the Later Roman Empire, A.D. 260–395*, Cambridge (1971), s.v. 'Apronianus' 9, 'Apronianus' 10, 'Secundus' 4, 5, and 6.
20. Jones *et al.* (eds.), *Prosopography*, s.v. 'Secundus' 4, 5, and 6; stemma 29.
21. Marriage with *manus*, which placed the wife in the legal position of a daughter in her husband's household, was displaced by marriage without *manus*; this tendency is noted already during the Roman Republic. Balsdon, *Women*, 17; Corbett, *Marriage*, *passim*; A. Berger, *Oxford Classical Dictionary*, repr. ed. (1976), s.v. '*filiae loco*', '*manus*'; B. Nicholas, s.v. '*patria potestas*'; Berger and Nicholas, s.v. 'marriage, law of'; T. J. Cadoux, s.v. 'names, personal'. Also, S. B. Pomeroy, 'The Relationship of the Married Woman to her Blood Relatives in Rome', *Ancient Society*, VII (1976), 215–27.
22. Visconti: L, 223.
23. The unlikely candidates are Fercia, Lercia, Percia, Ercia; Erica; Frecia, Precia; Fuercia, Puercia.
24. Jones *et al.* (eds.), *Prosopography*, stemma 29. The names of the wives, while not directly relevant to the monograms, might indicate possible names for other female children in the *gens* Turcia, according to observed Roman naming patterns.
25. Visconti: M–M, 11; Newton, *Blacas Collection*, 26; Dalton, *Catalogue*, 64. Dalton refers to one L. Turcius Rufius Apronianus Asterius and thus conflates two members of the family. For brief references, see A. Chastagnol, *Les fastes de la préfecture de Rome au bas-empire*, Etudes prosopographiques, II, Paris (1962), 105ff, 156ff; Jones *et al.* (eds.), *Prosopography*, s.v. 'Apronianus' 9 and 10.
26. Poglayen–Neuwall, '*Besitzer*', *passim*; also Buschhausen, *Metallscrinia*, 214. For brief reference Jones *et al.* (eds.), *Prosopography*, s.v. 'Secundus' 6.
27. *Corpus inscriptionum latinarum*, VI, no. 1773.
28. Poglayen–Neuwall, '*Besitzer*', 130; Buschhausen, *Metallscrinia*, 214. The age of the husband was stressed because data thought to concern Proiecta prevented a marriage before 379 when L. Turcius Secundus would have been well over sixty. This data on Proiecta is of questionable relevance to the treasure; see below, pp. 37ff.
29. *Corpus inscriptionum latinarum*, VI, no. 1772.
30. P. R. L. Brown, 'Aspects of the Christianization of the Roman Aristocracy', *Journal of Roman Studies*, LI (1961), 9ff. Jones *et al.* (eds.), *Prosopography*, s.v. 'Secundus' 4; also stemma 29. Turcius Apronianus, a Roman senator and member of the *gens* Turcia, was converted to Christianity by Melania the elder in the early fifth century: s.v. 'Apronianus' 8 and 'Melania' 1.
31. Galeani Napione, '*Lettera*', 41ff.
32. Chastagnol indicates Pelegrina (whom he names Peregrina) to be the daughter of Turcius Secundus and Proiecta, although he cites no evidence. Chastagnol, *Les fastes*, 296.

fig. 15 Seroux d'Agincourt, silver bowl found in 1632 in the grounds of S. Martino ai Monti. *L'Histoire*, II, p. 38.

fig. 16 Damasian epitaph for a Proiecta, buried 30 December 383. Museo Pio-Cristiano.

The Damasian Epitaph

Recent scholars observing the Esquiline inscriptions which refer to Turcius Secundus and members of his family have thought that the silver treasure marked the site of the *domus Turciorum*.[1] The location of the treasure, rather than the treasure *per se*, was accepted by earlier scholars as establishing a connection with the family of Proiecta, the wife of Turcius Secundus. In an effort to supplement the casket inscription and the (misunderstood) monograms, scholars turned to epigraphic materials, otherwise unrelated to the treasure, which had been discovered or located in the same general area of the city of Rome. These included an inscribed silver bowl, not part of the Esquiline silver, and an elaborate epitaph written by Pope Damasus (366–84) for a Christian woman named Proiecta. The proximity of the treasure and these inscriptions can be shown to be coincidental, but it nevertheless helped to fix them in the history of the silver.

While Visconti's references to the find site may seem casual and imprecise to the modern reader, it can be assumed that the location '*presso il monistero delle religiose Minime sull'Esquilino*' specified to his contemporaries the convent of S. Francesco di Paolo. When, in 1794, a Damasian epitaph, once the property of the church of S. Martino ai Monti, was introduced into a discussion of the treasure, the relative proximity of the treasure and the epitaph may have caused comment (see map, fig. 1). The discussion of 1794, however, is known to us only through the later report of Seroux d'Agincourt, who appears to have concluded that the discovery of the Esquiline Treasure occurred at S. Martino on the evidence of the epitaph and other material.[2] Seroux d'Agincourt's own researches had revealed that in 1632 a silver bowl had been found near the walls of the church of S. Martino and the oratory of S. Silvestro located in its grounds. One of the Carmelite friars furnished Seroux d'Agincourt with a drawing of the open-work bowl which bore the pointillé inscription SANCTO SILVESTRIO ANCILLA SVA VOTVM SOLVIT (fig. 15). Despite the differences in letter types, proportions, and techniques of execution, Seroux d'Agincourt wrote that the inscriptions of the Proiecta casket and the silver bowl matched one another and that therefore both pieces had originated in the same workshop, together with the rest of the treasure. Understanding the treasure to have indicated the site of the '*palais de Projecta*', he deduced that the Proiecta and the Ancilla of the two inscriptions were one and the same and that Proiecta had built the monastery of S. Martino over the ruins of her own home '*pour y rassembler des vierges consacrées à Dieu*'.[3]

This elaborate theory was never commented upon, but Seroux d'Agincourt's choice of a find site at S. Martino is reflected in the writings of all subsequent scholars. The epitaph, the inscription which first led Seroux d'Agincourt to the site, came to be closely associated with the treasure. It was the source of information concerning Proiecta's family and of the dates currently ascribed to the treasure.

The epitaph was originally introduced to prove to those who doubted the possibility of Christian ownership of objects of pagan or secular iconography that the owners of the treasure were in fact Christians. The verses of the epitaph were written by Pope Damasus and inscribed on a marble slab by Filocalus, his official letter cutter (fig. 16).[4] As was the case with most of the Damasian epigrams, the epitaph of Proiecta had first been erected in a suburban catacomb, possibly the *coemeterium* of Priscilla. It was brought into the city to S. Martino in the ninth century with at least one other Damasian epigram, that to the martyr Gorgonius, as part of the rebuilding by Pope Sergius II (844–7) of the early church dedicated by Pope Symmachus (498–514) to St Martin of Tours.[5] The two Damasian epigrams were recorded as set side by side into the floor of the Carolingian basilica of S. Martino and later immured to the right of its main door.[6] The epitaph of Proiecta was removed to the Vatican Library either during the rule of Pope Benedict XIV (1740–58) or immediately after 1780 when Cardinal Zelada began a major restoration of S. Martino.[7] In either case, the inscription, which seemed to confirm the find site for many, had been brought to S. Martino from a suburban catacomb in the ninth century and was no longer located in the church in the last decades of the eighteenth century when the Esquiline Treasure was discovered a short distance away at S. Francesco di Paolo.

Visconti knew of the epitaph in the Vatican, but he simply catalogued it along with other references to women who bore the name Proiecta. Seroux d'Agincourt, however, accepted it as evidence of Christian ownership of the treasure. Although he did not discuss it explicitly, such an acceptance implied that the Proiecta of the epitaph was the Proiecta of the treasure and that the dates associated with the one could be associated with the other. Sanclementi, writing within a few years of Seroux d'Agincourt, understood the possible interpretations; like Visconti, Sanclementi saw the two Proiectas as two separate individuals. Visconti stated, and others agreed, that the name was a humble one found frequently in reference to Christian women, even Christian women of the Roman aristocracy.[8] Most other scholars who have studied the treasure, however, have been understandably reluctant to surrender the secure dates provided by the epitaph. It is, they have said, too great a coincidence: the Proiecta recorded in a silver treasure of the late empire must have been the Proiecta of the epitaph written by Pope Damasus, found at a site near that where the silver was discovered.[9] Most scholars, following Seroux, have thought the silver was found 'near' S. Martino, and the art historians have apparently been unaware of the original provenance of the inscription in a suburban catacomb and its subsequent relocation to S. Martino only in the early Middle Ages. The epigraphers who have discussed the text— even those who understand the two Proiectas to be one—

have not mentioned the topographical relation of S. Martino to the find site of the silver, presumably because of their knowledge of the peregrinations of the epitaph. De Rossi, writing after and disagreeing with Sanclementi, argued that the identity of the names and the high social position of both Proiectas made their conflation possible and appropriate. But, he added, nothing could be proved. The epigraphers who followed de Rossi did so with no further comment.[10]

The text of the epitaph indicates its author, the person celebrated, the members of her family, her age at death, the date of burial, and the consuls for the year.

pride of place and that, while both husband and father might be named, a father would not be the sole personal reference while the husband lived.[14]

Sanclementi, followed by Ferrua, thought that the husband was named but that his name was not Turcius Secundus. '*Primo*' (line 3), understood as the dative of the *cognomen* Primus, was taken to identify the husband to whom Proiecta had been married.[15] Those who identify the Proiecta of the epitaph with the Proiecta of the treasure have read '*primo*' as a reference to the woman's first (and only) marriage.[16] De Rossi thought that '*fuerat primo quae*

QVID LOQVAR AVT SILEAM PROHIBET DOLOR IPSE FATERI
HIC TVMVLVS LACRIMAS RETINET COGNOSCE PARENTV̄
PROIECTAE FVERAT PRIMO QVAE IVNCTA MARITO
PVLCRA DECORE SVO SOLO CONTENTA PVDORE
HEV DILECTA SATIS MISERAE GENETRICIS AMORE   [5]
ACCIPE QVID MVLTIS THALAMI POST FOEDERA PRIMA
EREPTA EX OCVLIS FLORI GENITORIS ABIIT
AETHERIAM CVPIENS CAELI CONSCENDERE LVCEM
HAEC DAMASVS PRESTAT CVNCTIS SOLACIA FLETVS
VIXIT ANN+XVI+M IX+DIES+XXV+DEP+IIIKAL+IAN+FL+MEROBAVDES ET FL+SATVRNIN+CONSS   [10]

The consuls, Fl. Merobaudes and Fl. Saturninus, held office in AD 383 (line 10).[11] Proiecta was buried on 30 December of that year, having lived to the age of sixteen years, nine months, and twenty-five days (line 10). The epitaph states that Proiecta was a married woman (lines 3, 6) and implies that she was survived by her mother, father, and husband (lines 3, 5, 7). Roman law specified that a woman could enter into marriage at the age of twelve, so Proiecta, aged sixteen in 383, could have married in 379.[12] And the years 379 to 383 are those given to the treasure as dates within which the commissioning and giving of marriage gifts would have been appropriate. The reasoning is based on the sure knowledge that the Proiecta of the casket and the Proiecta of the epitaph were both married and on the assumptions that they were the same person and that the entire treasure consisted of wedding gifts. The conventional dates for the treasure are not derived from the silver but from the epitaph alone.

The Proiecta of the epitaph is mourned by her mother (line 5), who goes unnamed, and by her father, Florus (line 7). The contrast of named male and unnamed female parent conforms to the Roman pattern seen in the funerary inscriptions of children of any age who predecease their parents.[13] The absence of any reference to Turcius Secundus, however, does not conform to Roman practice. Inscriptions which commemorate the deaths of married persons indicate the fact of marriage, and most name surviving partners, identified by their role within the union: *uxor*, *convivia*, *coniuga*, *maritus*, *coniux*, etc. The inclusion of the title '*marito*' (line 3) but the omission of a personal name seems puzzling, especially in an inscription of the length and elaboration of the Proiecta epitaph. It is not surprising to find the father named in an epitaph for a married daughter: it is observed in other inscriptions and accords with the legal and social position of a Roman married woman. Observed convention, however, suggests that a surviving spouse had

iuncta marito', considered in combination with '*thalami post foedera prima*' (line 6), indicated that the marriage had only recently taken place. Certainly the phrase '*thalami post foedera prima . . . abiit*' (lines 6–7) conveys this impression. The allusion to the virginal state of the woman, '*solo contenta pudore*' (line 4), raises the possibility that the literal first vows of a Roman marriage—those of betrothal—might be the vows in question.[17]

A corresponding reading for '*primo . . . marito*' is difficult. As a reference of relative time, it indicates that Proiecta died after marriage to her first husband. The ordinal '*primo*' with its implicit sense of sequence actually suggests the unlikely (and superfluous) statement that Proiecta died after marriage to her first husband but before marriage to her second. Other vocabulary choices would convey the meaning 'one and only', and Latin epitaphs give the woman who had married only once the descriptive title '*univira*'.[18] They do not record the fact or number of multiple marriages for an individual, and neither first husbands nor first wives are noted as such.

In any event, it would be surprising to find Pope Damasus publicly eulogising someone 'who had been joined to [her] first husband', when the negative attitude of the early church toward second marriages was so clear. The early fathers were emphatic in favouring widowhood over remarriage in an apparent parallel to the preference given to virginity as opposed to marriage. Many, such as Ambrose, Clement, Augustine, and Gregory of Nazianzus, deplored remarriage but grudgingly tolerated it, following the teachings of Paul (1 Cor. 7:7–9). Others, such as Basil, understood remarriage as a form of bigamy or polygamy, believing that the union of the first marriage was not dissolved by the death of one of the parties.[19] Jerome, a close associate of Damasus, was severe in his rejection of remarriage, and it is possible that Damasus was as well. We know from Jerome (*Ep.* 22, 48) that Damasus wrote a treatise on virginity which Jerome approved and recommended. Knowledge that opinions on virginity and widowhood were tightly interconnected and commonly argued together in the early church allows the hypothesis that Damasus' lost tract on virginity might have contained statements on remarriage that would have pleased a Jerome.

For reasons doctrinal, philological, and epigraphic, therefore, 'Primo' seems best understood as the name of Proiecta's husband. De Rossi, who wished to combine the owner of the treasure with the subject of the epitaph, preferred his own reading but did not think the alternative incorrect.[20] The Proiecta of the epitaph remains a member of the Roman aristocracy about whom information can be recovered. It is possible to trace a history of her family following the lead given by the naming of her father, Florus. He has been discussed as the praetorian prefect of the eastern empire from 381 to 383 and as the patron of a basilica in Rome dedicated to the martyr Liberalis.[21] Both his public position of authority and his active participation in the cult of the martyrs, so closely associated with Damasus, suggest that Florus and Damasus could have known one another and that Damasus might appropriately have written the epitaph for the daughter of such a man. An intriguing but tenuous hypothesis links Damasus and Florus as uncle and nephew and thus explains Proiecta's epitaph as one of only three Damasian epigrams written for female contemporaries —all of whom may have been blood relations.[22]

The line of inquiry is fascinating but of no obvious relevance to a study of the Esquiline Treasure. Consideration of the epitaph in the context of conventions observed for Latin funerary inscriptions and in the light of Christian beliefs concerning marriage leads to the conclusion that the Proiecta of the epitaph, married at the age of sixteen and at date of death to one Primus, cannot be the Proiecta of the casket, wife of Turcius Secundus.[23] The association of these two inscriptions has furnished many generations of scholars with dates for the treasure. It has also introduced the treasure into the circle of Damasus and Filocalus and the commissions and works of art linked with their names. While an equivalent grouping of objects thought to have sympathetic affinities of style, iconography, and patronage is difficult to determine, the dating of the treasure formerly provided by the epitaph must now deduced be through the examination of other materials.

The eighteenth- and nineteenth-century scholars, while aware of the dates recorded in the epitaph, investigated the inscriptions for the primary purpose of obtaining names and identifying the families of the owners of the treasure. Their conceptions of dates for the treasure itself were vague and of obviously secondary importance. It is with the scholars of the twentieth century that the emphasis on dating grew stronger, and the fixed dates derived from the epitaph assumed an importance and an existence independent of the original search for the owners. While the conclusions of the earliest scholars must be emended, it is still possible to discuss ownership in terms of individuals, households, social positions, and religious affiliation. It is possible because of the eighteenth- and nineteenth-century fascination with and reliance on the objects in the treasure. For obvious reasons, the later scholarship interested in problems of dating drew

on the secure dates provided by the epitaph. When the epitaph is necessarily removed from consideration, the owners remain, but their chronology is open to investigation.

NOTES

1. Chastagnol, *Les fastes*, 107; Jones *et al.* (eds.), *Prosopography*, 750, 817; M. Arnheim, *The Senatorial Aristocracy in the Later Roman Empire*, Oxford (1972), 55.
2. Again the source of 1794 is the Roman ecclesiastical journal of 19 April 1794 cited by Seroux d'Agincourt; see above, p. 35, n. 11.
3. *L'Histoire*, II, 37, n.b.
4. G. B. de Rossi (ed.), *Inscriptiones christianae vrbis Romae septimo saeculo antiquiores*, 2 vols., Rome (1857–88), I, no. 329; F. Buechler (ed.), *Carmina latina epigraphica*, 2 vols., Leipzig (1895–97), I, no. 670; E. Diehl (ed.) *Inscriptiones latinae christianae veteres*, 3 vols., Berlin (1924/25–28/31), II, no. 3446; M. Ihm (ed.) *Damasi epigrammata*, Leipzig (1895), no. 53; A. Ferrua (ed.), *Epigrammata Damasiana*, Sussidi allo studio delle antichità cristiane, II, Vatican City (1942), no. 51; A. E. Gordon with J. S. Gordon, *Album of Dated Latin Inscriptions*, 4 vols., Berkeley (1958–65), III, no. 337.
5. An original location in the *coemeterium* of Priscilla, found in the writings of Sarazanius, is doubted by de Rossi who notes that the other Damasian epigram brought to S. Martino by Sergius was found in the *coemeterium ad duas lauras* off the Via Labicana (de Rossi (ed.), *Inscriptiones christianae vrbis Romae*, I, 146). The second epigram, for Gorgonius martyr: de Rossi (ed.), *Inscriptiones christianae vrbis Romae*, II, 64, 107, 437; Ihm (ed.), *Damasi epigrammata*, no. 31; Ferrua (ed.,) *Epigrammata Damasiana*, no. 32. The building programmes of the sixth and ninth centuries at S. Martino are discussed by Krautheimer *et al.*, 'S. Martino ai Monti', 90ff.
6. Early sources on their locations within the church are quoted by Ferrua, *Epigrammata Damasiana*, 165f, 201f. The two epigrams were brought from the catacombs along with other artefacts and inscriptions; Sergius decorated his church with lavish (contemporary) furnishings and, for both antiquarian and religious reasons, buried 'within it the relics of many saints taken from the catacombs' (Krautheimer *et al.*, 'S. Martino ai Monti', 90). For antiquarian attitudes and collections of inscriptions contemporary with Sergius, see A. Silvagni, *Nuovo ordinamento delle sillogi epigrafiche di Roma anteriori al secolo XI*, Dissertazioni delle Pontifiche Accademia Romana di Archeologia, ser. 2, XV (1921), 181–239; idem, 'Studio critico sopra le due sillogi medievali di iscrizioni cristiane milanesi', *Rivista di archeologia cristiana*, XV (1938), 107–22; idem, 'La silloge epigrafica di Cambridge', *Rivista di archeologia cristiana*, XX (1943), 49–112; See G. Ferretto, *Note storico-bibliographiche di archeologia cristiana*, Vatican City (1942).
7. Poglayen–Neuwall, 'Besitzer', 129; Ferrua (ed.), *Epigrammata Damasiana*, 202; Gordon, *Album*, III, 140. By the mid-nineteenth century the epitaph had been transferred to the Lateran collections, Museo di epigrafia cristiana, sect. vi, no. 34.
8. Visconti: L, 215, n. 1; Seroux d'Agincourt, *L'Histoire*, II, 37, n.b.; Sanclementi, *Numismata*, III, 206; Ferrua (ed.), *Epigrammata Damasiana*, 204.
9. The clearest statement of this logic is found in Tozzi, 'Tesoro', 286.
10. De Rossi, *Inscriptiones christianae vrbis Romae*, I, 146; those who follow de Rossi include Buechler, *Carmina latina epigraphica*, no. 670; Ihm, *Damasi Epigrammata*, no. 53; and Diehl, *Inscriptiones latinae christianae veteres*, II, no. 3446.
11. Jones *et al.* (eds.), *Prosopography*, 1045.
12. M. K. Hopkins, 'The Age of Roman Girls at Marriage', *Population Studies*, XVIII (1965), *passim*.
13. Many examples are found in *Corpus inscriptionum latinarum*, VI, 'Tituli sepulchrales et reliqui', nos. 10229–29680.
14. Ibid. The computer-generated vocabulary index for *Corpus inscriptionum latinarum*, VI, simplifies the search for comparanda. The various synonyms for husband and wife yield large numbers of epitaphs for married individuals, almost all of which conform

to the patterns discussed. It is far more difficult to work with Diehl's *Inscriptiones latinae christianae veteres*: there is no general index, and the categories whereby inscriptions are organised are neither exhaustive nor cross-referenced. Part II, section XXXIII (nos. 4214–55), where the terms *maritus*, *uxor*, etc. are referenced, does not, for example, include the Proiecta epitaph. (It is catalogued with references to '*lux aeterna*'.) This section includes only those inscriptions which contain the formula '*qui vixit annos* (number of years) *cum marito*' and its variations. The inscriptions organised by social class, titles, and professions (Pt I) provide a better, although random, selection. See also Pt II, sect. XXXI, '*Nomine defuncti et dedicantis*' (nos. 4039–4145).

15. Sanclementi, *Numismata*, III, 207; Ferrua (ed.), *Epigrammata Damasiana*, 204; Gordon, *Album*, III, 141. Gordon is emphatic if brief: 'Ferrua is undoubtedly right in taking Primo as the husband's name.'

16. 'First': de Rossi (ed.), *Inscriptiones christianae vrbis Romae*, I, 146 (for those who follow de Rossi, see note 10 above). 'First and only': Poglayen–Neuwall, '*Besitzer*', 129f; Buschhausen, *Metallscrinia*, 214.

17. Corbett, *Marriage*, 1ff; Berger, *Oxford Classical Dictionary*, s.v. '*sponsalia*'.

18. O. Marruchi, *Christian Epigraphy*, trans. J. A. Willis, Cambridge (1912), 12. The vocabulary index for *Corpus inscriptionum latinarum*, VI, indicates its use.

19. L. Godefroy, '*Le marriage au temps des pères*', *Dictionnaire de théologie catholique*, A. Vacant, E. Mangenot, and E. Amann (eds.), 15 vols. in 24, Paris (1909–50), IX, pt 2, 2077–123, esp. 2096ff. For the influence of Christian teachings on Roman marriage law, see A. L. Ballini, *Il valore giuridico della celebrazione nuziale cristiana dal primo secolo all'età giustinianea*, Pubblicazione dell'Università Cattolica del Sacro Cuore, ser. 2: Scienze giuridiche, LXIV, Milan (1939).

20. De Rossi (ed.), *Inscriptiones christianae vrbis Romae*, I, 146.

21. Ibid.; Marruchi, *Epigraphy*, 408ff; Diehl (ed.), *Inscriptiones latinae christianae veteres*, I, nos. 56, 57; Ferrua (ed.), *Epigrammata Damasiana*, 202; Jones *et al.* (ed.), *Prosopography*, s.v. 'Florus'.

22. Marruchi, *Epigraphy*, 362ff; idem, *Il pontificato del papa Damaso e la storia della sua famiglia*, Rome (1905), *passim*.

23. It might be argued that Turcius Secundus was the first husband of Proiecta, and Primus her second. The Damasian epitaph, far from indicating multiple marriages, implies a virginal state for Proiecta, the wife of Primus.

Observations of Style

In the literature on the Esquiline Treasure, dating has always been discussed in relation to style, but both dating and style have been dependent on the theories of ownership. The early scholars debating generations within the *gens* Turcia entertained dates ranging from the late third to the sixth century; Visconti mentioned the Proiecta of the Damasian epitaph with an emphasis equivalent to that given to a Proiecta recorded as the niece of the emperor Justinian. A concept of styles corresponding to specific points or periods of time does not appear to have been of prime importance. Many, like Visconti, entertained a general date in the fourth or fifth century because they favoured various owners whose dates accorded with that period.[1] At the time that the Damasian epitaph was accepted as proof of Christian ownership and a source of exact dates, art historical perspective had changed only slightly. The later scholars assumed a late fourth-century treasure to match their late fourth-century patrons and proceeded to investigate the origins of the style as though a general understanding of its character were given.[2] Both earlier and later groups of scholars understood the treasure to be a stylistic unit for which a single date would be appropriate. They spoke of *a* style, assuming there was but one which encompassed all, or almost all, the objects in the find. The two groups agreed in a general, vague definition of this style but differed as to its significance in an understanding of the treasure.

Scholars of both groups discussed the arts of the late empire as demonstrating a progressive deterioration of formal considerations, iconographic expression, artistic creativity, and technique. Many, however, pointed out that the Esquiline Treasure marked a singular if temporary arrest in this progression:

> ... *on peut conclure que ... non seulement ils* [Proiecta and Secundus] *employaient les meilleurs artistes contemporains, mais qu'ils avaient assez goût pour acquérir et destiner à leur usage, des objets exécutés avec la grace et la perfection qui charactérisent une époque de l'Art antérieur au siècle où ils ont vécu.*[3]

All agreed that the treasure demonstrated the continuation of what they termed hellenistic art: 'The tradition of earlier and better art may be recognised in the principal compositions'.[4] Eighteenth- and nineteenth-century scholars saw the treasure as marking a point in a linear progression from classical art to '*la seguente barbarie*'; it was a point variously described as being at the root of or just before the '*total decadenza d'arte che i monumenti de'seguenti secoli ci dimostrano*'.[5] Their dates for the treasure and for the eclipse of '*total decadenza*' varied with their dates for the patrons. The style in question was not characterised descriptively either in terms of the morphology of objects or details of their decoration. In retrospect, it was a style which was discussed for its transitional character. It stood between the good or classical style and the bad or barbaric and was fittingly referred to as '*non dispregevole mediocrità*'.[6]

The twentieth-century scholars of the treasure agreed with this general evaluation of the style but specified its origins: it was the result of eastern influences. These scholars, writing in the 1930s, were relatively more precise in their observations. Terms such as Roman, understood as late hellenistic, and oriental, understood as a mixture of iconographic, technical, and stylistic details, were used with little further clarification. What was clear was the positive connotation attached to things Roman and the negative attached to things oriental, a departure from the art historical conceptions of the 1920s.[7] These later scholars of the treasure did not wish to distinguish between the schools of Antioch and Alexandria, centres championed by their immediate predecessors. They did not think that the bulk of the treasure actually originated in an eastern workshop, although they did assign the objects with Greek inscriptions to Constantinople and certain other pieces to a '*byzantinischen Kunstkreis*'.[8] On the whole, they understood that the find site of the treasure indicated a western origin for most of the pieces and saw the eastern influences as indicative of *émigré* artists in the West or contact with imported goods from the generically labelled East. The indirect contact with eastern art was seen as resulting in any number of specific details: the use of stippling, gilding, and engraved ornament found on many objects in the treasure; the overall forms of the two caskets; the stocky proportions of the Erotes; the elongated proportions of the Venus figures; and the representation of curtained arcades, a domed building, and dalmatic costumes on the Proiecta casket. Eastern influences were also discussed as introducing abstract principles, specifically symmetry, at the expense of observed reality.[9]

Like the scholars of the nineteenth century, those of the twentieth understood certain pieces in the treasure to be earlier and less debased—the Paris patera and the Naples ewer (*nos. 3 and 18)—and some later and more debased—the eight plates with monograms (*nos. 5–12). These were judgements of quality relative to a general conception of the treasure. Those pieces whose workmanship was judged more or less adept than the core of the treasure were given dates correspondingly earlier or later. A certain uniformity of style and workmanship was clearly assumed for the majority of the pieces, and those which did not conform were explained as heirlooms or subsequent additions.

The conceptions of ownership must now be reconsidered, and the date, once thought secure, is no longer so. Dates cannot be derived from the patrons, for too little is known to fix them in time. In a reverse of the earlier pattern, dates for the patrons are necessarily dependent on observations of style and iconography within the treasure which allow individual objects or groups of objects to be placed in a relative chronology of art in the late antique period. The resultant dates are broad and imprecise, for the materials which can be adduced for comparison are themselves dated to general periods rather than to specific years. The loss of the Damasian dates has a positive side, however: the precise chronological reference must be surrendered, but so must any necessity to understand the collection as commissioned or purchased and presented within a tight, four-year period. The possibility remains that the treasure consists of pieces that are roughly contemporary, made within a limited period of time, but this must be demonstrated. The assumption of earlier literature that the collection conforms to a single style must be examined as well.

The evidence of the treasure is emphatic on the latter point. Within the twenty-seven pieces of the original find, several styles of decoration can be observed, each with a specific vocabulary of ornamental motifs. It is remarkable that the earlier scholars were able to conceive of the collection conforming to a single style while they worked with a corpus of sixty-one objects. The multiple styles of the treasure according to the logic of the previous literature would correspond to various dates, (foreign) influences, and different owners. The modern art historical expectation and acceptance of multiple, contemporary stylistic modes would allow for divisions based on style without requiring chronological or geographical factors for their explanation. It is possible to argue the contemporary dating of stylistically divergent works and to account for the bulk of the treasure as a heterogeneous but interrelated group. And the characterisation of the styles within the treasure is the necessary first step.

The observation of several different styles within the treasure results from the briefest review of its contents and is, to be more precise, a reaction to various definitions and uses of decorative ornament. Analysis of style in silver plate must, however, also include discussion of both the decoration and the general morphology of the objects. Art historical discussions of style in the decorative arts often dwell on the specifics of the surface ornament, especially on the representations of human figures where they occur, as though independent paintings, relief panels, and sculptures were the subject of analysis. The previous literature on the treasure is typical in this regard, discussing the proportional types of various figures, architectural backgrounds, and costume details. A few comments were made about the use of gilding, engraving, and stippling, but these techniques were simply labelled as eastern. Also eastern were the shapes of the two caskets, as though the geographical indication were sufficient characterisation. If these last comments were inaccurate and abbreviated, their area of concern was a valid one, for the shapes of the objects and their techniques of execution do indicate something of their stylistic relations and therefore their chronological references.

The observation of ornament on the Esquiline silver is informative but misleading in isolation, for if the decorations suggest multiple styles, the morphology of the pieces demonstrates a single underlying approach towards vessel design. By far the majority of the objects in the treasure can be seen to conform to a general taste for bold, angular geometric shapes, often combined to create complex polygonal forms. This is a fashion which has been noted as one

line of development in the silver plate of the fourth and fifth centuries.[10] Examples during this period include conical drinking-cups, six-sided pyxides, eight-sided jugs, hemispherical bowls with triangular rims, square, rectangular, and octagonal plates, and all manner of vessels with regularly faceted and/or fluted surfaces. Within the Esquiline Treasure, variations on this style are worked through the combinations of vessel forms and ornament; the major divisions are observed in the nature, degree, and position of decoration on the surfaces of these angular objects.

The Pelegrina ewer (*no. 17, pl. 31) is a clear example of the taste for polygonal forms. The body of the ewer is composed of seventeen broad facets which break at angles to form the foot and to define the shoulder and neck mouldings of the vessel. The spout is triangular in section, and the arching handle is faceted. The spare decoration of the piece allows an immediate perception of its planes and component parts. Less obvious examples of this style are found in the ornament-covered forms of both the Proiecta and Muse caskets (*nos. 1, 2). The plain, angular flask and canisters held within the Muse casket (pl. 17) are clearly fashioned to a style similar to that seen in the Pelegrina ewer, but the two caskets are also composed of bold geometric surfaces combined to create angular solids. The Proiecta casket (pls. 1–3) is composed of two truncated, rectangular pyramids with a broad, horizontal rim marking the division between lid and body. The Muse casket (pls. 12–16) is sixteen-sided with panels on both domed lid and body alternating flat and concave surfaces. Like the Proiecta casket, the Muse casket is divided with a broad horizontal flange whose moulding echoes the changing arcs and angles of the body.

The presence of this type of vessel design, as a style shared by both the simple and the heavily decorated objects in the treasure, is clearly illustrated by the close morphological relationship of the Muse casket and the large fluted dish (*no. 4, pl. 22; see pl. 16). However different their decorations, both pieces are composed of broad flat and fluted panels radiating from central medallions. The Muse casket medallion forms the top of its domed lid, while the dish medallion is centred on the bottom interior surface of that piece. Both objects consist of panels with alternating flat and concave surfaces which correspond in turn to alternating systems of decoration. A comparison of the fluted dish and the lid of the Muse casket reveals almost identical designs of polished flutes contrasting with planes covered with decorative motifs. The observation of these general forms shows the dome to be the inverse of the dish.

This taste for geometric forms in abrupt combinations is seen on a smaller scale in the design of the horse trappings (*nos. 36–41, pl. 46) where the clean outlines of the alternating circles and double peltae are emphasised by chased borders and punctuated with open-work. The tear-drop pendants of the trappings are simple, smooth, curved surfaces which contrast with the angled planes of the crescent pendants. Even the Paris patera (*no. 3, pl. 21) seems affected by this taste for defined surfaces and discrete component parts. Unlike the fluted Muse casket and dish, the faceted ewer, and the trapezoidal Proiecta casket, the patera belongs to a large family of objects whose basic design can be illustrated in a sequence dating from the Roman republic.

In contrast to earlier paterae, however, the piece in the Esquiline Treasure has a relatively broad horizontal rim attached to the bowl and decorated in relief as a distinct framing element. In addition, the handle of the patera joins the rim without the benefit of the transitional scrolls and curves which ease the junction of the handle and bowl in almost all earlier examples. The curvilinear terminals often seen on handles are replaced on the Esquiline patera by a blunt end.[11] Certainly, the traditional patera type can be recognised in this vessel, but the individual parts and the relations between them have been reinterpreted in the light of a style dating to the late empire.

The curving surfaces of the round monogram dishes (*nos. 5–8; see pl. 26) relate to other pieces in the treasure, not through observations of complex angular forms but of simple, cleanly defined, geometric shapes with crisply faceted rims. Their rectangular companion pieces (*nos. 9–12; see pl. 27) demonstrate the choice of an angular form for a function usually served by a circular format, and their bold horizontal flanges give another example of the taste for discrete component parts. The plates, the patera, the horse trappings, the fluted dish, the two caskets, and the ewer can all be understood as variations of a single approach towards vessel design.

There are exceptions within the treasure, but this style of geometric shapes and angular vessel forms defines the majority. Ironically, the single style observed by previous scholars resulted from an analysis not of forms but of surface decoration. This was their primary concern and only criterion in the evaluation of style. Observations of surface decoration do support a general late antique date for the Esquiline silver plate, but they also demonstrate several basic divisions within the treasure. The contrasts of decoration mentioned earlier between ewer and caskets and caskets and fluted dish give an indication of the possible divergences within a single style based on ornament. The decoration of the objects can be studied according to the techniques employed. The resultant divisions of pieces ornamented with niello inlay, pieces with engraved or chased designs, and those characterised by relief decoration, both cast and repoussé, are obvious and of limited analytical use. Technical details such as gilding cut across all three divisions, while others, such as stippling, occur only in distinct sub-groups (for example, objects with repoussé relief ornament). It seems more profitable to group objects according to the different combinations of form and ornament, in order to pursue the relations between the vessel design, which remains constant, and the surface decoration, which introduces a limited range of variables. Three major categories result: the two most obvious are apparent opposites, and the third can be seen as an intermediate.

One group of objects demonstrates a taste for largely undecorated, highly polished surfaces—silver for silver's sake. In this group, exemplified by the Pelegrina ewer (pl. 31) and the monogram plates (see pls. 26–7), angles, abrupt junctures of planes of contrasting curvatures, and shining surfaces act as form and decoration at the same time. Representational ornament occurs on these surfaces, but its use is limited and its forms are highly stylised. It is in this group that the abstract forms of individual letters and monograms are employed as ornament. The wreaths which surround the monograms on the eight plates (see pls. 26–7) are recognisable as such but are simultaneously understood as linear patterns. These decorative motifs are executed in niello inlay and gilding, resulting in sharply defined, brightly coloured ornaments which, despite their boldness, do not physically interrupt the smooth surfaces on which they are displayed. The horizontal borders of the rectangular monogram plates (see pl. 27) are pierced with simple pelta shapes lightly outlined with chased grooves. This open-work, in which polished surfaces are juxtaposed with dark voids, like the niello inlay, is an obvious negation of sculptural decoration. These ornaments have no immediate, three-dimensional boundaries, in contrast to other groups of objects in the treasure in which elaborate framing devices are employed. The black and gold forms set the decorative motifs apart from the silver surfaces which surround them. The visual distinction is sharp, the silver is enlivened by the introduction of colour contrast, and the planes of the objects are emphasised by decorative details which conform to the surfaces of the vessels. It is as though, by restricting decoration to two dimensions, the sculptural effects traditionally associated with silver plate are expressed by the geometric forms of the pieces themselves.

In marked contrast is a second style of decoration observed within the larger group of polygonal objects; it is characterised by the use of sculptural ornament on almost every surface. The prime example is the Proiecta casket with its four different border designs and four different figural 'scenes' distributed over nine relief panels (pls. 1–6, 8–9). It can be grouped with the Paris patera (pl. 21) and the Muse casket (pls. 12–16), although the three objects differ from one another in details and degrees of ornamentation. All are defined by decoration dominated by figural representations in relief. The figures are represented in spatial contexts with various levels of relief indicating, however summarily, the relationships of figures to one another and to their backgrounds. Raised borders are also characteristic of the group. The border designs are stylised by simplification and repetition, but they are all derived from the realm of naturalistic representation and appear to retain some of their original associations. A clear example is the generalised leaf-garland which is used as a framing device on both caskets and which appears on the top panel of the Proiecta casket as a proper wreath, tied with a ribbon and supported by two flanking figures (pl. 4).

Within a given framed panel, figural composition on these pieces is characterised by a filling of the available space either by the extension of limbs and draperies and the elaboration of architectural backgrounds as seen in the two caskets (see pls. 4, 6, 8), or by the enlargement of a texturally interesting attribute such as the shell in the bowl of the patera (pl. 21). The framing devices are broad and emphatically sculptural; they appear not to separate panel from panel but to unite them in an unbroken relief surface. All three pieces in this style also employ chased and engraved ornament with the result that the broad sculptural decoration in relief is enhanced by surface textures supplied through engraved and stippled details. The patera is the most conservative of the three with incised line and punch-work limited to details of jewellery, feathers, and hair, thus serving strictly within a representational framework. The Muse and Proiecta caskets are characterised by lavish use of these techniques for both the detailing of representational forms and for the general embellishment of relief surfaces (see pls. 10–11). The Proiecta casket adds the technique of gilding as another, primarily optical, decoration which enhances and competes with the sculptural forms. The inscription on the Proiecta casket rim is not picked out with gilding as are the closely related monograms on the eight rectangular and circular plates. The abstract, planar decoration associated with the first style seems to have been played down in the context of the casket, an emphatic example of the second style of plastic surface decoration. The overall taste for contrasts of colour and texture coupled with the sculptural character of the reliefs and their framing devices defines an exuberant style, as rich as the first style is austere.

The third or intermediate group is characterised by the use of areas of plain, highly polished silver in juxtaposition with areas covered with ornament. It can be defined as a hybrid or variant of the first two styles. The techniques of execution, the motifs represented, and the surface details differ from object to object, but the general decorative effect is uniform. The purposeful contrast of surface textures can be seen on a circular plaque from the horse trappings (pl. 46) where a lion's head, a sculptural form in high relief covered with incised lines to indicate texture, is juxtaposed with the smooth chased border which defines its outer edge. The plaque, in turn, contrasts with its neighbour in which a small gilded quatrefoil is centred with a plain silver field, outlined with a simple gilded groove and punctuated with pierced work. A final contrast of surfaces is supplied by the polished planes of the pendants on each horse trapping.

Perhaps the most obvious example of this hybrid style is the large fluted dish (pl. 22) in which plain flutes alternate with panels filled with curvilinear chased designs. Less immediately obvious as an example is the dome of the Muse casket (pl. 16). The body of the casket clearly belongs to the style of decoration seen on the Proiecta casket. But the lid of the Muse casket conforms to a taste for highly polished surfaces in its plain flutes in contrast with lavish ornament in its curving panels covered with inhabited vine scrolls. The Muse casket as a whole, considering both lid and body, combines two different approaches to surface decoration, which are used separately to define individual objects in the treasure. This combination in a single object causes a blurring of the divisions between the decorative styles, demonstrates their temporal and physical coexistence, and suggests their possible interrelation. The evidence of the Esquiline pieces indicates that the three decorative styles existed independently of one another, but that the different relations of form and decoration which they represent were not considered antithetical within the late antique taste for geometrically based, angular forms.

While most of the items in the treasure—nineteen of the twenty-seven pieces—conform to one style of vessel design and three styles of decoration, exceptions do exist. Two pieces in particular, the Naples ewer and the flask with Erotes (*nos. 18, 16; pls. 32, 30), are distinguished by virtue of their swelling contours and smooth transitions from foot

to body and body to neck, treated as three-dimensional, undulating curves. The decorative concepts of these two pieces are complementary to their forms. The spiralling relief of the flask (pl. 30), while confined to the body, expands and contracts with the contours of the vessel. The anthropomorphic treatment of the Naples ewer (pl. 32) results in a piece whose rounded body is translated into a female face, with a curving neck for the foot of the vessel and a fanciful head-dress for the spout. There are parallels for the Naples ewer in ancient ceramics and glass, but no examples which might indicate a specific date within the Roman period. In contrast, the Esquiline flask conforms to a jug/flask type well documented in the fourth and fifth centuries.[12]

Six other pieces, the two sets of furniture fittings, are not easily discussed in terms of the morphology observed for the majority of the treasure, and yet their decorations show them to be clearly related. In the case of both the arm ornaments (*nos. 34, 35) and the Tyche fittings (*nos. 30–3) it is difficult to follow the division of form and decoration observed in the analysis of the other pieces. The arm ornaments (pls. 44–5) are the arms of a chair: their tubular, right-angle design possibly dictated by the object to which they were attached. The Tyches (pls. 35–43) are conceived as statuettes. The relationships of the six to the main objects of the treasure are none the less clear. The abrupt junctures of the cylinders, the precise fluting of the orbs, and the stylised, radially symmetrical floral finials link the arm ornaments to the aesthetics of the geometrically conceived, angular forms. The abstract curves of the hands and fingers, in combination with the plain, polished, partly gilt surfaces, suggest an association with the first decorative style. The Tyches, with their plastic surfaces covered with stippling and punch-work and divided into areas of silver and gilding, seem to be the figural decorations of the panels of the Proiecta casket translated into three-dimensional sculpture. Close relations of figural types are shared by casket and Tyches, but there is also a more general, basic relationship in decorative approach. The two sets of fittings can thus be comfortably paired with two of the styles of decoration observed in the treasure.

The large group of nineteen objects related by a single approach to problems of form, and a group of twenty-five interrelated by three styles of ornamentation establish the treasure as a complex but coherent grouping. With only the knowledge that the geometric/polygonal style was one of several distinct styles in late antique silver, the pieces of the Esquiline Treasure appear to be a more conscious collection than is immediately apparent. It is difficult, nevertheless, to discuss the treasure as reflecting the specific taste of a single patron. The analysis of objects whereby a single underlying attitude towards vessel design is revealed is, after all, an academic exercise, however profitable. The objects themselves are design and decoration simultaneously, and, as such, they reflect several different tastes or styles. The stylistic relationships observed obviously do exist, however, among apparently diverse objects. If a single discerning patron is too simple an explanation for a set of complex interrelations, the hypothesis of a common workshop should be considered.

NOTES

1. Visconti: M–M, 3; Visconti: L, 215, n. 1; Seroux d'Agincourt, *L'Histoire*, II, 37, n.b.; Böttiger, *Sabina*, 62f; du Sommerard, *Les arts*, II, 139, n. 1; Newton, *Blacas Collection*, 24; Dalton, *Catalogue*, 61.
2. Poglayen–Neuwall, '*Besitzer*', and Tozzi, '*Tesoro*', *passim*.
3. Seroux d'Agincourt, *L'Histoire*, II, 39.
4. Newton, *Blacas Collection*, 27. A similar comment is found in Gardner, 'Countries and Cities in Ancient Art', *Journal of Hellenic Studies*, IX (1888), 77: '[the Tyches], as might be expected from the age of their production [are] poor, yet there are about them traditions of great beauty'.
5. Visconti: M–M, 6, 15.
6. Ibid., 15.
7. Prominent among the relevant scholars of the 1920s were L. Bréhier ('*Les trésors d'argenterie syrienne et l'école artistique d'Antioche*', *Gazette des beaux arts*, ser. 5, I, 1920, *passim*) and C. Diehl ('*L'Ecole artistique d'Antioche et les trésors d'argenterie syrienne*', *Syria*, II, 1921, *passim*). Dalton's later writings reflect a similar approach (*Early Christian Art*, Oxford, 1925, 326ff). For an early critique of this school see Poglayen–Neuwall's review of the Bréhier and Diehl articles in the *Byzantinisch-neugriechische Jahrbücher*, II (1921), 474–8.
8. Poglayen–Neuwall, '*Besitzer*', 132ff. The objects with Greek inscriptions are nos. 29, 59, and 60. Those given to the Byzantine sphere are *nos. 4 and 17 and no. 13.
9. Poglayen–Neuwall, '*Besitzer*', 135f; Tozzi, '*Tesoro*', 287f. Eastern influence and the symmetry which it introduced thus explained the discrepancies between the representation and the textual references of the *donum deductio*.
10. Strong, *Silver Plate*, 182 209. Strong must be consulted with caution in this period as he derives many of his general observations from the Esquiline pieces, including those which can no longer be considered part of the original find.
11. Strong, *Silver Plate*, 146. Note the diagram of patera handles; the Esquiline example is fig. 230, 1.
12. See Strong, *Silver Plate*, 188ff, fig. 37a, for comparisons for the flask.

The Esquiline Workshop

Silver workshops are well attested in ancient Rome. The large number of extant inscriptions which concern jewellery and plate has led some scholars to postulate that the city was an important centre for the production of artefacts in precious metals.[1] Indeed, while work done for specific commissions and sales transacted in the private homes of buyers (*Dig*. 19, 2, 31 and 19, 5, 20, 2) could take place in any city, in Rome certain streets and public buildings near the fora were apparently given over to the trade in silver.[2] Its manufacture may have been the work of slaves in the households of the very wealthy. At the opposite end of the spectrum, Pliny's references to *officinae* producing different styles of silver (*H.N.* 33, 139) have been interpreted to indicate that some silver plate was manufactured by freedmen and slaves in large factories.[3] Certainly, factories for the production of a limited number of goods are known in the late empire, but most historians of the ancient world stress the importance of small units of production throughout the Graeco-Roman period.[4] The owners of such shops could rise to great wealth and their enterprises swell to some size: a certain Fulvius, a maker of silver plate, listed on his tombstone the names of nineteen freedmen and women thought to have been craftsmen in his employ.[5]

Silver for a given vessel might be supplied by the customer (*Dig*. 19, 2, 31), or the prosperous owner of a shop could purchase refined silver himself from either independent mining contractors or state offices, although by the late empire this trade may have been controlled in large part by the government. Imperial silver stamps of the fifth, sixth, and seventh centuries clearly indicate that the processing and quality control of some silver for plate was supervised at that date by officials in the imperial bureacracy. The silver thus certified might be worked in either private or government workshops. Simple stamps which indicate a city of origin and certain decorative devices and inscriptions found on a few pieces of fourth-century silver suggest state control at an earlier date and the association of the manufacture of silver plate with the activities of the imperial mints—an association certainly supported by the evidence of the later stamps. Scholars have been quick to point out, nevertheless, that large numbers of unstamped silver vessels, datable to the fourth century but also to the fifth, sixth, and seventh, indicate the continuing efforts of private craftsmen and workshops even as state regulation appears to have increased.[6]

The Esquiline pieces are among the hundreds which do not bear stamps. Stamped pieces, however, give some evidence of workshop practice which helps in an understanding of the production of both stamped and unstamped objects. The placing of stamps on silver vessels and the relations of those stamps to surface decorations and to the final forms of finished pieces make it clear that stamps were applied after the silver had been cut out and only partially formed. The crude vessel shapes were then sold to private customers or finished in imperial ateliers. The stamps therefore provide material evidence of certain steps in the process and an accompanying division of labour in the manufacture of silver plate.[7]

Inscriptions identify by trade craftsmen who were *caelatores, tritores, toreuticenses, flaturarii, crustarii, auri nextrices, barbaricarii, inauratores*, and *aurifices brattiarii*, in addition to the general categories of *argentarii* and *vascularii*.[8] Clearly the presence of stamps cannot alone indicate a division of labour into such specialised tasks. Surviving silver plate does, however, bear witness to all the techniques in question, and single vessels often show a combination of four or five. Far more important, perhaps, ancient sources indicate that, while the concept and practice of division of labour may have been restricted to urban areas in the ancient world, it did exist and was thought to result in goods of the highest quality.[9]

Within the Esquiline Treasure, within the group of twenty-five objects which conform to the morphological and decorative styles previously discussed, it is possible to observe interrelations suggestive of a single workshop for many of the pieces. The identification of a workshop with its many craftsmen is a process different from the establishment of the *œuvre* of a single artist, although it is comparable to the definition of an artistic school. It might be hypothesised that the products of a single workshop would share similar materials, techniques of manufacture and decoration, a stock selection of fittings, a common vocabulary of forms and ornamental motifs, and perhaps a defined iconographic repertory, although the last is often presumed to be an area of interaction between patron and craftsman. In practice, ancient silver treasures present fragmentary evidence of workshop techniques. At best, the treasures represent a very small percentage of the products of any given workshop, and even the large treasures often cannot be expected or analysed to contain more than a handful of related objects.[10] The Esquiline Treasure may be a partial exception: the numbers involved are relatively small, but the interrelations are persuasive. The hypothesis of a common workshop for many of its pieces is based on the observation of specific details shared by many objects in the treasure.

The Proiecta casket (pls. 1–11) is an admirable introduction to the investigation and to the nature of workshop practice. The piece is generally well preserved with few and obvious restorations. Lid, body, hinge fittings, and handles were all found together, although the size and shape of the two main pieces would allow them to be matched even if separated.[11] The casket exhibits a polygonal form and rich decorative style seen in other pieces of the treasure, and yet, analysed in detail, it presents certain anomalies. For this very reason, the secure knowledge of its original state is of great importance. It is a complex object whose various component parts, and the motifs and styles they carry, can be assumed to originate in a single workshop.

Lid and body share a distinct form, a general style of decoration and techniques of repoussé relief with elaborate surface detail. Such basic observations demonstrate a coherent, overall design which would result from consistent workshop practice, while differences in hands are clearly visible in the representations of individual figures and whole relief panels. The decorative framework of raised borders surrounding relief panels was obviously planned as a whole, as was the alignment of the two toilet scenes of the casket lid and body (pls. 2, 11), the alignment of the top portrait panel with the two toilet scenes (pl. 4), and the significant omission of gilding from the back panels of both body and lid. All this speaks of a master plan, while details of execution indicate a division of labour. The choice of vine-scroll frames for the body of the casket and garlands for the lid might suggest a simple division into two halves. The toilet and procession of attendants depicted on the body of the casket are clearly the work of one hand, seen in the uniformity of drapery style, figural type, and physiognomy, even when the oversize figure of the main actor is considered (pls. 8–9). The figural representations of the lid, however, are far less uniform. There is a certain identity of physiognomy which links casket lid and body, but the proportional types of the lid are many. A maximum of three hands might be inferred for the lid: one for the portraits (pl. 4), one for the sea *thiasos* cum toilet (pls. 4–5), and one for the procession on the back panel (pl. 6). The minimum would be one craftsman working from three different models or in three different styles.

A further division of labour within a workshop might involve one or two craftsmen working solely on the decorative borders and an ordinator/engraver on the inscription of the casket rim. Certainly the solid-cast feet, hinges, handles, and soldering plates represent another effort, and the position and decoration of these fittings suggest the work of artisans other than those responsible for the repoussé reliefs. The handles are faceted and fluted, as are their ring mounts (pls. 8–9). The handles are simple but cleanly executed, in contrast to the surface decorations of their soldering plates which feature crudely engraved patterns resembling the veins of a leaf. The three hinges which attach lid to body are also engraved and chased, but their workmanship is precise (pl. 7). The overall geometric grid or diaper pattern incised on their surfaces is a marked contrast to the relief representations of figures, animals, and architecture which characterise the decorative panels of the casket.

More surprisingly, these fittings appear to have been applied with minimal regard for the relief ornament they obscure. The arc of the swing handles and the position of their ring mounts coincide with broad openings in the arcade on the short end panels of the casket body (pls. 8–9). The mounts are soldered directly on to the raised surfaces of twisted columns; the ring mounts rise to block parts of Corinthian capitals. Raised, the handles conceal the representation of rounded arches; lowered, they swing before standing figures. The hinges of the casket overlap the plain horizontal flange of the lid (pls. 6–7). On the back panel of

the body (pl. 9), however, the lower half of each hinge is soldered directly over an arch in the arcade on the body of the casket, obscuring both hanging curtains and the head of a female attendant beneath each arch. The result is awkward, but it must have been acceptable to the designers and artisans of the casket.

Thus in one securely documented piece there is evidence of a division of labour among a number of craftsmen and of the combination of different styles, techniques, and motifs. Certain details, such as the decoration of the hinges and their position, even appear discordant. While no other single object in the treasure can match the number and combination of the parts of the Proiecta casket, the eclectic character which it exhibits might be expected in other pieces and perhaps in the workshop as a whole. Certainly, single features of the Proiecta casket are repeated in diverse contexts within the treasure, and it is just this heterogeneous mixture and repetition of fittings, styles, techniques, and motifs which indicate a common workshop origin for many of the objects in the treasure.

It is quite easy, following the lesson of the Proiecta casket, to note the resemblance of the Muse casket (pls. 12–16), not only in general design and decorative style but also in detail. The garland borders which define broad areas of the Muse casket match those of the Proiecta casket in type, technique, and relative scale. The hinges of the caskets are identical, as are the soldering plates, down to details of their crude decoration. And the fittings of both are applied with equal finesse (see pl. 14). The figures under arcades common to the two caskets do not simply repeat a classical scheme; they share a simple drapery style and general figural type, including details of posture and physiognomy. All nine figures on the Muse casket (pls. 12–16) appear to be the work of one hand, most closely related to that seen in the bath procession on the back panel of the Proiecta casket lid (pl. 6). It seems a simple proposition that a single artisan might have been involved in the production of two pieces made in the same shop. Certainly the fittings for both caskets were supplied from the same source. Perhaps, however, the observed relations of figural style might be more cautiously understood as individual renderings of the same figural model—the standard model for that workshop.

The Proiecta casket figures, the work of as many as four hands (one for the body, three for the lid), and the Muse casket figures, probably the work of one, are strikingly similar. The figures are stocky with short necks, prominent bellies, relatively long torsos, and short legs. They have long, full faces with small foreheads, long, prominent noses and long upper lips, small mouths, close-set eyes, and broad cheeks. They are consistently represented in three-quarter views with garments modelled in soft curves in relief which correspond to shoulders, breasts, thighs, and other parts of the body understood as simple, rounded volumes. Drapery folds are indicated by patterns of engraved lines which most frequently echo the contours of the areas raised in relief. Drapery surfaces are stippled to indicate decorated hems, cuffs, and *clavi* on simple, long-sleeved tunics only occasionally varied by the addition of a mantle. This figural and facial type found on the two caskets is repeated in the four Tyche figures of the treasure (pls. 35–43) with slightly more elongated proportions. The draperies of the Tyches are plastically rendered, but it is as though the linear patterns of the casket reliefs were translated into three-dimensional sculptural passages.

The nudes of the Proiecta casket (pls. 4–5, 11) repeat the type established in the draped figures. The faces and the body proportions remain the same, but any sense of weight or volume and of the organic articulation of the body is removed with the clothing. The nudes appear hollow and inflated. The apparent proportions of the draped figures are translated into awkward representations of anatomy. The legs are short and stumpy; the lower torsos long and broad; the upper torsos narrow; and the arms long and rubbery. There is no sense of muscle or bone. The contrast offered by the Venus of the Paris patera (pl. 21) is striking in this regard, and the contrast helps to draw the definition and the boundaries of the Esquiline workshop style more clearly. The iconographic type of the Paris Venus, small breasted and heavy hipped, is the same as that of the casket Venus and Nereids. The proportional type, however, is distinct, with short torso and long legs, and the visual impression is one of solid forms of considerable weight. The Paris Venus stands apart from the figural style of the shop that characterises the caskets and Tyches, although the awkward understanding of her body, particularly in the breasts and shoulders, shows the Venus to be as obviously late antique as the vessel it decorates. Its forms recall the description of one style in the mid-fourth century, characterised by 'the importance of rounded lines and coherent forms, though clearly on a[n] . . . inorganic, non-classical basis'.[12]

The general conception of all the Esquiline figures, Muses, servants, Nereids, and Venuses, points to a late date. The uniformity of type observed for the two caskets and four Tyches, however, allows those six pieces to be securely grouped together. There is no question of a single hand: the relations are close, but not that close. While the figures of a single piece such as the Muse casket may be the work of one man, all six pieces, as finished products, represent the collaboration of many artisans in figures, frames, fittings, engraving and gilding. The resemblances among the six pieces suggest decorative motifs and figural types common to a workshop, seen through the productions of various contributing craftsmen-members.

It is possible to continue the chain by following other details, linking the inscription of the Proiecta casket (fig. 12, pl. 4) with the monograms found on the eight serving-plates (fig. 13; see pls. 26–7). It is an obvious relationship previously discussed and reinforced by the appearance on both the Muse casket and the round monogram plates of an eight-sided faceted and fluted wire of identical dimensions. A half-section of the wire forms a prominent convex moulding on the round plates (see pl. 26) and it functions as the ring from which the Muse casket is suspended (pls. 13, 17). The wire reappears as the handle of the Pelegrina ewer (pl. 31), which is linked in more general terms with the aesthetic of the monogram plates. Interestingly, the handle of the ewer terminates in a soldering plate crudely engraved to resemble a leaf—a detail shared by both caskets.

The clear connection of casket inscription and monograms brings together objects of radically different decorative styles. The visual shock of the combination, however, is no greater than that evoked by the juxtaposition of inscription, relief panels, handles, and hinges on the Proiecta casket itself. The casket teaches a singular lesson: its execution demonstrates the co-operation of artisans of different talents and tastes. The work of the ordinator of the casket inscription can be seen in the eight monogram plates where it is combined with the efforts of still other craftsmen. Certainly, it would be an over-interpretation to see the Esquiline workshop as a parallel to a modern factory, with one worker responsible for the hinges and one for the inscriptions. A model of a (relatively) small workshop is more appropriate, for, while there appears to have been a division of labour, the size of the workshop may have dictated that several different tasks were the responsibility of one craftsman: the engraver of inscriptions may also have been the engraver of decorative patterns. The varied titles whereby silversmiths are identified in inscriptions and texts indicate that certain activities were specific to certain craftsmen, but not every workshop could have consisted of such specialists. The division of labour discussed by the modern observer corresponds to perceived changes in style or technique which may or may not have distinguished the work of one individual from that of another. Changes can be observed, multiple workers are known to have constituted a workshop, but it is difficult to match the one with the other. Thus, for example, behind the pieces of the treasure one might hypothesise the figure of a merchant outside the workshop or a craftsman within responsible for the production and supply of octagonal faceted and fluted wire approximately one centimetre in diameter. It is obvious when used, its use unites dissimilar objects such as the Muse casket and the Pelegrina ewer, and it represents, as do the matching hinges and soldering plates, the stock fittings used by the workshop.

An octagonal faceted and fluted wire forms the buckles of the six horse trappings (pl. 46), but it is a wire distinctly smaller in diameter and therefore not an exact match with the other pieces. Another link exists, however, between the workshop group and the trappings in the form of the simple, clean open-work shared by the trappings and the rectangular monogram plates (pls. 27, 46). The crudely engraved finials, cast in one piece with the circular plates of the trappings, resemble the ring mounts of the two caskets and the soldering plate of the Pelegrina ewer. In addition, opposite the buckle on each trapping is a terminal covered with chased and engraved petal forms which are identical in scale and idiosyncratic details of execution to the myriad petal forms found on the surfaces of the large fluted dish (pls. 22, 46). It may be noted that the pattern which fills the central medallion of the fluted dish (pl. 23) is a diaper pattern similar to that on the casket hinges (pls. 7, 16). So popular was this motif on late silver plate, and so dissimilar the techniques of these two examples, that no close relationship is suggested by this detail.[13] Nevertheless, the large fluted dish is understood to be part of the workshop group through its decorative connection with the trappings and its morphological relationship to the Muse casket.

These relations of fittings, figural types, and decorative motifs are too close and too specific to be satisfactorily explained as aspects of a period style. Brief observation has been made that the caskets and the Tyche figures, and the rectangular monogram plates and the horse trappings formed two groups, the first related by figural style and the second by open-work decoration.[14] The two groups were correctly observed, but the perspective was limited. The two groups are related both to one another and to additional pieces in the treasure. A condensed statement of the relationships groups caskets and Tyches by figural style and decorative details; round monogram plates and rectangular monogram plates by inscription and decoration; rectangular monogram plates and horse trappings by open-work ornament; horse trappings and fluted dish by chased foliate designs; Proiecta casket and monogram plates by inscriptions; the two caskets, round monogram plates, horse trappings, and Pelegrina ewer by matching cast and engraved fittings.

The total in the workshop group is twenty-two objects. The Paris patera and the two arm ornaments bring to twenty-five the number of pieces grouped by design and decoration, but the patera and the arm ornaments fall outside the hypothesised workshop group. The Naples ewer and the flask with Erotes, distinct in their form and ornament, complete the treasure of twenty-seven pieces. The treasure can thus be understood to contain twenty-two objects from a single workshop dated to the late antique period by stylistic and technical criteria, four additional objects for which a late date is also appropriate, and the singular Naples ewer which might be late but whose date cannot be pin-pointed.

The definition of the workshop has many different results. It unexpectedly suggests something of the relationship between the two discoveries of silver which occurred in 1793. Of the second find of four pieces only two are known. While nothing can be said of the candelabrum and dish now lost, it seems significant that the remaining pieces, the Naples ewer and Paris patera, are among those which fall outside the Esquiline workshop group. At the least the discrete find sites noted by Visconti can be shown to correspond to separate assemblies of objects based on technique and style. Sufficient evidence does not exist either to include or exclude them from the family collection associated with the Turcii, but their special status within the treasure warrants some attention.[15]

The assembly of interrelated pieces in the workshop group gives an indication of the possible range of products which might originate in a given workshop. While the combination of stylistically distinct pieces may seem startling at first, the general concept of a functioning workshop which the collection conveys accords with a knowledge of the Roman economy and theories of workshop practices.[16] The relatively large group of interrelated pieces from the Esquiline Treasure forms an apparent contrast to the groups that can be observed in other finds datable to the late empire. The small, clearly related groups within the treasures of Mildenhall and Kaiseraugst and the five nearly identical dishes found together at Niš (Yugoslavia) indicate the size of workshop groups previously encountered even, as in the case of the Niš hoard, when the find site and the centre of manufacture are close.[17] While it is possible that further research on other treasures will demonstrate larger, related groupings, the Esquiline Treasure currently stands apart.

The association of the caskets and Tyches, which allowed

every scholar of the treasure to postulate an official career for the owner of the caskets, can be seen to be stylistic as well as archaeological. But a question is immediately raised with regard to the identities of the workshop patrons. Whose Tyches are they, the donor's or the owner's? Did the patron, who gave Proiecta and Secundus the casket on the occasion of their wedding, also present Secundus with insignia of high office? Tyche imagery was popular in the late empire, but its appearance is normally associated with the highest echelons of the imperial bureaucracy. And there is no evidence that Turcius Secundus, unlike some of his illustrious relatives, ever held a major office. Perhaps more than one donor and more than one owner are involved in the Esquiline silver.

The archaeological context and the domestic nature of the treasure would indicate that its goods are those of a single household, and its inscriptions provide some names, if not identities. The hypothesis of a common origin for twenty-two pieces might suggest that a single donor bestowed numerous presents on various members of the Esquiline household. It is possible that the married couple of Secundus and Proiecta, whose household it has always been assumed to be, frequented the same shop as the donor of their wedding gift for subsequent silver purchases for themselves and for others. Such solutions seem appropriate, but they do not exhaust the possibilities. The theory which interpreted the treasure as a trousseau eliminated the need to see Secundus and Proiecta as purchasing any silver at all. The theory resulted in the unlikely situation of their having been given new silver—not heirlooms—as wedding presents, inscribed with the names of third and fourth parties. It is also possible that Secundus and Proiecta were members of a household which included the donor of the casket and others, all of whose possessions formed the remainder of the treasure. As a family, they may have patronised a single silver workshop. Such a domestic arrangement would account for the roughly contemporary manufacture of many pieces and the presence of inscriptions referring both to Proiecta and Secundus and to others. It would allow the assignment of the caskets to the ownership of Secundus and Proiecta and the Tyches to another member of the *gens* Turcia, possibly but not necessarily of another generation, who was a documented holder of high office, which Turcius Secundus was not.[18] Other solutions might be suggested, but each must account for the presence of both Tyches and caskets and for at least one donor and four owners of silver manufactured within a limited period of time in a single workshop. In this light, the five pieces which cannot be placed in the same workshop provide welcome breathing space, but the puzzle remains.

One last result of the workshop grouping concerns the attempt to assign dates more specific than 'late empire' to the treasure. The observed interrelations are a potential boon for securing a date for a large number of objects, since information relevant to the dating of a single piece within the workshop group would indicate a date for twenty-two.

NOTES
1. H. J. Loane, *Industry and Commerce of the City of Rome, 50 B.C.–200 A.D.*, The Johns Hopkins University Studies in Historical and Political Science, ser. 56, II, Baltimore (1938),

86. Inscriptions referring to silversmiths, goldsmiths, and jewellers, of which 138 (out of 186) are from the city of Rome, are collected by H. Gummerus, '*Die römische Industrie*', *Klio*, XIV (1915), 129–89; XV (1918), 256–302. Calabi-Limentani, whose researches emphasise the legal, contractual aspects of artistic production, cites numerous passages from ancient authors, many of which concern the relative values of the precious raw materials and the labour involved in the manufacture of the finished products. *Studi sulla società romana: Il lavoro artistico*, Biblioteca storica universitaria, ser. 2, IX, Milan (1958).

2. The *basilica argentaria* (or *vascularia*); the shops along the *clivus argentarius*, so called in medieval times but probably a name of the Roman period; the shops along the Neronian *via sacra*. Loane, *Industry*, 133ff; E. Nash, *Pictorial Dictionary of Ancient Rome*, s.v. '*clivus argentarius*'. See also van Deman, 'The Sacra Via of Nero', *Memoirs of the American Academy in Rome*, V (1925), 115–26; idem, 'The Neronian Sacra Via', *American Journal of Archeology*, XXVII (1923), 383–424.

3. Loane, *Industry*, 87; T. Frank, *An Economic Survey of Ancient Rome*, 5 vols., Baltimore (1933–40), V, 212ff.

4. Loane, *Industry*, 89, 155 (5 or 6 workmen); A. Burford, *Craftsmen in Greek and Roman Society*, London (1972), 78ff (3 to 12 workmen); M. I. Finley, 'Technical Innovation and Economic Progress in the Ancient World', *Economic History Review*, ser. 2, XVIII (1965), 39 (4 to 6 workmen); A. H. M. Jones, 'The Cloth Industry under the Roman Empire', *Economic History Review*, ser. 2, XIII (1960–1), *passim* (8 to 12 workmen). Jones discusses the evidence for the state linen and wool factories. For a general survey see M. I. Finley, *The Ancient Economy*, Sather Classical Lectures, XLIII, Berkeley (1973); also F. M. de Robertis, *Lavoro e lavoratori nel mondo romano*, Bari (1967).

5. *Corpus inscriptionum latinarum*, VI, no. 33919. See Frank, *Economic Survey*, V, 210f.

6. The lex metalli Vipascensis (*Corpus inscriptionum latinarum*, II, no. 5181) of the Flavian period suggests state-owned mines rented to private contractors with the silver divided by contractor and state on a fifty-fifty basis. Loane, *Industry*, 45, n. 149. For imperial stamps see E. C. Dodd, *Byzantine Silver Stamps*, Dumbarton Oaks Studies, VII, Washington, D.C. (1961), 5ff. Fourth-century stamps are discussed in relation to the Cesena plate (P. Arrias, '*Il piatto argenteo di Cesena*', *Annuario della scuola archeologica di Atene*, N.S. VIII–X, 1946–8, 309ff; idem, *Bolletino d'Arte*, XXXI, 1950, 9ff) and to the Munich bank treasure (B. Overbeck, *Argentum Romanum: Ein Schatzfund von spätrömischem Prunkgeschirr*, Munich, 1973; Kent and Painter (eds), *Wealth of the Roman World*, nos. 1–9). A general discussion with an eye to workshop localisation is provided by F. Baratte, '*Les ateliers d'argenterie au bas-empire*', *Journal des savants* (1975), 202ff.

7. Dodd, *Silver Stamps*, 33f.

8. Loane, *Industry*, 91; see Gummerus, '*Industrie*'.

9. In a famous passage Xenophon, attributing the excellence of the food at the Persian court to the numbers and specialised tasks of those involved in its preparation, draws an analogy to craftsmen:

> . . . arts are developed to superior excellence in large cities. . . . In small towns the same workman makes chairs and doors and plows and tables, and often this same artisan builds houses. . . . And it is, of course, impossible for a man of many trades to be proficient in all of them. In large cities, . . . one trade alone, and very often even less than a whole trade, is enough to support a man: one man, for instance, makes shoes for men, and another for women; and there are places even where one man earns a living by only stitching shoes, another by cutting them out, another by sewing the uppers together, while there is another who performs none of these operations but only assembles the parts. It follows, therefore, as a matter of course, that he who devotes himself to a very highly specialized line of work is bound to do it in the best possible manner. (*Cyr.* 8, 2, 5)

Eight centuries later Augustine comments on the '. . . workmen in the street of the silversmiths [*vicus argentarius*] where one vessel, in order that it may go out perfect, passes through the hands of many, when it might have been finished by one perfect workman' (*De civ. D.* 7, 4). While Augustine would prefer the efforts of one workman, his statement shows that the vessel which is worked on by many does emerge 'perfect'. His negative attitude in this passage is clarified by its purpose as an analogy to the many, specialised deities of the pagan pantheon who are compared with Augustine's one, perfect god.

Finley ('Innovation', 38f) states that the division of labour, indicated by the passage in Xenophon, was not widespread but rather restricted to cities and courts. Burford (*Craftsmen*, 80, 96ff) is uncertain about such specialisation. Her doubt appears to be based on the premise that ancient objects were of (uniformly?) fine craftsmanship and that fine craftsmanship is not compatible with large workshops and specialised occupations. Xenophon, *Cyropaedia*, trans. W. Miller, Loeb Classical Library, 2 vols., London (1953); Augustine, *The City of God*, trans. and ed. M. Dods *et al.*, Edinburgh (1913).

10. In this context, the treasures of Berthouville and Traprain Law represent extremes. Berthouville consists of almost 100 separate votive gifts to a shrine of Mercury at Canetonum, dedicated by individuals over many years; Traprain is a pirates' cache of over 100 silver vessels assumed to have been taken during numerous raids on the Continent. The large treasures of Mildenhall and Kaiseraugst appear to contain only small groups of closely related objects (e.g. Kaiseraugst Inv., nos. 62.4, 62.23, and 62.26; Mildenhall, Brailsford, nos. 1, 2, and 3; 7, 8, 9, and 10). Neither has yet been examined, however, for indications of workshop practice. The forthcoming publication of Kaiseraugst, edited by H. Cahn, promises to address such questions. E. Babelon, *Le trésor d'argenterie de Berthouville*, Paris (1916); A. O. Curle, *The Treasure of Traprain: A Scottish Hoard of Roman Silver Plate*, Glasgow (1923); F. Drexel, '*Der Silberschatz von Traprain*', *Germania*, IX (1925), 122–8; J. W. Brailsford, *The Mildenhall Treasure*, 2nd ed., London (1955); T. Dohrn, '*Spätantikes Silber aus Britannien*', *Mitteilungen des Deutschen Archäologischen Instituts*, II (1949), 66–139; J. M. C. Toynbee, 'Some Notes on the Mildenhall Treasure', *Wandlungen christlicher Kunst im Mittelalter*, Forschungen zur Kunstgeschichte und christlichen Archäologie, II (1954), 41–57; K. S. Painter, 'The Mildenhall Treasure: A Reconsideration', *The British Museum Quarterly*, XXXVII London (1973), 154–80; idem, *The Mildenhall Treasure*, London (1977); R. Laur-Belart, *Der spätrömische Silberschatz von Kaiseraugst*, Katalog, Basle (1967); H. U. Instinsky, *Der spätrömische Silberschatzfund von Kaiseraugst*, Akademie der Wissenschaften und der Literatur, Mainz, Abhandlungen der geistes- und sozialwissenschaftlichen Klasse, V, Wiesbaden (1971). Also Kent and Painter (eds.), *Wealth of the Roman World*, Mildenhall, nos. 54–79; Kaiseraugst, nos. 80–7.

11. The first published drawings of the casket in Seroux d'Agincourt's *L'Histoire* (fig. 4) omit the feet and swing handles. No view is given where the hinges might be seen. It might be argued from the nature of the drawings that their true subjects were the individual relief panels, not the casket *per se*, and that fittings were inappropriate in that context. An engraving in the Montagnani-Mirabili edition of Visconti is the first perspective rendering of the casket: both feet and handles are clearly shown. Another engraving in the volume provides a view of the cover, showing two hinges. The texts of both Visconti and Seroux d'Agincourt mention only two hinges. The Dalton engraving represents the three hinges as they now appear. Comparisons of the engravings and examination of the casket suggest that a third hinge has been added between the two fittings shown in the engravings (see pl. 7). Dalton commented that 'one [hinge] has been restored' without specifying which one. The workmanship and wear are almost identical on all three. One can only hypothesise that the middle hinge is original, that it was found separated from the casket and later replaced. Visconti: M–M, 5, pls. I, III; Seroux d'Agincourt, *L'Histoire*, III, 8; IV, pl. IX, 1–2, 4–5; Dalton, *Catalogue*, 61, 63.

12. Hanfmann, *Seasons Sarcophagus*, I, 51.

13. See G. L. Brett, 'Formal Ornament on Late Roman and Early Byzantine Silver', *Papers of the British School at Rome*, xv, N.S. II (1939), 33–41; Strong, *Silver Plate*, 196, fig. 39.

14. Poglayen-Neuwall, '*Besitzer*', 131.

15. The question arises as to whether the two lost pieces, like the patera sold to Gossellin and the ewer sold to Stefano Borgia, were also sold to private collectors soon after the discovery. If so, do the separate sales of these pieces reflect an awareness on the part of the early owners that the four pieces of the second find constituted a group apart?

16. See, for example, Frank, *Economic Survey*, v, 210ff:

    'If in such shops the principle of division of labor had been introduced so that each workman performed a set task instead of producing entire articles, we can explain why . . . on certain pieces the engraving, the molded design, and the emblemata often fail to harmonize.'

    Recent investigations by the British Museum Laboratory support the Esquiline workshop grouping. The laboratory efforts were directed toward the analysis of compositional differences between various late antique hoards and therefore do not address the Esquiline question directly. Nevertheless, the results strengthen the workshop hypothesis; see M. J. Hughes and J. A. Hall, 'X-ray Fluorescence Analysis of Late Roman and Sassanian Silver Plate', *Journal of Archaeological Science*, 6 (1979), 321–44.

17. For the Mildenhall and Kaiseraugst groups, see above, n. 10. For the Niš treasure see Baratte, '*Ateliers*', 200f, n. 23; Kent and Painter (eds.), *Wealth of the Roman World*, no. 10; A. Oliver, Jr., *Silver for the Gods: 800 Years of Greek and Roman Silver*, Toledo (1977), no. 118.

18. See the stemma of the Turcii, fig. 14. The evidence for domestic arrangements of joint (as distinct from conjugal) families is slender. Each husband is presumed to have brought his bride to a 'new' dwelling; actual practice is difficult to identify. For a discussion of republican patterns see J. A. Crook, '*Patria Potestas*', *Classical Quarterly*, xvii (1967), 113–22.

The Date of the Treasure

The treasure provides no evidence for precise dates comparable to those once thought to have been furnished by the Damasian epitaph. The morphology of most pieces suggests a date in the fourth or early fifth century. Details of decoration—the use of gilding and niello inlay, the figural types, the geometric designs—simply agree with a late antique date; they do not help to narrow it. Certain pieces and decorative passages can be matched with silver from other treasures. In almost every instance, however, the dates associated with the other treasures are derived from numismatic evidence and are indicative therefore of dates of burial rather than manufacture. As examples of silver apparently commissioned and owned by private individuals, the Esquiline and related treasures lack the inscriptions which refer to imperial anniversaries and thus allow the close dating of some pieces of late Roman plate.[1]

It is possible to hypothesise a burial date for the Esquiline Treasure, and previous scholars did so. The theories were based on a general consensus of a late date for the silver, an assumption that the treasure was a purposeful burial, and basic knowledge of the history of the city of Rome. Visconti suggested a burial during the fifth century, a time when internal and external problems made life in the capital difficult for many. Later authors were more specific, emphasising that the treasure was buried in great haste in the face of barbarian attacks; the 410 sack of Rome by the Visigoths and the sixth-century struggles of the Lombards and Ostrogoths were discussed.[2] The violent papal politics of the 360s, the sack of 455, the arrival of the Huns in Italy, and other disturbances of the fourth and fifth centuries provide plausible occasions, but there is no evidence at all to suppose that the burial, if indeed it was purposeful, was carried out in haste. Since the composition of the treasure is indicative of silver produced in the fourth or early fifth century, any number of specific events or a general attitude of unrest might account for burial at any time from the fourth century onwards. Nor can the possibility of accidental burial be completely eliminated.

Although no evidence exists to secure an exact date of burial, a suggestion of its relative chronology can be made: the pieces of the treasure were buried within a generation or two of their manufacture. While individual objects in the treasure have been damaged, the damage on the whole is the result of burial, not wear. Surfaces of vessels have been scarred by chemical corrosion and staining, and parts, now restored, were deformed and broken under pressure. When such damage is discounted, the evidence of wear is minimal. The horse trappings (especially *nos. 38 and 41) have lost plates, pendants, tongues of buckles, and portions of attached ornaments. Such damage, however, may correspond to relatively limited wear; the potential for damage and breakage for trappings in active use must have been great. Three of the Tyches have lost applied fittings; the

hasp on the Muse casket and the handle of the Paris patera are worn. The objects have been used, but the period of active use cannot have been of long duration. These observations of wear, or its absence, in combination with the style of the pieces lends credence to Strong's thesis that the treasures of the late empire contained silver of the late empire with only scattered heirlooms.[3]

However interesting a relative chronology for the burial of the treasure, it lacks reference to an absolute date of manufacture, for such a date is difficult to establish. Previous scholars noted various details of the silver which indicated dates parallel to but independent of their theories of ownership. Precisely because of their indirect bearing on questions of patronage, the details were only casually mentioned and developed. The areas of investigation ranged from monogram types to fibulae, and many of them repeated the pattern of suggesting general rather than specific dates.

The hortatory inscriptions of the Proiecta casket and the Pelegrina ewer (figs. 11, 12) were explained as formulaic acclamations of a type used from the third to the fifth centuries.[4] The Chi-Rho monogram was discussed as an early form found in fourth- and fifth-century inscriptions.[5] The monograms on the eight serving-plates (fig. 13; see pls. 26-7) were compared with Latin monograms found on art works ranging in date from the mid-fourth to the mid-sixth century.[6] Certainly the monograms and inscriptions, and the letter forms with which they are composed, are late antique types, but the general dates for the treasure suggested by stylistic considerations are still more precise than those derived from the epigraphic evidence.

Many scholars commented on the costumes represented on the panels of the Proiecta casket (see pls. 4, 6, 8–11). Tozzi argued that the depiction of dalmatics and tunics with long sleeves provided a terminus post quem of the midfourth century, by which time the costumes introduced in the late second century had become common for the Roman upper classes. It is a weak argument which accounts for the costumes represented but certainly cannot be used to establish a limiting date for the decoration of the casket. Similar claims were made for the crossbow fibula worn by Secundus and the large jewelled collar worn by Proiecta on the top panel of the Proiecta casket lid (pl. 4). The fibula, tunics, and dalmatics are items of costume which were introduced early and which had achieved currency by the third and fourth centuries. The necklace is indeed a late antique type, but again only a general date in the fourth, fifth, or sixth century is indicated.[7]

Certain details of costume and fashion, however, do aid the establishment of firmer chronological bounds, narrowing the broad date of fourth to early fifth century to the middle decades of the fourth. Precisely because the arguments rest on observations of personal fashions, they must not be pushed too far and corroborative evidence must be sought.

Nevertheless, an observation of the hair-style of the woman and the beard of the man from the portrait panel of the Proiecta casket (pl. 4) suggests a date in the fourth century when the two are considered together. Visconti observed that Proiecta wore a hair-style similar to that worn by Helena, and Secundus a beard '*non dissimile da quella di Massimiano, o . . . di Giuliano Apostata ed Eugenio*'. Later scholars repeated the observation, simplifying it by limiting the male reference to Julian.[8] Visconti's listing of Maximian, a member of the first tetrarchy, Julian the Apostate, Augustus in the 360s, and Eugenius, usurper in the West in the 390s, gives a more accurate indication of the intermittent popularity of the style from the late third until the end of the fourth century.

The adoption of a clean-shaven physiognomy by the Constantinian house following the tetrarchic period would appear to have been a purposeful evocation of first- and second-century styles and a rejection of the imperial images of the immediate past. Equally purposeful was the choice of a bearded image by Julian, the last heir in the Constantinian line, who became emperor only after years of strained relations with the more powerful members of the family and open civil war with his predecessor (and co-ruler) Constantius II. Upon assuming independent power, Julian resumed wearing the beard of his early years. Addressing the city of Antioch which had ill-treated him as 'Μισοπώγων', Julian identified himself synecdochically as 'the beard' and discussed his beard and the reactions it drew in an extended analogy to the vicissitudes of his stay. It was clearly a personally significant style with strong links to a distinctly different past.[9] After the tetrarchy, only two other fourth-century rulers, Procopius and Eugenius, wore beards, and both were usurpers whose official images were probably intended to refer to Julian. Two other usurpers in the fifth century, John and Avitus, followed the same style, while the official rulers of the period, specifically Honorius, Theodosius II, Marcian, and Leo I, were characteristically clean shaven with only occasional bearded images recorded in the coinage.[10]

It would appear that during the fourth and fifth centuries both clean-shaven and bearded styles were acceptable, alternating with one another as current fashions. Within the imperial circle, however, the beard seems to have been the singular mark of one emperor, Julian, and several pretenders to the throne who styled themselves after him. As a fashion imitated by the Roman aristocracy, the beard may have passed in and out of favour following customs at court and may have carried the general connotation of allegiance to a leader. As such, it might be presumed that beards would have been worn by sympathisers of the usurpers and by a larger, necessarily less partisan group which supported Julian, a legitimate heir in the Constantinian line. The fortunes of the Turcii were specifically linked with Julian. Like other Roman families who had held public office during Constantine's rule and in the years immediately following his death, the Turcii had been passed over by Constantius, only to be raised up again by Julian.[11] L. Turcius Apronianus was named prefect of the city of Rome by Julian, and the bearded Turcius Secundus might well have been a minor office holder in his administration. It certainly would seem

possible to grow a beard as a matter of fashion at any time during the fourth century without betraying personal politics. Nevertheless, a Roman family of aristocratic office holders such as the Turcii was undoubtedly influenced by imperial taste. For this reason Turcius Secundus and his beard might be happily dated to the decades of the mid-fourth century and the reign of Julian.

Proiecta, with her hair like Helena, can be seen to corroborate this date. In the three depictions of the Roman matron on the Proiecta casket, two variations of the same hair-style are represented (pls. 10–11). Both feature hair parted in the middle, swept up, braided, and coiled on the crown of the head. This is the so-called *Haarkranz-Frisur* worn by the various females associated with the first and second tetrarchies.[12] Variations of the style contrast the manner in which the hair is drawn back, above the forehead and over the ears. The two representations on the casket lid (pl. 10) show the hair relatively loose and waved, while the hair-style represented on the casket body (pl. 11) is more compact and more closely curled. It has been wisely argued that individual female hair-styles remained popular after their fashion at court can be attested through coin portraits, and that variations of the *Haarkranz-Frisur*, including those seen on the Proiecta casket, remained popular and therefore characterised female portraits during the second quarter of the fourth century.[13]

Such observations of mid-century fashions suggest the general period from approximately 330 to 370 for the execution of the casket reliefs. These dates agree with two additional aspects of the treasure which furnish termini post. Questions of generations and conversion to Christianity within an aristocratic Roman family would suggest, at the earliest, a date after the so-called Edict of Milan (313) for Secundus to be recorded as a Christian, while a more conservative date at the mid-century would accord with patterns observed for the aristocracy in general.[14] The second detail is an obvious one: the presence of a statuette representing Constantinople requires that the group of Tyche figures date to the period after the foundation of the city. Constantine began construction of the city in 324, and references to activities of 328 suggest that there may have been a personified image at that time. The first representations of the Tyche of the new capital, however, are found on silver medallions struck at the mint of Constantinople to celebrate the consecration of the city on 11 May 330. Further, it has been pointed out that representations of Constantinople as the equal or sister city of Rome are innovations of the vota coinage of Constantius II, with the earliest examples dating to 343.[15]

The iconography of imperial cities, the pattern of religious conversion in the Roman upper classes, and the dissemination of court fashions all indicate a date in the fourth century. The Tyches point to a date in the second half of the century, while the portrait panel of the Proiecta casket suggests the middle decades. There is no conflict, but rather a latitude which allows these workshop products to have been commissioned at different times, by different individual patrons, for different occasions within a limited period. The general date suggested by the five objects can be applied to the other seventeen pieces in the workshop group. The bulk of the treasure, therefore, might be dated to the mid-fourth century, and the burial of the entire collection, on the evidence of wear, might be placed at the end of the fourth or the beginning of the fifth century.

NOTES
1. For anniversary dishes in general, see Strong, *Silver Plate*, 199ff. The Munich treasure, found after the publication of Strong, contains several additional examples. Overbeck, *Argentum Romanum, passim*. See Oliver, *Silver*, no. 118.
2. Visconti: M–M, 13, 17f; Newton, *Blacas Collection*, 27; Poglayen-Neuwall, 'Besitzer', 136.
3. Strong, *Silver Plate*, 182f.
4. Visconti: M–M, 5; Seroux d'Agincourt, *L'Histoire*, III, 9.
5. Seroux d'Agincourt, *L'Histoire*, III, 4; V. Schultze, *Archäologische Studien über altchristliche Monumente*, Vienna (1880), 111f.
6. Visconti: M–M, 10.
7. Tozzi, 'Tesoro', 283ff. See M. G. Houston, *Ancient Greek, Roman and Byzantine Costume*, London (1947), 97f, 120ff; Higgins, *Jewellery*, 192.
8. Visconti: M–M, 4; Böttiger, *Sabina*, 64; Tozzi, 'Tesoro', 285, n. 1.
9. In his satire, Julian praises Cato the Younger, the Greeks, laudable for having maintained their ancient virtue, and the Celts, whose company and culture, though crude, were preferable to those of the citizens of Antioch. No source or reason is given for his beard, although Julian describes himself in general as 'Greek in [his] habits' (*Mis.* 367, B). No specific Roman imperial reference is made, although modern writers see an allusion to Hadrian and the Antonines as well as to a Greek philosopher type in Julian's bearded image. 'Misopogon or Beard Hater', in *The Works of the Emperor Julian*, trans. W. C. Wright, The Loeb Classical Library, 3 vols., London (1913–30), II, 420–511. See R. Browning, *The Emperor Julian*, Berkeley (1971), 158; G. W. Bowersock, *Julian the Apostate*, Cambridge, Mass. (1977), 11, 13, 60f., F. D. Gilliard, 'Notes on the Coinage of Julian the Apostate', *Journal of Roman Studies*, LIV (1964), 135–41; R. Calza, *Iconografia romana imperiale da Carausio a Giuliano*, Rome (1972), 364ff.
10. The portrait types for the period can be traced in the following publications: J. P. C. Kent *et al.*, *Die Römische Münze*, Munich (1973); *The Roman Imperial Coinage*, H. Mattingly (ed.) *et al.*, 8 vols. (1923–), vols. VI, VII, IX; A. R. Bellinger *et al.*, 'Late Roman Gold and Silver Coins at Dumbarton Oaks: Diocletian to Eugenius', *Dumbarton Oaks Papers*, XVIII (1964), 161–236.
11. R. Edbrooke, 'The Civil Officials of the Emperor Julian', *Prosopographical Studies in the Roman Empire in the Fourth Century A.D.*, Ph.D. dissertation, University of Chicago (1970), 137f. While it is clear that Julian encouraged the pagan aristocracy in the West, Christians were among the office holders of his administration. Edbrooke, 'Officials', *passim*.
12. K. Wessel, '*Römische Frauenfrisuren von der severischen bis zur konstantinischen Zeit*', *Archäologischer Anzeiger* (1946–7), 70f.
13. H. von Heintze, '*Ein spätantikes Mädchenporträt in Bonn: Zur stilistischen Entwicklung des Frauenbildnisses in 4. und 5. Jahrhundert*', *Jahrbuch für Antike und Christentum*, XIV (1971), 71ff.
14. Brown, 'Christianization', passim; A. H. M. Jones, 'The Social Background of the Struggle between Paganism and Christianity', *The Conflict between Paganism and Christianity in the Fourth Century*, A. Momigliano (ed.), Oxford (1963), 17–37.
15. A. Alföldi, 'On the Foundation of Constantinople: A Few Notes', *Journal of Roman Studies*, XXXVII (1947), 15f; J. M. C. Toynbee, 'Roma and Constantinopolis in Late Antique Art from 312 to 365', *Journal of Roman Studies*, XXXVII (1947), 135–44, *passim*; G. Dagron, *Naissance d'une capitale: Constantinople et ses institutions de 330 à 451*, Paris (1974), 43ff.

The Esquiline Workshop and Related Treasures

While evidence internal to the Esquiline Treasure furnishes approximate dates for the silver, there is no suggestion in the style or iconography of the pieces as to its place of production. The treasure was buried in Rome, and that fact has always been taken to indicate that the pieces were manufactured there as well. Certainly, local manufacture for the treasure is possible, but proof is lacking. If there was an active trade in Rome in the late empire, roughly equivalent situations might be argued for other major metropolitan centres. The attribution to Rome, like most attributions of late antique plate, is based on general probability[1]: Rome had a flourishing silver trade, the treasure was buried in the city, and its owners were members of the Turcii family, well attested in Rome from the third century onwards.

A working hypothesis of a mid-fourth century date and provenance for the Esquiline collection in the city of Rome allows a hypothesis of an equivalent date and place of origin for pieces of silver comparable to those in the treasure. This process would have been appropriate even when the Damasian epitaph supplied the dates, but it was seldom followed. Scholars of the treasure tended to view the vessel shapes, decorative motifs, and techniques shared by objects from other treasures as foreign in origin and, therefore, apart from the core of the treasure. This reasoning caused the large fluted dish (*no. 4), for example, to be grouped with pieces from the Scottish treasure of Traprain Law as examples of Byzantine workmanship.[2] The observation that the Esquiline Treasure contains a large group of objects from a single workshop discourages any attempts to disperse the objects to various locales. The observation actually reverses the process by indicating that pieces such as those from Traprain Law might be best understood as Roman, mid-fourth century.

The earlier scholars can hardly be found wanting: workshop production was a minor concern of theirs, and the available materials for comparison were limited. By the 1930s, the last period of active scholarship on the Esquiline Treasure, only a few late antique hoards had been recovered. Several singular pieces, such as the Missorium of Theodosius and the Corbridge lanx, had been known for some time, as had a few smaller treasures.[3] The treasure of Traprain Law, discovered in 1919 and published in 1923, was the largest, most clearly comparable find known to the last scholars of the Esquiline silver. In recent decades, when numerous treasures have been recovered, there has been no new literature from the perspective of the Esquiline material. The great treasures of Mildenhall and Kaiseraugst, found in 1946 and 1962 respectively, do contain pieces comparable to ones in the Esquiline find. But, while the stylistic resemblances have been discussed, the potential date and provenance indicated by the Esquiline silver have not.[4] More tellingly, the Damasian dates of 379 to 383 for the Esquiline Treasure could not be made to match the mid-fourth century

dates of burial indicated for both the Swiss and British treasures. The scholars of Kaiseraugst, but more specifically of Mildenhall, have noted the distinct morphological and decorative parallels of the Esquiline silver but have declined to pursue the chronological implications. Now that earlier dates for the Esquiline material can be entertained, the new chronology allows the parallels observed among the Mildenhall, Kaiseraugst, Traprain Law, and Esquiline Treasures to be considered as aspects of style in Rome in the middle of the fourth century.

Placing the Esquiline Treasure in the city of Rome in the middle decades of the century gives a sense of satisfaction but does not substantially help to clarify matters of regional style and production in the late empire. Many more pieces would have to be localised and dated within the period before the centres usually mentioned—Rome, Antioch, Alexandria, Constantinople, Naissus, Thessalonica, and Milan—could be accurately and profitably characterised. A consistent style, or group of styles, has been observed in silver of the second and third quarters of the fourth century, with certain of these aspects of vessel design and decoration continuing much later. Unfortunately, the contents of many late treasures give no clue to the origin of their silver, and their find sites, often on the borders of the empire, point instead to complex trade patterns. The number of objects in question is enormous: only the first century AD with its Augustan 'court' silver and Campanian hoards offers comparable material.[5] While the numbers involved give added credence to the general stylistic trends discussed for the period, they simultaneously discourage hopes of isolating one centre from another on formal criteria alone.

There are discernibly new tastes for multangular forms, for chased geometric patterns, and for abstract designs in niello and gilding; there is also continued appreciation of figural decoration in relief, documented in example after example, scattered in finds throughout the Roman world. For this reason, it is hardly surprising that fittings and vessels similar to those in the Esquiline Treasure are found in variously dated and widely separated collections of late antique plate. It is interesting to note the presence of silver horse trappings, different in articulation but remarkably similar in appearance to the Esquiline set, in tombs at Qustul in Lower Nubia. The Nubian tombs are dated from between the mid-fifth to the end of the sixth century by pottery remains and inscriptions.[6] A large plate from the tomb of the Queen of the Golden Mask near Kerch in southern Russia has in its centre a wreath and a niello monogram like those on the Esquiline plates; it has been suggested that the Kerch plate dates to the late third or early fourth century.[7] These comparisons, however, like others for the Esquiline ewer, flask, patera, and fluted dish, are only general. They unfortunately add little to our knowledge of late Roman material and of the Esquiline find in particular.

By the same token, the figural types seen in the treasure are indicative only of a general late antique style. The small-breasted, heavy-hipped Venus of the Paris patera and Proiecta casket is found repeatedly on monuments of the period. The squat, large-headed Erotes of the Esquiline patera, casket, and flask illustrate a generic type, not in itself indicative of any relationship beyond a common late date for the objects on which it is found. The same is true of the stocky, full-faced figures which appear as Muses and attendants on the two caskets of the treasure. Rumpf and others have compared the Erotes of the patera with those of the Missorium of Theodosius as though there were a significant resemblance, one indicative of more than separate reflections of the same broad style.[8] But the visual evidence will not support such a close connection. The observation of vessel design allows the pieces of the treasure to be understood as examples of late Roman silver plate; similarly, the presence of these figural types allows the decoration of the pieces to be understood, along with figural compositions in many media, as aspects of a late antique style. Such proportional types, repeated with minor variations, are an integral part of any definition of the style of this period.

To clarify the nature of the Esquiline collection further, it should be added that there are types of decoration and vessel design considered characteristic of the period but not characteristic of the Esquiline Treasure. Whole classes of objects, such as chalices and flanged bowls, are not represented in the treasure but included in many others. Such omissions indicate little except the categories of terracotta, pewter, or bronze vessels which might have been expected at the time and at the site of the discovery of the Esquiline silver. More important, several major decorative styles of fourth-century silver are also missing from the treasure. The treasure lacks, for example, pieces of the apparently ubiquitous heavily beaded ware and, closely related to it, vessels characterised by elaborate figural borders and by emblemata in high relief. Are these the styles of centres outside the city of Rome? The bold use of niello and silver gilt seen in the Esquiline monograms accounts for one of the polychrome effects popular in late metalwork, but there were others. The combination of niello, silver, and gilding was employed on numerous vessels, spotted in detailed figural scenes or in intricate border and emblema designs based on floral and geometric motifs. Are these the styles of shops inside the city of Rome but outside the Esquiline workshop? These decorative styles, like those within the Esquiline Treasure, do not appear to have been mutually exclusive. Single objects, such as the Cesena dish or the Ariadne plate from Kaiseraugst, suggest that styles documented within the Esquiline Treasure (for example, chased foliate patterns) could be combined with others not represented (for example, gilt and niello figural scenes).[9] Sharp regional divisions, therefore, are not suggested. The vessel designs and styles of decoration contained in the Esquiline Treasure seem to be a selection from the variety known for the silver of the fourth century. It is tempting, although possibly misleading, to see the styles within the Esquiline Treasure and within the Esquiline workshop group as indicating the repertory of a single Roman workshop which featured wares in some contemporary styles but not in all.

Prevailing opinions on the scale of workshop production would support this limitation and help to explain the difficulties which arise when close comparisons are sought from the large pool of fourth-century materials in silver. It is only occasionally possible to draw comparisons between objects in the Esquiline Treasure and other pieces of silver plate indicative of relationships more specific than those of similar examples of broad stylistic trends. The number of close comparisons is extremely small and limited to silver, for the comparisons are based in part on similarities in technique. It is a necessary restriction in the face of the large number of objects in many media which share a general style at the mid-century. In addition, it is a restriction based on the premise that it might be possible to isolate other products of the Esquiline workshop and that such products, according to known patterns of Roman workshops, would be limited to works in precious metals.

Despite the large numbers of objects available for comparison, only a handful can be seriously considered. Certainly, no group of interrelated objects in silver related, in turn, to the Esquiline pieces is now known to exist. Indeed, the probability is small that such a group will ever be recovered. The result is that objects from the Esquiline Treasure must always be compared with single pieces of plate for which a workshop context cannot be demonstrated. Only details which match exactly are acceptable comparisons, and objects which may be related may not appear to be so. If this seems obscure, it must be remembered that the rectangular monogram plates could not be grouped with the Muse casket had they been found separately. The necessary intermediary links of hinges, inscriptions, figural style, and wire fittings supplied by the Proiecta casket and the circular monogram plates would be lacking. This said, it is conceivable that single objects exist which might supplement the workshop group of the Esquiline Treasure. The process of their discovery, however, is extremely difficult, and the results are necessarily tentative. Distinctive fittings such as the hinges and handles of the caskets do not apparently recur.[10] The comparisons must therefore be based on more subtle criteria.

As previously mentioned, the diaper pattern which fills the medallion of the fluted dish (pl. 23) is a popular motif in late antique silver, commonly discussed as part of a repertory of chased designs based on foliate forms. An indication of this repertory is given by the six different motifs used in the decoration of the flat panels of the fluted dish (pl. 22). The motifs are found in many media and continue into the medieval period. Late Roman examples of the designs in silver can be quickly divided according to the techniques of their manufacture. The pattern found on the hinges of the two caskets (pls. 7, 16), for example, is executed with a series of punches: the curved lines and the circular and oval depressions which compose the pattern are identical in length, curvature, and depth of impression each time they are employed. Other examples of diaper patterns executed in punch-work can be found in various treasures, including those of Traprain and Coleraine,[11] but no two pieces match exactly. No two would appear to have been struck with the same set of dies.

The quatrefoil and foliate designs of the Esquiline fluted

dish demonstrate a different method of execution in which a pointed engraving tool and a broad gouge were employed. The examples of this technique are numerous, and, in each, it is possible to discuss the individual style and skill of the hand responsible. The quatrefoils and petal forms, which are the basis for the patterns of the Esquiline dish, are idiosyncratic, consistent, and easily recognised. For this reason, the appearance of identical motifs executed in the same scale and manner, with the same small details, allows the identification not simply of the same workshop but of the same hand. Such is the case of a fragment of a large fluted dish from the treasure of Traprain Law (pl. 23).[12] The Traprain fragment preserves part of a central medallion almost identical with that of the Esquiline dish, with a square inscribed within a circular field. Canopies of petals fill the resulting lunettes, and a right-angle grid of oval petals is set at forty-five degrees to the vertical and horizontal axes of the square. The stippling applied to the Esquiline quatrefoils and canopies is omitted from the Traprain example, but all other details match. In both, the quatrefoil patterns are executed with double outlines and running diagonal channels; the petal forms in the lunettes are open-ended, freehand curves, with blunt, tapering grooves in the centre. The size of the tools employed, the length and depth of the curves and channels, and the articulation of the framing devices are the same for both dishes. The close match of these two pieces serves to highlight the difficulty of assembling pieces made in the same workshop, for, while exact matches are clear, they are few.

More general comparisons of patterns are numerous but of little value. Several other fragments from Traprain, a lanx from Mileham, spoons from Mildenhall, bowls and dishes from Kaiseraugst, and spoons from Great Horwood indicate only a portion of the pieces similar in technique and motifs to the fluted dish from the Esquiline Treasure.[13] The existence of an intermediate class of objects, more closely related than these examples of a common period style, is difficult to demonstrate. The search is for objects possibly made within the Esquiline workshop but not necessarily made by a hand attested in the Esquiline Treasure. One example of this class can be illustrated by the fluted dish from the Mildenhall Treasure (pl. 24).[14] Only slightly smaller than its counterpart in the Esquiline Treasure, the piece from Mildenhall follows the same pattern of internal organisation and decoration. Its central medallion, filled with geometric and foliate forms, is surrounded by a plain border and a series of alternating panels which radiate like the spokes of a wheel. Where the Esquiline dish has twelve decorated panels, the Mildenhall has fourteen. The Esquiline repertory of six designs, however, can be compared with the Mildenhall selection of two, both of which are variations of designs found on the Esquiline dish. Overall, the workmanship of the Mildenhall plate is less polished: engraved lines and grooves are broken and angular where equivalent passages in the Esquiline patterns are smooth. A comparison of the two series of engraved lines which circle the central medallions, capping the narrow ends of the flat and fluted panels, is instructive. In the Esquiline dish, this incised border is clearly legible as a spoked wheel. In the Mildenhall dish, the individual line segments are ragged and their junctions

awkward, with the result that the many parts do not resolve into a circular figure. The suggestion that the two dishes are related, however, is not based on the technical superiority of one piece over the other. The resemblance of the two in design and decoration is striking and might be explained by the modelling of one on the other or by the dependence of both on a common model. The differences in execution simply indicate the work of two distinct hands.

Observations of chased ornament thus allow the identification of the Traprain fragment to be a piece made by a craftsman of the Esquiline fluted dish and the Mildenhall plate to be a piece modelled after objects from the Esquiline workshop or possibly produced in the Esquiline workshop itself. In view of the attention given to the figural compositions in the treasure, it would be helpful to an understanding of their place in late Roman silver to find comparisons and relationships like those discussed for the vessels with foliate ornament. Unfortunately, even the closest comparisons of figural decorations are qualified. Further investigation of the Mildenhall Treasure suggests that, while the fluted dish is related to the Esquiline workshop, the figural material of Mildenhall is not. The eight pieces from Mildenhall with Bacchic and hunt imagery are fourth-century products with border motifs, proportional types, and compositional principles shared with objects in other treasures but not with objects in the Esquiline.

No one object, let alone a group, provides a parallel for the combination of specific facial and figural types, draperies, architectural backgrounds, and border motifs, executed in repoussé with gilding and stippling, which is seen in the two caskets of the Esquiline Treasure. The flask with Erotes and the Paris patera fare no better, although, as late antique works which fall outside the Esquiline workshop group, they are pursued with less zeal. Again, comparisons must be based on matching details, but, in contrast to the pieces with chased designs, the figural pieces cannot be matched so securely.

The solid-cast Corbridge lanx (pl. 19) has been thought to be related to objects within the Esquiline Treasure. It provides numerous parallels in the raised and engraved vine-scroll borders, the architectural backgrounds, the costumes with stippled details of *clavi* and hems, and the simple linear formulae whereby drapery folds are indicated. Such details can be compared with passages on the two caskets. There are, however, more dissimilarities than similarities. On balance, the lanx is best understood as a piece distinct from the products of the Esquiline workshop.[15] A second late antique plate, the Parabiago patera (pl. 19), bears far closer comparison with the Esquiline material.[16] Like the lanx, it is solid-cast in contrast to the repoussé relief of the Esquiline caskets. Comparisons with the Parabiago patera, however, involve both the caskets and the solid-cast Tyches from the treasure, and therefore questions of differences in technique seem of lesser importance. Like the Proiecta casket and Tyches, the relief surfaces of the Parabiago patera are heavily stippled and gilded to accent textures and decorative borders and to provide a visual counterpoint to the sculptural decoration. Draperies are soft and simple with the linear formulae seen on the caskets used to represent folds and hem-lines. The figures are stocky. With few exceptions, the faces are represented in three-quarter view with pupils and nostrils indicated with points. The faces are related to those on the caskets, but they are remarkably close to the faces of the Tyche figures (pls. 35–43) with an overall triangular shape, small forehead, close-set eyes beneath sloping brows, straight nose, small mouth and chin.

The postures of most of the figures on the Parabiago patera are comparable to those on the Esquiline reliefs. Some postures, however, such as that of the male river personification to the lower left and Abundance or Tellus to the lower right, appear more spatially complex and perhaps more successfully realised than those depicted on the casket panels. The three-dimensional Tyche figures are not an exact comparison, but they do demonstrate that craftsmen capable of conceiving and successfully constructing figures in the round were present in the Esquiline workshop. The postures of the male and female personifications of the Parabiago patera are perhaps best understood as examples of the classical quotations or topoi which survive into the Byzantine period. The observation of these persistent types lies at the base of studies, such as Matzulevitch's, which understand late antique and Byzantine art to have strong components inherited from the Roman.[17] Hardly classical in style, the Parabiago patera figures are nevertheless clearly descended from Graeco-Roman models. The apparent association of certain iconographic types with fixed postures of classical origin accounts for figures such as Tellus, which appear throughout the history of Roman art in the midst of company less classically inclined. The resemblance of the other figures of the Parabiago patera, their forms, features, and draperies, to those of the caskets and Tyches is compelling. But the precise nature of the relationship of the patera to the Esquiline shop is puzzling. A feasible answer is found with difficulty, for, while the majority of the figures of the patera can be understood as products of the Esquiline shop, the personifications require another hand, possibly of greater skill, versed in classical types. The literal combination of two or more hands for the Parabiago patera, and the consequent addition of at least one craftsman to the Esquiline shop, is a possible but inelegant solution. The relationship stands observed if unexplained.

One last comparison for the figural silver can be made with fragments of a flagon from the treasure of Traprain.[18] Four pieces remain from a depiction of Ulysses identified by Eurykleia (pl. 18). Four female figures, two standing, one kneeling, and one seated, are preserved on the two largest fragments of the repoussé relief. Two fragments of faces complete the surviving pieces of the vessel. The large fragments were found crushed flat, and the present restoration would appear to err in the direction of exaggerated breadth, with sharp juxtapositions of different levels of relief.[19] Only general observations seem appropriate in this context: the figures are stocky and their draperies are softly and simply handled, detailed with rows of stippled ornament as are the costumes represented on the Esquiline caskets. The two small fragments which preserve female faces have not been restored and, as a result, they give an indication of the original facial types of the figures on the flagon. Their small foreheads, sloping brows, close-set eyes, small mouths and chins reproduce the Esquiline type exactly (and match

the faces of the Parabiago patera as well). Therefore, despite the poor state of preservation of the vessel as a whole, portions of the Traprain flagon provide evidence of a close relationship between it and the reliefs and Tyches of the Esquiline Treasure.

Of the comparisons discussed, only one object—the fragment of the chased fluted dish from the Traprain Law treasure—matches so closely as to be automatically included in the Esquiline workshop group. The repoussé flagon from the Traprain treasure is another possible match, but its damaged condition requires a qualified, cautious acceptance. Both the Mildenhall fluted dish and the Parabiago patera appear to be closely related to pieces in the Esquiline Treasure, but the nature of the relationships is not clear. The agency of additional craftsmen or the process of copying models must be called upon to account for certain differences in both. Such explanations may not, in fact, correspond to historical reality. In essence, such explanations serve to indicate a small group of objects with common stylistic traits and to isolate them from the large numbers of fourth-century vessels which compare with the Esquiline objects, but only in a most general way. The observed relationships are close, but the resulting attributions to the Esquiline workshop number only two. Those pieces associated by style but not necessarily attributed to the workshop bring the total to four.

NOTES

1. J. M. C. Toynbee, *A Silver Casket and Strainer from the Walbrook Mithraeum in the City of London*, Leiden (1963), 15:

   'We know virtually nothing of local styles in silver under the Late Empire, if indeed, such styles existed; . . . there is not a piece in the Mildenhall treasure, for instance, of which we can do more than guess the origin, basing our guesses on nothing more compelling than argument from general probabilities'.

   The very few fourth-century pieces with stamps or signatures which indicate places of origin are discussed by Baratte, '*Ateliers*'.
2. Poglayen-Neuwall, '*Besitzer*', 133ff.
3. The Missorium was found in 1847, the lanx in the 1730s. The treasure of Great Horwood was found in 1872; the Coleraine and Hardenburg collections of scrap or '*Hacksilber*' were recovered in 1854 and 1849 respectively. The large treasures of Petrossa (1837) and Berthouville (1830) were exceptional for their size. J. R. Mélida y Alinari, *El disco de Teodosio*, Madrid (1930); O. J. Brendel, 'The Corbridge Lanx', *The Journal of Roman Studies*, XXXI (1941), 100–27; H. Waugh, 'The Hoard of Roman Silver from Great Horwood, Buckinghamshire', *The Antiquaries Journal*, XLVI (1966), 60–71; H. Mattingly *et al.*, 'The Coleraine Hoard', *Antiquity*, XI (1937), 39–45; E. Munksgaard, 'Late Antique Scrap Silver Found in Denmark: The Hardenburg Høstentorp and Simmersted Hoards', *Acta Archeologica*, XXVI (1955), 31–67; A. Odobesco, *Le trésor de Petrossa*, Paris (1889–1900); Babelon, *Berthouville*.
4. See above, p. 51, n. 10, for bibliographic references for Traprain, Mildenhall, and Kaiseraugst.
5. Strong, *Silver Plate*, 182.
6. W. B. Emery, *The Royal Tombs of Ballana and Qustul*, 2 vols., Cairo (1938), I, 27ff, 50ff, 251ff; II, pls. 55–57 A and B; idem, *Nubian Treasure: An Account of the Discoveries at Ballana and Qustul*, London (1948).
7. Strong, *Silver Plate*, 194f, pl. 63A; E. H. Minns, *Scythians and Greeks*, Cambridge (1913), 384, 433f, fig. 326. Minns would date the plate far earlier, but Baratte ('*Château d'Albâtre*', 128f) demonstrates that the monogram agrees with a late third-, early fourth-century date.

8. A. Rumpf, *Stilphasen der spätantiken Kunst*, Arbeitsgemeinschaft für Forschung des Landes Nordheim-Westfalen, Geisteswissenschaften, Abhandlung, XLIV, Cologne (1957), 22; similarly, the Theodosian Erotes are compared with the Parabiago patera: A. Levi, *La patera d'argento di Parabiago*, Opere d'arte, V, Rome (1935–44), 21.

9. Arrias, 'Cesena'; Laur-Belart, *Kaiseraugst*, Inv. no. 62.252. For a survey of the major stylistic trends with brief bibliography of the treasures involved, see Strong, *Silver Plate*, 182–209, esp. 194ff.

10. The recurrence of a rare and distinctive pattern, for example, allows Baratte ('*Ateliers*', 207) to suggest a workshop relationship between Kaiseraugst Inv. no. 62.252 (Ariadne plate) and Traprain Law, Curle no. 19.

11. Curle, *Traprain*, no. 137, fig. 63; Mattingly, 'Coleraine', 45, pls. I, V.

12. Curle, *Traprain*, no. 32, pl. XIX, A.

13. Ibid., no. 31, pl. XIX, B; no. 87, fig. 39; no. 100, fig. 44; no. 107, fig. 54; no. 110, fig. 58; Strong, *Silver Plate*, 196, pl. 62A; Brailsford, *Mildenhall*, no. 13, pl. 6; nos. 32–4, pls. 8e,d; Laur-Belart, *Kaiseraugst*, no. 5, pl. 12; no. 10, pls. 14, 15; no. 12; Waugh, 'Great Horwood', nos. 1, 2, fig. 1, pl. XVII. See Kent and Painter (eds.), *Wealth of the Roman World*, nos. 77–9, 100, 103.

14. Brailsford, *Mildenhall*, no. 13; Painter, *Mildenhall*, no. 13. The Mildenhall dish was discovered without the two handles which are now attached. One assumes that traces of solder or the like dictated the current restoration. No such traces can be found on the Esquiline dish, although two swing handles (nos. 57–8) are part of the present treasure and are often assumed to have been attached.

15. See, for example, Dohrn, '*Spätantikes Silber*', 17. The elongated proportional types of the lanx, the precise, small beaded borders, the use of stippling and engraved line, not only as decorative touches but as elements of representation, and the marked preference for faces depicted in profile are all at variance with the reliefs of the Esquiline caskets. It is noteworthy, nevertheless, that the one profile head in the Esquiline panels, the Nereid on the left panel of the Proiecta casket lid (pl. 5), is strikingly similar to the Corbridge profiles with the large, long nose with straight bridge, fleshy tip and distinct nostril, a compact mouth and chin, and a firm jaw.

16. Levi, *Patera*, pls. I–III, figs. 1, 5–7, 10; A. Alföldi, '*Die Spätantike*', Atlantis, XXI (1949), 68ff.

17. L. Matzulevitch, *Byzantinische Antike*, Berlin (1929).

18. Curle, *Traprain*, no. 8, pl. XII, fig. 9.

19. A description of the restorations is given by Curle, *Traprain*, 99f.

The Esquiline Workshop in the Fourth Century

The association of four additional pieces with the Esquiline workshop has numerous implications. The identification of a workshop group in Late Antiquity is welcome for its documentation of diverse though related products, and each additional piece associated with the group provides new information to test or confirm hypotheses of workshop production and trade. Obviously, the perceptions of the pieces added are affected in this process. In the case of the Esquiline group, the four objects to be considered are ones which, by themselves or in their archaeological contexts, are thought significant for the late antique period. Involved are the treasures of Mildenhall and Traprain Law, two extremely different but equally important silver hoards, and the Parabiago patera, the style, but more frequently the iconography, of which, receives discussion in studies of the period.

The association of these objects with the Esquiline workshop group suggests mid-century dates and provenance in the city of Rome for all four. In no instance does either the date or the provenance conflict with previously accepted theories. The Parabiago patera is usually cited as a late fourth-century work, but a reading of the Alföldi essay, which established its fourth-century date, shows that Alföldi's stylistic comparisons simply indicate a general date in the second half of the century.[1] Mildenhall is thought to have been buried in mid-century,[2] and, in view of the minimal wear and the excellent state of preservation of most of the treasure and certainly that of the fluted dish, a date of manufacture shortly before the date of burial satisfies the archaeological evidence. Traprain Law was probably buried in the late fourth or early fifth century. As a treasure, it represents a barbarian hoard of over 160 pieces, most of which are fragments of vessels broken, flattened, and folded in preparation for melting and recasting or for use as currency.[3] The association of a mid-century date with the Traprain fluted bowl and flagon would indicate an approximate date for the beginning of the migration of these two vessels which ended in a pirates' cache half a century later.

This migration presumably began in Rome and ended in central Scotland. Southern Gaul is commonly understood as the origin of the Traprain Law silver; this provenance, however, results from inconsistencies in Curle's text on Traprain. Southern Gaul was discussed as the probable source of the pieces of 'Teutonic' manufacture and as the apparent immediate source for the booty. Curle understood the inhabitants of Traprain Law to have been Saxons or Celts and their loot to have been the product of numerous raids on the Continent. Rome, along with several other Mediterranean centres, was discussed by Curle as a possible source for pieces in the Scottish treasure.[4] The association of the Esquiline material partly confirms his hypothesis by suggesting a Roman origin for at least two of the pieces in the hoard.

A similar situation exists with regard to the provenance of the silver in the Mildenhall Treasure. Although far smaller than the treasure of Traprain, Mildenhall can also be understood as a collection of objects from various workshops.[5] The identification of the Mildenhall fluted dish with the Esquiline workshop group indicates a possible place of origin for that piece and something of the nature of silver trade and travel in the western empire, for the Mildenhall dish formed part of the silver service of a (Roman) landowner in southern England. In fact, chased foliate ornament such as that found on the fluted dishes of the Esquiline, Traprain, and Mildenhall Treasures would appear to have been an international style in late antique silver. As mentioned previously, surviving examples are numerous. Related materials from the treasure of Kaiseraugst are executed by one Euticius Naisi[6] and accompanied by a plate signed ΠΑΥϹΥΛΥΠΟΥ ΘΕϹϹΑΛΟΝΙΚΗϹ[7]—Greek artisans from eastern cities were working for both Latin- and Greek-speaking markets. If Kaiseraugst gives an indication of eastern production, the Esquiline and its workshop relations from Traprain and Mildenhall demonstrate its western complement.

The Roman provenance indicated for the fourth addition to the Esquiline group, the Parabiago patera, also agrees with the accepted theories concerning the origin of that piece. Its north Italian find site carries little weight in the context of late antique trade patterns and fits comfortably with an attribution to the city of Rome. The stylistic parallels commonly discussed for the plate—Esquiline, Traprain, and Corbridge—reflect the influences of various artistic spheres as understood by previous scholars. Esquiline and Traprain have commonly been treated as western products; Corbridge is usually, if unnecessarily, associated with the East.[8] Ultimately, however, the conventional attribution of the Parabiago patera to the West has been based on its iconography. The striking stylistic similarities of figural and facial types identified in the Esquiline Treasure serve to strengthen this attribution. But the argument concerning the western iconography of the patera is grounded in beliefs concerning 'Kunstpropaganda' in the 'Kulturkampf der Spätzeit'.[9] The argument would see the Parabiago patera with its imagery of Cybele and Attis as an example of an aggressively anti-Christian art sponsored by pagans in Rome at the end of the fourth century. The introduction of such an object into the workshop which produced the Proiecta casket with its Christian inscription clearly raises numerous questions.

The issues are complex. Theories of artistic production in the ancient world are involved, specifically theories concerning the origin of (and responsibility for) significant religious imagery. Closely connected are necessarily retrospective definitions of what did or did not constitute significant religious imagery in the fourth century AD and, perhaps, what did or did not represent imagery considered neutral by craftsmen, patrons, and the more distantly involved purchasers of ready-made, manufactured goods. Ultimately involved are questions of the religious climate of fourth-century Rome and the nature of the relationship posited between something so broad and diffuse as that climate and the particular imagery found on the sculpted surfaces of silver caskets and plates.

For a long time it has been thought that some workshops in Late Antiquity produced works for a clientele which included both pagans and Christians, each group requesting and receiving imagery suited to its religious affiliation. However, the model of such a purposeful relationship between craftsman and patron, basic to most hypotheses of significant religious imagery, has its complement in the far less active involvement to which unfinished, or nearly finished, works testify. One thinks of sarcophagi, complete but for portraits of the deceased. Indeed, many of the Dionysiac, Muse, and Seasons sarcophagi from the period raise the issue of craftsmen, working essentially independent of patrons, creating finished works through variations and combinations of fixed classical types.[10] The role of personally significant but publicly neutral themes is perhaps best seen in these market conditions. In addition, many allegorical themes, while perhaps pagan in origin, were clearly of general application by the late empire. It is in this context that the popular themes of Muse and Venus imagery, represented on the Esquiline silver, are best understood.

An allegorical interpretation of the Parabiago patera would be possible. The elaborate imagery of the plate, however, is virtually unique, and the popularity of the cult of Magna Mater in fourth-century Rome was such that an interpretation of the patera as a votive gift or testament of the cult seems most appropriate.[11] If the iconography of the patera suggests a singular, unusual commission, the Esquiline caskets represent pieces purchased, and perhaps commissioned, for a specific occasion but decorated with common, predictable classical imagery. The association, discussed in the scholarly literature, of the *iconography* of the Parabiago patera with a western pagan reaction does not therefore necessitate the removal of the patera from the Esquiline workshop. The association of the *style* of the Parabiago patera with a western pagan reaction, however, immediately causes the Esquiline workshop to be understood as an agent of the so-called 'Roman Renaissance', for the pagan reaction as an art historical concept involves the revival of classical style as well as pagan imagery.

Those scholars who would see the Parabiago patera as visual evidence of a pagan polemic in the fourth century group it with other objects whose iconography, according to their interpretation, is unequivocally pagan. The group is discussed as including the contorniates, the Corbridge lanx, the Concesti amphora and situla, the Dumbarton Oaks Seasons sarcophagus, the Achilles plate from Kaiseraugst, the Bacchic dishes from Mildenhall, the Vatican Virgil, consular diptychs of the fourth and fifth centuries, the diptych of Asclepius and Hygieia, and that of the families of the Nicomachi and Symmachi. The group is often expanded; it is most commonly represented in discussion by the Nicomachi and Symmachi diptych (pl. 20).[12] This representative piece is well chosen for purposes of argument, for its subject concerns pagan cult, it is securely dated in the fourth century, and it was commissioned for aristocratic Roman families closely associated with the pagan reaction. Similar statements regarding date, iconography, and patronage are made for the other pieces in the 'Renaissance' group, but none has the pedigree of the diptych. The imagery of many pieces can be understood to be political, allegorical, or neutral. Previous literature, however, would appear to treat all art after 313 which is not Christian as pagan. And that which is pagan is tacitly understood to be anti-Christian. This assumption of propagandistic subject matter has allowed scholars to postulate pagan owners for objects which lack any such documentation. Following this to its logical extreme, scholars have suggested the emperor Julian, the perfect pagan patron, or members of his entourage to have been owners of the Mildenhall and Kaiseraugst Treasures. Such patronage has been thought appropriate and perhaps necessary to account for the representations of Bacchus, Alexander, Hercules, Venus, and Achilles found on vessels in the two treasures.[13] Classical imagery has been seen to indicate a pagan owner. It is in this context that surprise has been continually expressed that Christians would have owned the Proiecta casket with its Venus and sea *thiasos*.[14]

It is somewhat ironic that the Esquiline caskets and patera have always been discussed with the works associated with the pagan reaction. In a sense, their imagery would appear as appropriate as any in the 'Renaissance' group, and, although the caskets were produced for Christians, these Christians were members of, if converts within, the same senatorial aristocracy responsible for other commissions. But the style of the works, which is clearly late antique, was thought or perhaps assumed to be representative of the classical revival of the fourth century. Classical style and pagan iconography need not go hand in hand. The long life of some classical topoi, in which aspects of original meaning and style are preserved together, suggests a match of idea and form not seen in all monuments. The Nereids of the Proiecta casket (see pl. 5), which preserve a classical type in far from classical style, serve to indicate the nature of the possible stylistic variants and give the lie to theories of typological or generic style applied without consideration of the deviations witnessed in many individual monuments.

The literature on the mid-century 'Renaissance' seems to see pagan iconography and classical style as inextricably linked and tied in turn to contemporary political events. The term 'Christian' is used to indicate aspects of religious imagery, religious affiliation, and consequent political stance. The term 'pagan', extremely broadly defined, is applied to imagery, religion, political parties, and, in addition, to style where it is clearly synonymous with classical. It is not obvious that such definitions were native to the fourth century, and the oppositions inherent in the choice of terms can cause distortion. It is from a background of such oppositions, for example, that the adoption of a classical (read pagan) style for Christian subject matter appears to be more dramatic and more necessarily purposeful than it may have been in fact; and the use of a non-classical style for a pagan subject does not fit the pattern and is therefore often overlooked. The patera from the Esquiline Treasure provides an example of a scene, the toilet of Venus, thought to be pagan on an object thought to be pagan in a style thought to be classical. The identifications are conventional but misleading. The toilet of Venus is so common in the late empire as to be stripped of any specific cultic meaning it may have once carried; the Esquiline patera is a vessel inelegantly termed a 'saucepan' by modern scholars of silver plate.[15] But even if both the image and the vessel *were* pagan, the Venus of the patera is clearly executed in a non-classical, late antique style not identical with but quite comparable to that seen in the caskets and Tyches.

The caskets from the Esquiline Treasure do compare closely with the Parabiago patera, another product associated with the Esquiline workshop and a member of the conventional fourth-century grouping. Perhaps a more general stylistic relationship exists among the Esquiline caskets and patera, the Parabiago patera, and the numerous other pieces in the 'Renaissance' collection. Nevertheless, it is questionable whether all these objects relate to one another as common products of a revival of classical style. Basic to any definition of classical style is the representation of the ideal, organically functioning, balanced human figure. Such a concept is also basic to the definition of a revival of classical style.[16] For this reason alone, it is difficult to accept the Esquiline caskets and patera as illustrative of any properly defined renaissance movement. And what is the nature of the 'Renaissance' and the classical style which can encompass the Concesti amphora, the Vatican Virgil, and the Nicomachi-Symmachi ivories?

It is a problem of a singularly ill-chosen exemplar: the Nicomachi-Symmachi diptych (pl. 20) misrepresents the larger group. While spatial conceptions and isolated awkward passages in the representation of human anatomy indicate a late date, the figures, the draperies, and the border ornaments of the Nicomachi-Symmachi ivories do appear to reflect a conscious study of earlier models. With some qualification, this observation can be extended to include the Asclepius and Hygieia and Probianus diptychs conventionally associated with the Nicomachi-Symmachi plaques.[17] Considering the known patrons, the families of Q. Aurelius Symmachus and Nicomachus Flavianus, it is reasonable to assume that a retrospective, classicistic style was expressly chosen for these pieces. The larger collection of objects grouped with these diptychs as commissions of the Roman aristocracy in the fourth century does not exhibit the same style. Theirs is an unconscious, irregular, and extremely distant reflection of classical style simply typical of the late empire. The greater part of the group may be western, fourth century, and even Roman. The pieces are not necessarily pagan in any active sense, and they do not represent a single, coherent revival drawn from classical models.

Recent historical research has shown the group of Romans who actively supported the pagan reaction to have been quite small[18]; the small number of objects which might be linked by truly pagan themes and classical style is therefore an appropriate correspondence. The art historical concept of a 'Roman Renaissance' would appear to be based on historical perceptions of the fourth century which are themselves exaggerated. The conversion of Constantine has been understood as causing an immediate and unified reaction in the pagan Roman aristocracy. The building of Constantinople, the transference of the capital, and the various imperial decrees concerning pagan cult were thought to have provoked public defiance on a grand scale and to have created a power vacuum in Rome which was immediately filled by the (pagan) Senate.[19] The broad outlines are possibly accurate, but the numbers discussed and the violence and swiftness of the reaction reflect an over-interpretation of the sources. Constantine did convert and he did cause Constantinople to be built. The building of Constantinople, however, did not cause a sudden change in the fortunes of Rome: Rome had gradually relinquished its primacy during the third century. Throughout the fourth century it continued as one of the imperial residences along with Nicomedia, Milan, Trier, Sirmium, and Antioch. The imperial constitutions regarding paganism, issued by Constantine and his sons and expanded by Theodosius, decreed pagan ceremonies banned, temple treasuries and estates confiscated, and temple precincts closed. Throughout the fifth century the laws had to be reiterated and penalties re-enacted, for paganism continued. With few exceptions, pagans appear to have persisted rather than resisted, and pagan cult is documented in the East in the sixth century and in the West in the seventh. The senatorial aristocracy in Rome was largely pagan into the fifth century.[20]

Relations between pagans and Christians during this period appear to have been fluid and often determined by events outside the religious sphere. However striking the polarities envisioned by Jerome, the necessity of choosing to be either Ciceronian or Christian (*Ep.* 22, 30) was not acknowledged by all. In 394 Nicomachus Flavianus, leader of the pagan opposition, did battle against Theodosius in the name of Jupiter and Hercules, but he did so in league with the usurper Eugenius, a Christian and teacher of classical rhetoric. And ten years before, Q. Aurelius Symmachus, prefect of the city of Rome and leader in the fight over the altar of Victory, was defended on charges of exploiting Christians before the Christian emperor Valentinian by Pope Damasus himself.[21] Co-religionists were not necessarily allies, nor pagans and Christians enemies.

Recent historical studies have discussed this period as one of gradual diffusion and transition. A parallel for the visual arts would be appropriate. Questions of pagan and Christian imagery are best treated with caution: the lesson of the Esquiline Venus with its Christian inscription should finally be committed to memory. In addition, despite the attractive match of patron, iconography, and style seen in the Nicomachi-Symmachi ivories, it should be realised that insufficient evidence exists to correlate reactionary movements and classicistic styles as a general phenomenon.

An alternative paradigm has been suggested by Rumpf and followed in various art historical studies of the late empire. Rumpf's analysis of styles in the fourth century moved away from problems of causation and in so doing ignored any arbitrary boundaries between works of pagan and Christian content and/or patronage.[22] He also discussed artistic developments as operating independently of historical events. So, while Rumpf detailed the stages of a classical revival following the early Constantinian period, he discussed the last quarter of the fourth century as a waning of the mature revival of the middle decades. This is in obvious contrast to the theory of the pagan Roman reaction, the visual parallels for which are discussed as reaching a peak in the 390s with a full-blown classicistic style coinciding with the battle of Frigidus and the last great pagan offensive. Rumpf's analysis thus accords with theories of a 'Constantinian Renaissance' but conflicts with a large body of literature which discusses the last quarter of the fourth century as another revival movement, the so-called 'Theodosian Renaissance'.[23] It is curious to observe that the same group of monuments is cited to illustrate differing interpretations of style in this period. For Rumpf the Missorium of Theodosius, the Corbridge lanx, the Esquiline patera and caskets, the Parabiago patera, and the Nicomachi-Symmachi diptych are examples of a style which he characterised as feeble, decadent, and degenerate. The same objects are discussed by others as illustrating the high point of the fourth-century classical revival. It would appear that what is being debated is the eye of the beholder.

When the Constantinian and the Theodosian revivals are combined with the 'Roman Renaissance' at the mid-century, these movements seem to define the entire fourth century as a series of independent revivals located in various centres and fostered by diverse groups of patrons. In the literature, the Constantinian and Roman renaissances are understood as different expressions of one revival movement, and the 'Theodosian Renaissance' is assumed to be linked to the earlier effort at the mid-century, although the agency of transmission is not known.[24]

A possible key to an understanding of the fourth century and to the revival theories considered appropriate and necessary to its explication lies in art historical perceptions of the preceding period. An element in the definition of any revival movement is its observed difference and distance from that which went immediately before. In discussions of the fourth-century revivals, the preceding period is always identified as that of the tetrarchies, and the monuments are those associated with the individual members and the celebration of their joint rule. Writing in the 1930s, Gerke discussed fourth-century materials as harking back, not to Periclean, Augustan, or Trajanic antecedents but simply to the third century.[25] Gerke's comments have been echoed by numerous scholars to whom the tetrarchic style appeared to be a complete break with the past. Any resemblances between monuments of the fourth century and those from periods before the tetrarchies could only be conceived as conscious revivals. The barrier represented by the Venice and Vatican porphyry groups, the tetrarchic coinage of the mints of the eastern empire, the historical panels from the arch of Constantine, and the decennial monument in the Roman forum prevented any sense of continuity between the arts of the third and fourth centuries.

The coinage of the western mints, the Arcus Novus of Diocletian, the recarved Constantinian heads on the Hadrianic roundels, and other related materials provide an antidote and an illustration that styles documented in the third century persisted into the later years of the reign of Constantine and the fourth century as a whole.[26] A renais-

sance may seem a necessary theoretical structure to explain the distance from the decennial monument to the sarcophagus of Junius Bassus. Monuments exist, however, which indicate that neither the early nor the mid-fourth century is accurately represented by models such as these. The renaissance solution gives a false impression by characterising the arts of the western empire as dominated by a single style during this period. The theory implies a uniformity seldom seen or suggested for other periods of Roman art.

It has been argued that the revival of classical style is a recurring phenomenon in Roman art; that each successive revival is conditioned by contemporary period style(s); and that these revivals are based in a current of 'perennial hellenism' which preserves, continues, and adapts classical style. These theses cannot be documented with a series of incontestable monuments; rather they represent an effort to explain an apparent continuity and development of a style based in hellenistic art, the parallel development of a style characterised by abstract, anti-classical considerations and the periodic interruption of both by classical revivals.[27] Such a schema, while open to debate and further clarification, allows for a clearer and more flexible understanding of observed artistic processes. Its application to the fourth century would extend the theories applied to Roman art in general to the late empire in particular.

Certainly the Esquiline pieces were strange choices for the illustration of a classical revival. In the context of the existing literature, redating the treasure from the late to the mid-fourth century would simply serve to move the pieces from one renaissance to another. Observation of the proportional types, the treatment of the draperies, and the spatial concepts in the compositions of the figural reliefs suggests rather that the Esquiline caskets and patera show the interpretation of classical types in a late antique style. It is significant that of the twenty-seven pieces in the treasure only the caskets and patera were ever mentioned in discussions of a renaissance movement. The choice was obviously, if tacitly, based on iconographic considerations. The Muses and the Venus figures with their attendant Erotes, Nereids, and Tritons were understood as pagan subjects treated in an appropriately classicistic style. The Tyche figures which exhibit the very same figural style as that of the caskets have never been selected. Apparently the Tyches were not considered to be pagan, and they therefore were not assumed to reflect the revival of classical style. The remaining twenty pieces of the treasure, most of which are non-representational, have been consistently omitted from discussion, further indicating that the classical revivals of the scholarly literature were considered solely in relation to figural style to the exclusion of ornament and vessel design.

Visconti and Seroux d'Agincourt were the first to express the opinion that the treasure indicated a revival of earlier (and better) standards of art. Their comments were vague and their criteria unstated, but in so characterising the treasure they succeeded in elevating it above the 'decadenza' then associated with the arts of the late empire. Although it is difficult to trace the stages in the growth of the renaissance theory, it is possible that its origin, or at least its application to the Esquiline Treasure, can be located in eighteenth- and early nineteenth-century notions of artistic decline, as an explanation of those objects perceived as being of unusually high quality. With the general acceptance of Riegl's positive evaluation of the late Roman/late antique period, the theories might have been expected to pass away: on the contrary, they appear to have multiplied.[28] The reasons are not clear. Many scholars saw motivations for classical revivals in the activities of individual patrons, in contrast to the supra-personal, ahistorical *'Kunstwollen'* posited by Riegl. More important, the renaissance solutions offered an explanation for the many elements of classical figural style observed in late works, less satisfactorily dealt with by Riegl whose aesthetic characterisation of the period appears to have been largely drawn from compositions (abstract, hieratic) and techniques (polychrome, open-work) which, if not new in the later period, achieved a prominence not seen in the early empire. Elements that speak of a survival or revival of classical types and styles, however modified, were not easily accommodated within Riegl's theory which still postulated a single style for the period no matter how positive its evaluation.[29] Works such as the Esquiline Treasure continued to be perceived as exceptions to such uniform rules, although the non-figural silver and certain aspects of the figural compositions are best considered within the general period style as first articulated by Riegl.

The term 'late antique' has come to be understood and applied in many disciplines as a general term whose most common reference is a chronological one, a historical period which begins with the fourth century or, for some, the third. As such, it might be expected to designate objectively those monuments produced during this period of time; its art historical application, however, still reflects in some measure its original usage. Works thought classicistic are seldom labelled late antique. The term is reserved for those works which are thought to demonstrate continuous developments from the antique, from styles derived from hellenistic concepts and abstract considerations understood as constant components of Roman art.

Following this usage, it seems best to consider the Esquiline Treasure as a whole as a product of these late antique styles; the renaissance theories possibly appropriate to some fourth-century work seem ill-suited to an understanding of the treasure. Admittedly, the renaissance theories originated in stylistic considerations of the treasure, but these were buttressed by other materials. The ownership of the treasure by an aristocratic Roman family and the iconography of some of its pieces served to link the silver with an ill-understood pagan reaction as an agency of a classical revival. The Christianity of two of the owners, even when associated with Pope Damasus in the earlier literature, posed no apparent impediment to the assumption that the treasure illustrated a movement understood to be pagan in origin. The late antique styles of the silver were overlooked as the treasure was gathered into a collection characterised as classicistic.

The Esquiline Treasure would appear to have been consistently, if not consciously, misinterpreted and misrepresented. The find site of the silver was relocated, monograms on eight objects cursorily deciphered, and an epitaph misread and subsequently introduced into the literature all by way of establishing a family for the female owner of the treasure and a date for its contents. This date in combination with male and female aristocratic patrons and late antique representations of mythological figures formed a constellation firmly associated with a 'Roman Renaissance'. The silver was in fact owned by Roman aristocrats, some of whom were newly converted to Christianity at the mid-century. Despite assumptions concerning their social class and pagan forebears, these Romans purchased or commissioned silver in contemporary styles. And they purchased twenty-seven pieces, not three. The two caskets and the patera cannot be divorced from the rest of the Esquiline Treasure, the majority of which appears to have been produced within a limited time span in one workshop characterised by a distinct repertory of vessel forms and decorative motifs which would tax the definition of any classical revival.

The lesson drawn from a study of the Esquiline Treasure suggests that the 'Roman Renaissance' requires reconsideration and that the individual pieces conventionally associated with the concept deserve careful re-examination. In addition, the validity of current perceptions of the fourth century as a series of revival movements must be seriously questioned. The evidence of the Esquiline Treasure indicates that the hypothesis of multiple coexisting modes, applied to earlier periods of Roman art, would yield a less dramatic solution than a renaissance theory but one better supported by surviving evidence from the fourth century.

NOTES
1. Alföldi, *'Spätantike'*, 70ff.
2. Painter, *Mildenhall*, 22f.
3. Curle, *Traprain*, 5, 101ff.
4. Ibid.
5. Brailsford, *Mildenhall*, 21ff; Painter, *Mildenhall*, 12ff.
6. Laur-Belart, *Kaiseraugst*, Inv. nos. 62.4, 62.23, 62.26. No. 62.4 is the signed piece.
7. Ibid., no. 62.1. For the nationalities of artisans see J. M. C. Toynbee, *Some Notes on Artists in the Roman World*, Collection Latomus, VI, Brussels (1951). For the 'international style' see Brett, 'Formal Ornament', *passim*.
8. See Brendel, 'Corbridge', 126.
9. Alföldi, *'Spätantike'*, 68ff.
10. Ward-Perkins provides a brief discussion of the possible relations between patron and craftsman as seen in the Dionysiac sarcophagi at the Walters. J. B. Ward-Perkins, 'Workshops and Clients: the Dionysiac Sarcophagi in Baltimore', *Rendiconti della Pontificia Accademia Romana di Archeologia*, XLVIII (1975–6), 191–238.
11. H. Bloch, 'The Pagan Revival in the West at the End of the Fourth Century', *The Conflict between Paganism and Christianity in the Fourth Century*, A. Momigliano (ed.), Oxford (1963), 202ff; idem, 'A New Document of the Last Pagan Revival in the West', *Harvard Theological Review*, XXXVIII (1945), 199–244; J. Matthews, *Western Aristocracies and Imperial Court, 364–425*, Oxford (1975). For a general survey of the imagery see M. J. Vermaseren, *The Legend of Attis in Greek and Roman Art*, Leiden (1966).
12. The literature is voluminous; among the studies, A. Alföldi, *Die Kontorniaten*, Budapest (1943); new ed. with E. Alföldi, *Die Kontorniat-Medaillons*, Antike Münzen und geschnittene Steine, VI, Berlin (1976); idem, *'Spätantike'*, 61ff; Bloch, 'Pagan Revival', 212f; Dohrn, *'Spätantikes Silber'*, 115ff; E. Kitzinger, *Byzantine Art in the Making*, Cambridge, Mass. (1977), 7–4; idem, 'A Marble Relief of the Theodosian Period', *Dumbarton Oaks Papers*, XIV (1960), 39ff; idem, 'On the Interpretation of Stylistic Change in Late Antique Art', *Bucknell Review*, XV

(1967), 2; idem, 'The Sutton Hoo Ship Burial: The Silver', *Antiquity*, XIV (1940), 51f; D. E. Strong, *Roman Art*, ed. J. M. C. Toynbee, Baltimore (1976), 163ff; W. F. Volbach, '*Silber- und Elfenbeinarbeiten vom Ende des 4. zum Anfang des 7. Jahrhunderts*', *Beiträge zur Kunstgeschichte und Archäologie des Frühmittelalters*, Akten zum VII Internationalen Kongress für Frühmittelalterforschung (1958), Graz (1962), 22ff.

Of these authors Alföldi, Dohrn, Strong, and Volbach define the movement most broadly, including almost every object of the minor arts and many examples of monumental works which can be dated to the fourth century. Strong, for example, includes the Ambrosian *Iliad* which is Greek and generally dated later (R. Bianchi-Bandinelli, *Hellenistic-Byzantine Miniatures of the Iliad*, Olten, 1955), the calendar of 354 with its Christian inscription (H. Stern, *Le calendrier de 354: Etudes sur son texte et son illustration*, Paris, 1953), the Milan ivory of the Marys at the tomb (W. F. Volbach, *Elfenbeinarbeiten der Spätantiken und des frühen Mittelalters*, 3rd ed., Mainz am Rhein, 1976, no. 110) and many other works, which he feels demonstrate classical style and iconography. Strong and other authors understand Christian works to have been affected by a classical style carried by those objects with pagan imagery. Bloch is far more conservative in his discussion; Kitzinger is the most selective.

13. Laur-Belart, *Kaiseraugst*, 3ff; Painter, *Mildenhall*, 18ff. Instinsky (*Kaiseraugst, passim*) argues for Magnentius, or a member of his entourage, as owner of the Kaiseraugst Treasure.

14. Visconti was the first to record his surprise, followed by many including du Sommerard, Kraus, Schultze, and Dalton. See above, pp. 31f. The sentiment is reflected in Strong's 1976 survey of Roman art. A similar reaction is evoked by the now-missing Risley lanx which bore a 'pagan' representation of the hunt and an inscription naming its owner EXSVPERIVS EPISCOPVS [ECCLESIAE BOGIENSI DEDIT XP]. In both cases, the iconography is not so much pagan as secular. Strong, *Roman Art*, 167; idem, *Silver Plate*, 185f. A welcome contrast is provided by some recent literature which characterises the Venus of the casket as 'having purely ornamental significance' (R. Bianchi-Bandinelli, *Rome: The Center of Power*, trans. P. Green, New York, 1974, 102) and other mythological subjects as drawn from a 'pagan background that was taken for granted' (J. Huskinson, 'Some Pagan Mythological Figures and their Significance in Early Christian Art', *Papers of the British School at Rome*, N.S. XXIX, 1974, 69).

15. The Roman patera was a shallow dish without foot or handle derived from the Greek phiale and used for libations (H. Luschey, *Die Phiale*, Bleicherode am Harz, 1939). Strong, in his survey of silver plate, classes the Esquiline vessel under the heading 'saucepans'; the ancient term is not known. It is a vessel found in contexts which suggest domestic use 'in the service of liquids'. Imagery of Graeco-Roman deities and the dedication of examples of the vessel in some sanctuaries also suggest occasional use in pagan cult (*Silver Plate*, 145ff.) Five 'saucepans', four of which bear images of Neptune, have been found to carry imperial stamps dating to the reigns of Anastasius I (491–518; Dodd, *Silver Stamps*, no. 1), Justinian I (527–65; Dodd, no. 14), Mauricius Tiberius (582–602; Dodd, no. 30), Heraclius (610–41; Dodd, no. 50), and Constans II (641–51; Dodd, no. 77). Dodd, interestingly, refers to the vessels as trullae, a term which Strong considers for the 'saucepans'. It is doubtful that the imperial workshops of the fifth, sixth, and seventh centuries were producing objects for pagan cult. The Neptunes, bathing Venuses, Nilotic scenes, fish and fishermen found on the late vessels may indicate an association with water. The archaeological context of the Esquiline patera indicates domestic use; perhaps Böttiger was correct to associate the Esquiline patera with the bath (see above, pp. 26f). It should be noted that the Parabiago patera is not a patera but a shallow footed plate.

16. The criteria for the definition of a classical style are numerous; figural style is but one. The general problem of classical style and its revival(s) is discussed in E. Panofsky, 'Renaissance and Renascences', *Kenyon Review*, VI (1944), 214ff; idem, *Renaissance and Renascences*, Stockholm (1960).

17. Volbach, *Elfenbeinarbeiten*, nos. 55, 57, 62; 51ff.

18. See A. Cameron, 'The Friends of Ammianus', *Journal of Roman Studies*, LIV (1964), 15–28; idem, 'The Date and Identity of Macrobius', *Journal of Roman Studies*, LVI (1966), 25–38; Matthews, *Western Aristocracies*; B. Croke, 'The Editing of Symmachus' Letters to Eugenius and Arbogast', *Latomus*, XXXI (1976), 533–49; B. Croke and J. Harries, *Christians and Pagans in the Late Roman West: A Documentary Study*. I am grateful to Brian Croke for allowing me to read the *Latomus* article in page proof and the text of the *Documentary Study* in typescript.

19. The art-historical interpretations draw most heavily on the corpus A. Alföldi. See for example, *Kontorniaten*, and *The Conversion of Constantine and Pagan Rome*, trans. H. Mattingly, 2nd ed., Oxford (1969). A reflection of Alföldi is found in Bloch ('Pagan Revival') who also draws on his own early researches ('New Document'). A critique of the approach is found in the bibliographic essay of S. Mazzarino, '*La propaganda senatoriale nel tardo impero, 1939–1951*', *Doxa*, IV (1951), 121–48.

20. For a general survey see A. H. M. Jones, *The Later Roman Empire*, 3 vols., Oxford (1964), I, 37ff, 366ff; II, 687ff, 938ff.

21. Matthews, *Western Aristocracies*, 210, 238ff.

22. Rumpf, *Stilphasen, passim*; Lavin, like Rumpf, sees change beginning in the Constantinian period, but sees its ultimate origin in a 'limited and reactionary segment of the society' (I. Lavin, 'The Ceiling Frescoes in Trier and Illusionism in Constantinian Painting', *Dumbarton Oaks Papers*, XXI, 1967, 111).

23. Kitzinger ('Marble Relief') provides a survey of the literature; a postscript in a re-edition of Kitzinger's essays cites the most recent bibliography: *The Art of Byzantium and the Medieval West*, W. E. Kleinbauer (ed.), Bloomington (1976), 389.

24. Kitzinger, 'Marble Relief', 21, 39f; Lavin, 'Ceiling Frescoes', 110f. Kitzinger discusses classical values growing gradually in the course of the fourth century; see his *Byzantine Art*, 22–44.

25. F. Gerke, *Der Sarkophag des Junius Bassus*, Berlin (1936), 8ff.

26. See, for example, E. Harrison, 'The Constantinian Portrait', *Dumbarton Oaks Papers*, XXI (1967), 79–96.

27. For periodic and non-periodic aspects of classical art in the Roman period, see G. Rodenwaldt, '*Das Problem der Renaissancen*', *Archäologischer Anzeiger*, 1931, 318ff; O. Brendel, 'Prolegomena to a Book on Roman Art', *Memoirs of the American Academy in Rome*, XXI (1953), 60ff; E. Kitzinger, 'Byzantine Art in the Period between Justinian and Iconoclasm', *Berichte zum XI. Internationalen Byzantinisten-Kongress*, Munich (1958), 3ff; R. Brilliant, *Roman Art*, London (1974), 211ff; P. H. von Blanckenhagen, 'Elemente der römischen Kunst am Beispiel des flavischen Stils', *Das neue Bild der Antike*, H. Berve (ed.), 2 vols., Leipzig (1942), II, 310–341. The difficulty of distinguishing a revival conditioned by contemporary styles from a classical revival is raised by E. Garger, '*Zur spätantiken Renaissance*', *Jahrbuch der Kunsthistorischen Sammlung in Wien*, N.S. VIII (1934), 1, 10f.

28. A. Riegl, *Spätrömische Kunstindustrie*, 2nd ed., Vienna (1927), reprint ed. Darmstadt (1973). Many of the renaissance theories were published in the early decades of the twentieth century, before Riegl's publications of the 1890s and 1900s had been widely accepted. Garger ('Renaissance', 1ff) quotes and refers to many; see also, D. Levi, '*L'Arte romana: Schizzo della sua evolusione e sua posizione nella storica dell'arte antica*', *Annuario della Scuola Archeologica di Atene*, N.S. VIII–X (1946–8), 279ff, n.2. The renaissance theories continue in relatively recent literature, however; see p. 67 and above, n. 12. A bibliography of critical writings on Riegl is provided by R. Bianchi-Bandinelli, *Enciclopedia dell'arte antica*, s.v. 'Riegl'.

29. See, for example, Riegl on the sarcophagus of Junius Bassus, *Kunstindustrie*, 175ff. Matzulevitch, writing in 1929, divides the objects of his study into vessels '*mit klassisch-antiken Darstellung oder mit Ornamenten spätantiken Charakters*', thus indicating the class of objects and the type of decoration most successfully understood within Riegl's characterisation. *Byzantinische Antike*, 2.

Conclusion

In the summer of 1793, workers digging a well at the foot of the Esquiline hill in Rome accidentally uncovered a large collection of silver vessels. The find occurred in the grounds of the convent of S. Francesco di Paolo, in the ruins of a Roman building filled with the debris of later structures that once stood on the site. The accidental discovery of over twenty pieces of silver led to more systematic digging about the grounds and the subsequent find of four pieces of silver at a spot near the first site. Each discovery appears to have uncovered a collection of vessels, one much larger than the other, but insufficient evidence remains to identify the exact purpose and nature of the two burials. Within weeks of the first find, Monsignore Giulio Maria della Somaglia, a high-ranking church official and trustee of the convent, called in Ennio Quirino Visconti to publish the material. Visconti, a prominent antiquarian, then head of the Capitoline Museum, quickly completed his essay before the discovery of the second collection of silver, which he briefly discussed in a postscript appended to his main text. Bits and pieces of silver were found in the following years, consisting primarily of fragments from the damaged vessels. These fragments, along with pieces of modern silver, were used to restore those objects which had been broken and deformed under pressure or stained and pitted from chemical corrosion during their centuries of burial.

The restorations took place within thirty years of the discovery. During this period the silver changed hands several times. By 1800 della Somaglia had sold the treasure to the Baron von Schellersheim who, in turn, sold it to the Duc de Blacas in 1827. By 1866, when the Duke's son sold large parts of the family collections to the British Museum, the treasure was thought to contain some sixty pieces of silver. Four pieces discussed by Visconti had been lost and apparently forgotten for years, while two pieces had been sold to other private collectors, one to Stefano Borgia, another to P. F. J. Gossellin. The fifty-nine pieces sold to the British Museum included thirty-four that had been added to the treasure over the intervening years. The silver vessels that can now be securely matched with the finds of 1793 number twenty-seven.

This silver represents the domestic goods of a wealthy Roman family and includes tableware, horse trappings, furniture fittings, and toilet silver, consisting of caskets and flasks. Many of the objects are decorated with common scenes from the classical repertory of Muses, Nereids, vintaging Erotes, and Venus figures. The iconography of the furniture fittings, however, is less common and carries associations with high office in the late empire. An identification of the family and thus an indication of the offices held can be derived from inscriptions found on objects in the treasure. These name the Turcii, prominent in Rome, whose various members rose to the offices of *corrector*, governor, suffect consul, consul, and urban prefect during the fourth

and fifth centuries. A previously unknown male member, Turcius Secundus, a convert to Christianity within this pagan family, is named along with his wife Proiecta. Their inscription occurs on a casket probably presented to the couple as a wedding present. Two other females are attested: one a member of the *gens* Turcia and another, one Pelegrina, whose exact relation to the family is not specified. The nature of the domestic arrangement of the two females, the Christian couple, and the pagan office holder(s) is not known. Their valuables were found together; the objects, according to stylistic criteria, are roughly contemporary in date; and stylistic and technical details indicate that most of the pieces were made in a single silver workshop. The interrelations of objects in the treasure further indicate that the shop was patronised by several members of this household over a limited period of time.

With the exception of one object—the only bronze vessel, sold at an early date to Stefano Borgia—the pieces of the treasure can easily be matched, both in overall design and surface decoration, with other examples of various late antique styles of silver plate. Of these twenty-six vessels, twenty-two are associated with the so-called Esquiline workshop, while among those not included in the workshop collection are pieces from the second find of 1793, further emphasising their existence as a group apart. The styles displayed by all twenty-six, however, indicate a general late antique date in the fourth or early fifth century for the treasure as a whole. More specific dates, once supplied by an epitaph erroneously thought to be Proiecta's, are now derived from evidence internal to the treasure. The presence of a Tyche figure of Constantinople requires a date after the year 330, and a constellation of four Tyches suggests a date at the mid-century. Aspects of personal fashion depicted in relief decorations confirm this date, while vicissitudes in the official careers of the Turcii family further reinforce it. A broad date from 330 to 370 accommodates all the evidence, permits a (relatively) late conversion for Turcius Secundus, and allows the workshop products to have been commissioned and purchased in celebration of various events in the lives of the household members.

A date in the mid-fourth century also agrees with dates associated with objects from the treasures of Mildenhall and Traprain Law and with the Parabiago patera. These appear closely related to the Esquiline silver, so closely that specific relations with the Esquiline workshop are suggested. The patrons of the workshop thus potentially include the pagan office holder(s) and Christian couple of the *gens* Turcia as well as the pagan owner of the Parabiago plate, with its imagery of Cybele and Attis. This evidence of a religiously heterogeneous clientele agrees with existing theories of workshop production in the ancient world, but the specific associations of the Esquiline pieces carry additional implications. According to older literature, such associations would cause the workshop, and the treasure with it, to be understood as part of the 'Roman Renaissance', a movement discussed as originating in the West, reviving significant pagan, anti-Christian subject matter in the wake of the conversion of the emperor and the transference of the capital to Constantinople. The revival of pagan iconography is thought to be tied to a revival of classical style, following a theory of typological styles (*Gattungsstile*) applied to Roman art since the 1930s. The Parabiago patera may indeed be a testament to the cult of Magna Mater, but the common classical iconography found in the Esquiline silver hardly signals pagan cult. More important, perhaps, the style of neither Esquiline nor Parabiago could ever be called classical: the late antique renderings of figures and their spatial interrelations which first led to their association also causes them to be removed from any 'Renaissance' group. The Esquiline Treasure offers striking evidence of the survival of classical imagery, its treatment in a late antique style, and its easy acceptance by both pagans and Christians in the late empire. The Esquiline silver also demonstrates the contemporary manufacture of objects of distinct formal styles by craftsmen within a single workshop and, equally important, the purchase of these distinct styles by the members of a single family of the Roman aristocracy in the mid-fourth century.

Catalogue

The catalogue which follows provides descriptions and discussion of the individual objects in the Esquiline Treasure. Details of technique, restoration, and iconography specific to single vessels and of limited relevance to the arguments of the preceding text are recorded in the catalogue entries. All sixty-one pieces currently understood as the Esquiline Treasure are included, while the twenty-seven which can be securely identified with the original find are designated by asterisks. Brief discussion of the four pieces missing since the early nineteenth century completes the catalogue. Bibliographic references for the individual entries are limited to the Visconti essay of 1793 and the British Museum guide of 1901 written by O. M. Dalton; a select bibliography for the treasure as a whole can be found on p. 99.

*No. 1 Proiecta Casket (figs. 6, 12, 17, pls. 1–11)
Silver with gilding.
L 55.9 cm (22 in); W 43.2 cm (17 in); H 28.6 cm (11¼ in).
BM M&LA 66, 12–29, 1.
Inscription (fig. 12): On the horizontal rim of the casket
lid, before the front panel, in large engraved capitals:

P
A|ω SECVNDEETPROIECTA VIVATIS INCHRI [STO] (*Secunde
et Proiecta vivatis in Chri* [*sto*]: Secundus
and Proiecta, live in Christ)

Inscription (fig. 17): On the vertical rim of the casket lid,
to the left, before the front panel, in pointillé capitals:

ꝑ XXII—III Ꞅ

(*P*(*ondo*) *XXII, III* (*Unciae*), *S*(*emuncia*): Twenty-two
(Roman) pounds, three and one-half (Roman) ounces)[1]

fig 17. Weight inscription from Proiecta casket (*no. 1). *Scale* 1:1

The oblong casket has a body in the form of a truncated
rectangular pyramid whose sides are isosceles trapezoids;
the lid is a similar shape, smaller in overall size. The sides of
the lid are recessed from the edge of the casket and surrounded by a horizontal rim with a narrow vertical lip. There
are three hinges connecting the rim of the lid to the back
panel of the body (pl. 7). The casket once rested on four
corner braces of which three remain; the brace at the rear
right corner is gone. The object was presumably carried by
the two swing handles which are attached to the short ends
of the casket body by means of circular soldering plates with
eight-sided ring fittings. The handles are octagonal in section
with each facet carrying a running groove. Ring mouldings
mark the centre of the arcs; the handles taper towards each
end, terminating in several fillet mouldings and a knob finial.

Every surface of the casket, with the exception of the
bottom, is defined by decorative frames. Where two panels
meet, two borders run parallel; and, in the case of the lid,
where three panels meet—top and two sides—three borders
do also (pl. 4). The panels of the lid are framed with
borders of stylised floral motifs; the panels of the casket
body are framed with vine scrolls. All borders on the casket
are raised above the plane of the fields which they enclose.
The horizontal bottom band on the casket body is raised an
additional step above the side borders (pls. 8–9). The scroll
depicted on the bottom band circles the entire casket body
without interruption, running from left to right. The top
border of each panel on the casket body also runs from left
to right and continues down the right side; the scroll on the
left of each body panel runs from top to bottom.

The divisions of the lid are made more complex by a
multiplication of elements. The horizontal rim is ruled on
both inner and outer edges with engraved lines, and an
inscription is engraved within the reserve space along the
front of the casket (fig. 12, pl. 4). The top rectangular panel
is framed with a stylised floral motif which runs continuously

around the four sides with awkward transitions at the
corners (pl. 4). This border is itself framed with narrow
convex mouldings to either side. At the corners of the
panel, the outer convex moulding extends downwards,
separating or marking the joints between adjacent surfaces.

The trapezoidal panels of the lid are framed with a garland
motif with narrow convex mouldings running along the
inner and outer edges on the sides and across the tops of the
panels (pls. 4–6). Unlike the casket body, there is no continuous bottom moulding on the lid. The garlands on the
lower borders of the back and side panels of the lid run from
right to left; that on the front runs from left to right. The
vertical mouldings of the front and side panels are symmetrical garlands which rise from the bottom horizontal
moulding and continue across the top, meeting at the centre.
The garland mouldings on the back panel meet at the upper
left corner.

The five panels of the lid represent three related mythological scenes, a double portrait, and a scene from daily
life—a procession to a bath. The portraits occupy the top
panel; the procession, the back. The three mythological
scenes, which combine a Toilet of Venus with a sea *thiasos*,
are arranged with the main scene or toilet on the front and
the accessory figures on the side panels. Below the Toilet of
Venus, there is a second elaborate toilet scene on the casket
body whose main figure is aligned with the Venus on the lid.
This scene, with its eleven attendant figures, occupies all four
decorated panels on the casket body.[2]

On the top panel of the lid there are two half-length
portraits enclosed in a wreath supported on either side by
two standing Erotes (pl. 4). The wreath is the same garland
motif which frames the panels of the casket lid. It is bound
at the bottom with fillets and topped with a rosette or jewel.
The portraits are those of a richly dressed man and woman.
The woman wears a large jewelled collar over what appears
to be a long-sleeved tunic girdled below the breasts; she
holds in front of her a decorated scroll in both hands. The
man wears a long-sleeved tunic beneath a *chlamys*, fastened
at his right shoulder with a bow or crossbow fibula. His left
arm is covered, and his right gestures in front of his body,
with thumb raised and two fingers extended indicating
speech. The woman's hair is parted in the middle, brushed
back in wavy sections, and brought up in a braid circling
the crown of the head. The man's hair is short and curly as is
his beard with moustaches. The man is depicted as being
slightly taller and larger than the woman; both have heads
and hands relatively large for their bodily proportions. The
woman to the left overlaps and therefore appears to stand
in front of the man. The faces of the figures are turned
towards one another in three-quarter views; their bodies are
frontal.

The Erotes which flank the portraits are nude except for a
decorative band which crosses the chest from the shoulder
to the waist. Their hair is short and fringed in comma curls
at the brow; their wings are hatched to indicate feathers.
They are symmetrically paired with inner arms reaching up
and outer arms crossing the body to grasp the wreath.
Uneven ground-lines provide a base for the figures. The
lower torsos and legs are represented in three-quarter
postures turned out towards the frame. The upper torsos

are frontal, and the faces are turned inwards in three-quarters views towards the centre. Both figures have stocky proportions, but the Erote on the left is rendered less awkwardly than that on the right. Its easier relationship to the frame, the more volumetric rendering of its shoulders, even the detail of the rinceaux design on its chest band where the other has none, all are signs of greater attention to modelling and detail.

Comparing the faces of the Erotes with the faces of the couple, it is difficult to determine whether there has been an attempt to individualise the so-called portraits. The scheme of half-length figures framed by a wreath is a portrait convention, but the features of the faces are found elsewhere on the casket. The straight nose, small mouth, prominent eyes with dotted pupils, full cheeks, and heavy jaw of the Erotes are repeated in the faces of the couple. The woman's nose is narrow and short, while the man has the same broad nostrils as the Erotes. His beard and the consequent lengthening of his face, their hair-styles, and their clothing constitute the main 'portrait' features.

The side panels of the lid differ from the top in placing figures in definite spatial settings: the mythological scenes take place in the sea; the procession takes place in an urban architectural context. Like the top panel, however, the side panels preserve and combine numerous proportional types in a single scene. The front panel has two stocky Erotes, two small-headed, heavily-muscled Centaurotritons, and an elongated, small-breasted, heavy-hipped Venus (pl. 4). The facial types of the top panel are also repeated, and the Venus, with her short, narrow nose, resembles the female portrait figure.

The nude Venus is seated in a large cockle shell supported by two flanking Centaurotritons. Her upper torso is frontal; the lower torso and legs are turned three-quarters to the left. She holds a straight pin in her right hand with which she dresses her hair, which is brushed back and down her neck. Her face is turned three-quarters to the right where a mirror with her faint reflection is held by a Centaurotriton. The left arm of the Venus is obscured by the mirror and by the drapery which falls from her left shoulder and continues across her left thigh and over her right leg. She wears a small conical cap topped with a circular finial and a jewelled collar with a pendant which reaches to her navel.

The Centaurotritons are depicted with lower bodies in profile and torsos turned three-quarters towards the centre. They wear short capes of animal skin knotted below their necks and flying out behind them. An Erote stands on the coiled tail of each. The Erotes turn three-quarters towards the centre and offer gifts; segments of drapery flutter behind them. The Erote to the left, with short curly hair, holds a footed rectangular casket; that on the right, with more abundant hair, offers a basket filled with fruit.

The panel on the right side of the casket lid depicts a Nereid riding a *hippocampus* (pl. 5); the panel on the left depicts a Nereid on a *ketos* (pl. 5). Both figures are represented as moving towards the front panel and are easily understood as parts of the main scene. The scale of the figures is larger, but the elongated proportions of the Venus are repeated in the Nereids.

Extensive restorations to the right panel reflect a later taste (fig. 6, pl. 5). In the area of original silver, the head of the *hippocampus*, a duck depicted above it, and the head, upper torso, and right arm of the Nereid are preserved. The Nereid is turned three-quarters towards the left; her head is in profile. It is the only profile head on the casket. The body of the *hippocampus* and that of the Nereid are restored. In the restored area below and to the right of the *hippocampus* are a dolphin and a strangely Napoleonic Erote.

The better-preserved left panel represents two dolphins swimming before a *ketos* and an Erote behind, gesturing towards the Nereid (pl. 5). Her body lies across that of the *ketos*. The legs and lower torso of the Nereid are turned three-quarters to the right, the upper torso is frontal, and the head is turned back three-quarters to the left. Drapery twisted around each arm billows in an arc above her head, and a long pendant of the type worn by the Venus hangs around her neck to a point above the navel.

The scene of the back panel of the lid takes place before an arcade of alternating round and pointed arches depicted as springing from spirally fluted columns with Corinthian capitals (pl. 6). Six figures, in two groups of three, flank a large building in the centre of the panel. The building is represented as having a front entrance with an entablature supported by corner piers and two spirally fluted columns; there are arched openings in its sides. Above the entrance are four round-headed windows and two ridged mouldings possibly to be read as balustrades or as rows of tiles on a sloping roof. The building might therefore be understood to have an entrance porch, distyle in antis, preceding a plain, fenestrated wall. Recessed from this façade is a large dome flanked by what appear to be four small domes to the left and five to the right.

Each group of three figures is composed of an adult woman walking towards the centre preceded by a youth and followed by a girl. The women wear dalmatics with *clavi*, mantles, and soft boots; the youths wear tunics, and the girls dalmatics—in the case of the figure to the far right over a long-sleeved tunic. The women wear their hair in a fashion similar to that of the woman in the top portrait panel. The youth on the left has a specific hair-style with short bangs and long hair at the sides and back, while the other three figures have indistinct caps of curls.

All figures are represented in three-quarter postures open towards the centre; the lead figures, the two youths, turn their heads back in three-quarter views towards the other figures. The first figure from the left carries an oval casket, the fourth figure a candelabrum, the fifth a large rectangular casket, and the sixth a ewer and a patera or trulla. To the right of the sixth figure is a situla with an arched handle. Movement towards the centre is indicated by the striding postures of the figures, especially those of the young men who step up, as if entering the central domed building. The bath procession, like the portrait panel, depicts figures with costumes and hair-styles contemporary with the manufacture of the casket.

The theme of the bath is echoed on a general level by the Toilet of Venus on the lid and elaborated in the representations on the casket body. The four decorated panels of the body can be understood as one large scene (pls. 8–9). All four panels are unified thematically; they are also unified spatially by a system of alternating round and pointed arches carried on spirally fluted columns with Corinthian capitals. Pairs of curtains hang in the arched openings tied back to reveal human figures. The outermost arches of the two long sides contain peacocks with bodies facing outwards and heads turned back. The spandrels of the short sides contain two baskets of fruit, two birds, and two rosettes symmetrically displayed.

The chief actor in the scene, the woman at her toilet, is placed under the wider central arch of the front panel of the body (pls. 8, 11). The head of the figure, which is seated frontally on an elaborate chair, is on a level with the heads of her standing attendants. In addition to her dominance by position and scale, hers is the most lavish costume: she wears a large *colobium* with necklaces over a long-sleeved tunic. Hers is also the most lavish hair-style, a large braided coil on the crown of the head. Her gestures mimic those of the Venus on the lid as she dresses her hair with a pin and inclines her head to the left where an attendant holds a mirror. In her left hand she holds a pyxis.

The eleven attendant figures of the casket body are similar in proportion to the adult women of the back panel of the casket lid (pls. 6, 8–10). The attendants are modelled far more subtly, however, and, therefore appear less awkward. All but one of the attendant figures stand in three-quarter postures, although there is some variation in direction. The nine female attendants wear either long-sleeved tunics girdled beneath the breasts or dalmatics, both with *clavi* and decorated cuffs and borders. Their hair-styles are less exactly rendered than that of the main figure, but all consist of hair gathered into buns or coils on the crown of the head. There are two male servants dressed in long, tight-sleeved tunics with *clavi* and *orbiculi*. They both wear the hair-style of bangs with long hair to the sides and back, similar to that seen on the youth from the back panel of the casket lid.

The two female attendants who flank the main figure face in towards the centre: the figure to the right holds the mirror; that to the left holds a rectangular casket (pl. 8). Starting on the right end panel and continuing around to the opposite side, the impression is one of figures in procession from left to right. Seven of the nine figures on the three panels turn to the left; one figure turns back to the right, and one faces out. All carry attributes. On the right end panel a female servant carrying a large square object with elaborate borders and surface design—possibly a second casket—is flanked by women carrying a patera or trulla, a ewer, and a situla (pl. 8). The three female servants of the back panel carry, from left to right, a third rectangular casket, a circular casket suspended by chains from a ring, and a large, smooth surfaced basin or mirror (pl. 9). In addition, there is a vase at the foot of the first servant. On the left end panel, the two male servants carrying flaming candles in simple candlesticks flank a female servant who holds yet another rectangular casket in front of her (pl. 9).

The decoration of the casket is executed in repoussé. Visual evidence suggests that the outlines of decoration were pounced with evenly spaced points on the surface of the casket and then raised in relief from the back. Engraved line is used to outline and to embellish areas of relief. There is internal modelling in passages of drapery and on the torsos of the bodies, but it is most commonly complemented by line and outline. Line does function independently of relief in background areas, such as the arcade of the back panel of the lid (pl. 6). Line also has a purely decorative function as in the spirals of the columns, the 'faceting' of the architectural arcade, and the gratuitous outlining of most attributes—mirrors, caskets, and baskets. The framing devices of both body and lid are worked in relief with all detail supplied by engraved line. Crudely engraved line veins the four soldering plates, and the three hinges which join lid and body are decorated with a linear, geometric pattern (pl. 7).

There is a limited use made of shallow grooves on the surface of the casket. The sea of the three mythological panels is the most obvious and extensive area of its use (pls. 4–5), but the device also appears on the tails of the Centaurotritons and on the inner surfaces of the Venus' shell.

There is a fourth important technique, that of stippling for decorative effect (as opposed to the evenly spaced pouncing mentioned above). Decorative stippling occurs on every panel. Circles of stippled dots, groups of semicircles, and circles of punch-work decorate the fabrics of the portrait figures' costumes, the drapery of the Erotes, and the bodies of the various sea creatures. Hatching imitates animal skins and bird feathers, torque mouldings, and basket weaving. Stippling dots every eye and every grape; it echoes the tendrils of the vine scroll. It decorates the *clavi, orbiculi*, cuffs, and borders of all costumes; it is the jewellery of the Venus and Nereid. It embellishes most of the attributes carried by the various attendant figures.

All the devices which have a decorative function, such as line, grooving, and stippling, are secondary in visual effect to the gilding which is used on seven of the nine relief panels of the casket. Where gilding is omitted, as on the back panels of the lid and body, the other devices appear more prominent, but the two panels are dull in comparison with the others. Gilding is used compositionally as in the top panel (pl. 4), where it is concentrated within the portrait medallion, and in the front panel of the body (pl. 8), where the heavily gilded drapery of the central figure helps to define its visual importance. The primary use of the gilding, however, is decorative.

Gilding is used with the frequency of stippling and, in fact, often coincides with its appearance. Gilding picks out all grape clusters and leaves on the borders of the casket body and appears at roughly regular intervals on the garland borders of the lid. All capitals and bases, all *clavi, orbiculi*, jewellery, cuffs and borders of drapery, all hair-styles, manes, beards, wings, hooves, and paws are gilded. Every object carried by an attendant figure is edged and decorated with gilding. The bodies of the sea creatures, the shell on which the Venus sits, and the incidental draperies of the Erotes, the Centaurotritons, the Venus, and the Nereids are gilded. Almost every object represented is partially gilded, and gilding is therefore fairly evenly distributed on every panel.

The consistent use of these decorative devices renders restorations to the casket easily discernible. The restored silver is a close colour match to the original, but the restored gilding is not; it is pale and of a slightly different tint. As a result, its restoration is obvious. The new pieces also show a misunderstanding but, more commonly, a total lack of stippling, which appears practically everywhere on the original surfaces.

The restorations are composed almost entirely of new silver. A few old pieces are restored to the panels of the casket (fig. 6), and several fragments from the horizontal rim are integrated into what is largely new material (fig. 12, see pl. 4). Three pieces of ancient silver, including the weight inscription, remain from the vertical lip of the rim, restored along the front face of the casket. The four bottom corners of the casket are all restored, while the single largest area of restoration covers the right panel of the lid and crosses into the front panel on a diagonal. There are repairs along the bottom borders of the body panels and incidental restorations on the back and left panels of the lid. There are numerous cracks on the surfaces of the casket. These cracks, as well as the seams between old surfaces and new restorations, are backed with silver strips and occasionally secured with solder. There is some surface pitting on the casket body; the surfaces of the lid are relatively free of corrosion.

Visconti: M–M, 3ff, pls. I–VI; Dalton, *Catalogue*, no. 304, 61ff (with figs. 61, 177), pls. XIII–XVIII.

*No. 2   Muse Casket (fig. 18, pls. 12–17)
Silver.
D 32.7 cm (12$\frac{7}{8}$ in); H 26.7 cm (10$\frac{1}{2}$ in).
BM M&LA 66, 12–29, 2.

The circular casket has a domed cover approximately equal in height to the body of the vessel. The dome is recessed from the edge of the lid, surrounded by a plain horizontal rim with a narrow vertical lip. The body and cover are joined by a hinge (pl. 14), and the entire casket is suspended from three chains attached to a large ring. The ring is octagonal in section with a shallow groove in each facet. The chains are fastened to the body by means of three soldering plates with eight-sided ring fittings. A narrow tapering tab for raising and lowering the lid is attached to the rim opposite the hinge by means of another soldering plate with ring (pl. 12).

The surfaces of both the body and the dome have been divided into sixteen panels with alternating flat and concave faces; the rim of the lid echoes this alternation. The flat surfaces of both halves are decorated with vases, vine motifs, and birds. The fluted panels of the dome are undecorated, while those of the body contain standing female figures under

fig. 18 Muse casket (*no. 2). *Scale* $\frac{1}{4}$:1

arches. There is a circular medallion at the top of the dome which contains a female figure seated in a landscape setting (pl. 16).

There are multiple systems of organisation within and among the surfaces of the casket and its decorative motifs. The dominant system is that established by the alternating panels, since the concave and the flat surfaces of the body are aligned with those of the dome. The effect is one of verticals radiating downwards from a central medallion. A definite front and back are established through the opposition of hinge and tab. In addition, the flat panel below the tab is distinct in design from the other decorative panels, featuring two birds below a large wreath tied with a ribbon and topped with a rosette (pl. 12). The suggestion of emphasis and of the creation of a 'façade' is further strengthened by the alignment of the top medallion, whose vertical axis is a continuation of that established by the tab and its associated panel (pl. 16).

In contrast to the vertical accents there are horizontal bands of garland mouldings circling the casket at both the top and bottom of the body, on the vertical rim of the cover, and surrounding the top medallion. Each successive garland reverses the direction of the previous garland moulding. A further horizontal division into halves is suggested by the decoration of every panel on the casket body in contrast to the sharp alternation of decorated and plain surfaces on the domed lid.

Smaller systems of organisation can be seen in the relationships between panels. The decorative panels of the dome are grouped in symmetrical pairs according to the spirals of the rinceaux and the postures and attributes of the birds contained within them. The related panels on the casket body have spindle motifs with spiral flutes which reverse direction in each successive panel. Each dome rinceau consists of four major spirals, which diminish as they grow upwards in the narrowing trapezoidal field. The rinceaux rise out of stylised kantharoi with fluted bodies and wide mouths; two secondary spirals grow downwards, with leaves and grape clusters flanking the vases. The first of the main spirals contains a small bird in profile, the second a five-lobed leaf, the third a flower, and the fourth spiral ends with a furled leaf. There are additional leaves and grape clusters in the spaces between the spirals and the narrow incised lines that define the edges of the fields.

The decorative panels of the body repeat the same motifs in a different, internally symmetrical arrangement. Each panel contains a wide-mouthed, fluted kantharos out of which grow two symmetrically curving vines. A spindle-shaped shaft rises out of the centre of the vase. Each vine has a major spiral which curls up and out from the base and then in towards the centre; within this spiral, there is a small bird in profile facing the spindle. There is a secondary spiral on each vine which curves downwards, carrying a grape leaf and grape cluster or a rosette and furled leaf. As mentioned above, the first panel below the tab is distinct in design, clearly set apart from this scheme. For purposes of discussion, the panels aligned on axis with the tab will be designated the first panels of both dome and body, and numbering will proceed to the right. Two decorative panels on the casket body, the fifth and fifteenth, are partially obscured by

two of the three soldering plates for the chain mounts; the top of the ninth panel serves as a base for the lower half of the hinge.

The concave surfaces of the body carry representations of female figures identified as eight of the nine Muses. Although distinguished from one another by costume and attributes, the figures are represented as variations of a single type (pls. 12–15). All stand under shallow arches supported by symmetrically fluted columns with simplified bases and Corinthian capitals. The figures are a uniform proportional type with full faces, prominent bellies, and short necks. The faces are characterised by a straight, narrow nose, a long upper lip, a small mouth, and full, rounded cheeks. There is a single hair-style of locks parted in the middle and brushed back in sections. A second, smooth area is visible encircling the crown of the head; it is difficult to determine whether it represents hair or a head-dress of some type. The lack of surface detail suggests the latter, in which case it may be associated with a pointed tab which stands upright at the centre parting. The tab is a stylised version of the feather head-dress worn by the Muses, an attribute alluding to their victory over the Sirens.[3]

Six of the eight Muses have a uniform stance with weight carried on the left leg and the right leg extended from the body with a break forward at the knee. The figures of the second and fourth panels differ in bearing their weight on the right legs: the figure of the second panel leans her left arm on an abbreviated column and crosses her left leg before her (pl. 12); the figure of the fourth panel supports her left leg on a step or pedestal, with the knee sharply bent (pl. 13). Three of the eight figures turn their faces three-quarters to the left (panels six, eight, and twelve); the other five face forward.

Variations of dress should be noted, and specific attributes can be seen to identify the individual Muses.[4] The figure of the second panel, Urania, the Muse of astronomy, is wrapped in a long and complexly draped mantle with the right sleeve of a tunic showing (pl. 12). She wears soft boots, as do the other seven. The figure leans on a column with spiral flutes and rectilinear mouldings at the top and bottom. She holds a short rod in her right hand, gesturing over a globe marked with two intersecting equators; the sphere rests on a simple rectangular base.

The figure of the fourth panel, Melpomene, the Muse of tragedy, wears a long, tight-sleeved tunic with a wide girdle beneath the breasts and two panels of equal width passing over the shoulders (pl. 13). She carries a gnarled club in her right hand and a large tragic mask in her left. There is an unfurled scroll to the right.

Clio, the Muse of history, on the sixth panel, wears a full-sleeved short tunic over a long undergarment (pl. 13). Her left hand grasps a codex or writing diptych, while the right gestures before her body in speech. There is an open scrinium filled with scrolls to the right of the figure.

The figure of the eighth panel wears a long, tight-sleeved tunic with a short cloak or scarf crossing the body from her left shoulder to her right hip where it is held out from the body by her right hand (pl. 14). A short-haired, closed-mouth mask, considerably smaller than that held by

Melpomene on the fourth panel, is held in the figure's left hand. The nature of the mask suggests an identification of the Muse as Polyhymnia in her role as the Muse of mime.[5]

The tenth panel is partially obscured by a soldering plate which covers the figure's left arm and any attribute possibly carried on that side (pl. 14). The figure wears an ankle-length, tight-sleeved tunic with a swirling hem. A short, thick, pointed rod, most probably a plectrum, is carried in the right hand. The Muse might be identified as either Erato with a cithara or Terpsichore with a lyre. The hem of the garment might be understood to indicate a dancing posture, and the Muse in question would therefore be interpreted as Terpsichore, Muse of the dance.

The Muse Euterpe on the twelfth panel is dressed in a long, tight-sleeved tunic girdled below the breasts (pl. 15). A short mantle falls behind the figure, apparently attached to the girdle by two small panels which pass over the shoulders. The figure holds a pipe or end-blown flute in each hand.

The fourteenth panel represents Thalia, the Muse of comedy, in a similar tunic with an ankle-length swirling hem (pl. 15). Two panels pass over the shoulders, but there is no mantle depicted. The figure holds a *pedum* in her right hand and a grotesque comic mask in the left.

The sixteenth panel probably represents Calliope, Muse of epic poetry, wearing a mantle over a long tunic; a scroll is held in both hands in front of the body (pl. 12). To the right of the figure is a ewer on a spirally fluted stand.[6]

The female figure in the centre medallion of the dome wears a simple tunic girdled below the breasts (pl. 16). Unlike the eight figures on the casket body, she lacks the hair ornament and does not pose conspicuously displaying attributes. It would be difficult to identify the figure with any one of the Muses despite the temptation to see the full complement of nine Muses in the nine female figures represented. It might be suggested that the ninth figure represents the owner of the casket (Proiecta?), on the analogy of similar groupings found on sarcophagi. The head and face of the medallion figure are unfortunately creased and abraded, although a hair-style with a braided coil on the crown of the head, similar to styles on the Proiecta casket, can be recognised. The figure is seated on a folding stool in a three-quarter posture to the right, with head turned back towards the left. Sitting beneath the branches of a tree which grows to the right, she holds what appears to be a garland in her left hand and reaches towards a large basket of fruit with her right. A bird in profile rests on the figure's right wrist. The medallion is worn, and details of representation are difficult to discern.

The original fittings of the casket have been mentioned: a hinge, a tab mounted on a ring, three chains with soldering plates, and a large ring to which the chains are attached. In addition to the faceting of the various wire rings, there is surface decoration on several of the fittings. The two halves of the hinge are covered with a grid of incised ovals set at forty-five degrees to the edges of the hinge; the four-sided reserve spaces are marked with circular depressions (pl. 16). The tab, whose surface is worn, is decorated with a bead and reel motif. One soldering plate (panel ten, pl. 14) has an irregular shape reminiscent of a serrated leaf. The other two plates (panels five and fifteen) are circular and crudely marked as if to indicate veining. All three, as well as the hinge, are affixed to the body of the casket with solder and silver rivets.

The interior of the casket is fitted with a bronze plate with circular fittings for five vessels. The central and largest is a silver flask with a cylindrical lower body and a smoothly sloping neck which terminates in a convex moulding and angular rim (pl. 17). A continuous break between the two main sections of the flask suggests a major repair; the possibility exists that the top is not original to the body, for the fit is far from exact. The other four vessels are identical cylindrical silver canisters with tightly fitting lids (pl. 17). Just below the lids, the bodies have an angular moulding, and the lids themselves flare outwards at the top. All five vessels are decorated with numerous engraved lines in successive circles on the cylindrical surfaces and in concentric circles on the tops of the lids. The decorative lines are not simple incised horizontals but minute vertical strokes which resolve into horizontal lines at a distance while simultaneously producing a glittering effect.

The techniques employed in the decoration are relatively few. The motifs, with the exception of the incised designs on the various fittings, are executed in repoussé. Some, but not all, of the motifs are outlined; incised line is also used decoratively as flutes on vases, veins on leaves, and spirals on columns. Stippling appears repeatedly—on vine tendrils, drapery borders, grape clusters, birds—to the extent that the restorations can easily be distinguished by their lack or fumbling use of stippling.

In general, the casket is relatively well preserved. The most obvious addition is a modern key lock placed behind the first panel of the casket body.[7] The interior of the casket shows silver strips at the base of the seventh and ninth panels, although there are no exterior repairs at these points. Panel ten, with the irregular soldering plate, is heavily reinforced. There is only one restored piece on the casket body: it is found at the top of the third panel, above the paired birds (fig. 18). The repair continues into the garland moulding above the panel. There are ten pieces of restored silver on the lid. Nine lie along a horizontal crack running across the front of the casket from panel fourteen to panel three (fig. 18). A tenth piece restores the feet of the figure in the top medallion and the stool on which she sits.

The surface of the casket body is in excellent condition, in marked contrast to the generally pitted surface of the domed lid. The restorations to both lid and body lack the surface corrosion of the original silver. The modelling of the motifs is sharper and more angular, and, as mentioned, stippling is most commonly omitted. There are cracks in the horizontal rim surrounding the dome near the hinge, incidental cracks in the dome panels aside from the area of major damage, and a sharp crease across the face of the female figure in the central medallion. There are two chisel marks on the vessels contained inside the casket: one on the bottom of one of the canisters and one on the bottom of the flask.

Visconti: M–M, 7ff, pls. VII–XI; Dalton, *Catalogue*, no. 305, 64ff (with figures, 65f), pl. XIX.

*No. 3 Paris Patera (pl. 21)
Silver.
D 24.2 cm (9½ in); L (with handle) 37 cm (14⁹⁄₁₆ in).
Paris. Musée du Petit Palais. Dutuit Collection.

The patera has a flat bottom, curving sides, a high flaring foot ring, a horizontal rim, and a horizontal handle which extends from the rim. The exterior decoration is limited to an engraved circle within the foot ring; the interior of the patera, its rim, and its handle are richly decorated. The narrow rim is elaborated with a border motif of sea shells with alternating interior and exterior faces. The shells are all arranged with ribs radiating outwards and alternate not only with regard to surface but also with regard to type. The shells shown as exterior surfaces are scallops; those shown as interior surfaces are cockles.

The handle is occupied by a standing figure and, below its feet, a recumbent animal. The figure is a beardless, short-haired nude male in three-quarter stance to the right with his head turned three-quarters to the left. His left hand grasps a spear which extends the length of his body. The animal is a long-tailed dog with body in profile to the right and head turned sharply back to the left.

The shallow bowl of the patera is interpreted as a large cockle shell with broad, smooth surfaces alternating with shallow grooves capped with semicircular ridges. Above the umbo, or beak, of the shell, a partially draped female figure is depicted, flanked by two Erotes. The figure is seated in a three-quarter pose to the left with ankles crossed; no physical support for her posture is represented. The figure is shown tying a fillet in her hair and turning her head to the right where a mirror is held by a flying Erote. The Erote to the left carries a cloth and offers a flower. The female wears a small crescent ornament in her hair, which is loosely brushed back into a knot with tendrils falling down the neck and over the shoulders. A chain of pointillé ornament crosses between her breasts, and a pendant hangs from the crossing. Drapery covers her right leg and curves back and over an implied but unrepresented support from which it hangs in folds. The Erotes are both represented as flying or hovering with torsos in three-quarter view, heads and wings in profile, and outer legs forward, crossing inner legs which extend backwards. The subject is the Toilet of Venus and, therefore, the male figure with the attributes of a young hunter might be identified as Adonis.

The figures are modelled in relief with strong swelling forms defining arms, thighs, and torsos. Several different proportional types are represented from the stocky Erotes to the elongated, heavy-hipped, small-breasted Venus. The faces are all distinguished by prominent brow ridges, long noses, long upper lips, small mouths, and heavy jaws. Figures are in three-quarter pose with outer limbs fully modelled and some inner limbs reduced to engraved line.

Incised line is also used for surface articulation and embellishment. The hair of the figures and the dog, the wings of the Erotes, and the borders of the drapery are all indicated with engraved line. In addition, stippling decorates the drapery and such attributes as the mirror, the crescent hair ornament, the fillet, and the jewellery on the breasts of the Venus figure.

The patera is well preserved. There is a small fragment missing from the rim to the left of the handle, and there are patches of surface discoloration scattered over the entire vessel. The handle has been worn, especially in the area of the legs and the lower torso of the male figure where a smooth surface now obscures the original modelling and surface detail. The underside of the object is covered with lacquer now brown with age. The lacquer covers, but does not obscure, a chisel mark, approximately 2.5 cm (1 in) long, on the right side of the handle opposite the representation of the dog.[8]

Visconti: M–M, 21f, pl. XXIII.

*No. 4 Fluted Dish (fig. 5, pls. 22–3)
Silver.
D 56.2 cm (22⅛ in).
BM M&LA 66, 12–29, 3.

The large dish has a flat circular centre and twenty-four radiating panels with alternating flat and concave surfaces. There is a circular foot ring which echoes the central panel and a narrow rim which caps the straight and semicircular ends of the radiating surfaces.

Decoration of the underside of the dish is limited to three incised concentric circles within the foot ring. The upper surfaces of the dish, which are distinguished from one another by decoration, direction, and curvature, are additionally defined by systems of engraved lines and grooves. The central medallion is enclosed within two engraved concentric circles flanking a broad shallow groove. Each flat radiating panel is framed with an engraved line which runs approximately 0.6 cm (¼ in) from its edge on the sides and outer border and by a faint groove which runs in the resultant margin. The decorative patterns which occupy these reserve fields do not extend to the border of the central panel but end a short distance from it. This inner edge of the decorative fields is defined by engraved line; there is no accompanying groove. This engraved line is simultaneously part of the framing device of the flat panels and part of a larger radial composition. The straight lines are joined to the engraved semicircles which define the ends of the fluted panels. The resultant figure resembles a spoked wheel whose cusps lie tangent to the central circular panel. The fluted panels are otherwise undecorated.

Engraved decoration fills the central medallion and the outlined areas of the flat panels. There are six motifs in all, five of which are based on combinations of petal or leaf shapes. A square is inscribed within the central circular panel; its sides are composed of parallel incised lines which flank a shallow groove (pl. 23). While not defining a structural member of the plate, the device divides the circle effectively into a square and four lunettes. The lunettes are filled with petals which fan in canopy or shell shapes. The square is decorated with a right-angle grid pattern set at forty-five degrees to the vertical and horizontal axes of the square. A line within the decorative grid is composed of oval petals linked tip to tip to form a chain. Where two lines intersect, four petals join. In the overall design, the grid pattern of petals creates negative shapes: four-sided forms defined by four equal concave sides. There is a circle of stippled dots at each intersection or meeting of four petals and within each reserve space.

The patterns of the radiating panels show two types of surface organisation. Six of the twelve panels are covered with overall designs which fill the elongated trapezoidal fields with motifs growing larger towards the outer borders. The other six panels are divided along their long axes by two parallel incised lines with a shallow groove running between; identical, symmetrically disposed motifs flank the division. Although the individual fields are distinctly narrower, the motifs of these panels also increase in size towards the outer edge.

There are six patterns for twelve panels: each pattern appears twice, and the two panels which feature the same pattern lie next to one another, separated only by an intervening flute. These groups of two are further organised along an axis which is roughly perpendicular to two sides of the central square. To one side are grouped those panels which feature motifs symmetrically flanking a central division; to the other are those with overall patterns and no internal division. Analysis of restoration, which follows, demands that the panels—both flat and fluted—be easily identifiable. The dish is therefore illustrated with divided panels to the left and undivided panels to the right. The undecorated flute which lies on the dividing axis above the central square will be designated the first panel; numbering continues clockwise.

The second and fourth panels are filled with a garland motif with the petal or leaf tips pointing inwards. The sixth and eighth panels feature superimposed canopies of petals, smaller but similar to those which appear in the lunettes of the central panel. The tenth and twelfth panels repeat the diagonal grid of ovals with stippled circles found in the central square. The fourteenth and sixteenth panels, the first of the divided format, show petals curving inwards towards the central groove. The eighteenth and twentieth panels represent a pattern in which petals curving inwards alternate with petals curving outwards in groups of three. The relative complexity of this pattern and the free-hand technique of execution result in less than perfect symmetry across the central divider. The last two decorative panels, the twenty-second and twenty-fourth, feature rows of superimposed heart-shaped leaves with tips pointing towards the centre of the dish. Small stippled spirals flank each leaf at the tip.

The techniques employed include incised line, chasing, and stippling for decorative accent. There is no need to elaborate on the organisation of the surfaces, but the execution of the leaf or petal motifs is distinct and noteworthy. The two long sides of each petal are incised in smooth, curving lines; a blunt-ended groove with a mild taper is worked from the narrow to the broad end of the petal; and, apparently last, fine stippling is applied in an arc, completing the rounded tip of the petal for which there is no incised line. In certain patterns, such as the garlands and petal canopies, the stippling forms an unbroken line of scallops, capping numerous petals in a row.

The execution of the grid of ovals, seen in the pattern that fills both the centre square and the tenth and twelfth panels,

is only somewhat different. It has been mentioned that the ovals are outlined with two incised lines, but, as with the petal motifs, the lines do not actually meet at either end. An additional detail concerns the blunt-ended grooves which run the long axes of the ovals. Rather than radiating outwards from points of intersection, the grooves run systematically from lower left to upper right on one diagonal and from lower right to upper left on the other. These small details of technique become important in discerning areas of restoration.

The plate has been heavily damaged.[9] Although the central area and large portions of the radiating panels are perfectly preserved, at one time two-thirds of the outer edge was broken off to a depth ranging from approximately 5 to 12.7 cm (2 to 5 in) from the rim. The damage occurred along two series of cracks: one running from the first panel to the eleventh; the other from the fifteenth to the nineteenth panel (see fig. 5). There are incidental repairs to the rim, cracks near the foot ring, and small chips out of the surface in other areas.

The two areas of major damage have been restored using both new and original pieces of silver. Like the restorations on the Proiecta casket (*no. 1), the colour match of the new pieces of silver is extremely close, but the understanding of the style being imitated is not without error. The petal motifs, where restored, are executed with engraved lines which are deeper and more angular than the original work; the lines are filled with a niello-like substance unlike the original engraved but unfilled patterns. Stippling is rarely used in the restorations. Its omission is linked to a misunderstanding of the petal forms in which engraved line forms both the sides and the rounded tip, and in which the central groove is more sharply tapered, ending in a round tip which echoes the engraved line. In the restoration of the grid motif in panel ten, the grooves radiate outwards from points of intersection, rather than following the two diagonals established in the unrestored areas.

Observations of errors in style are reinforced by the awkward integration of the new silver into a restoration which also contains some fragments of old silver. The old pieces have highly irregular outlines and extremely fragile edges which spawn many hair-like surface cracks. The new pieces are angular and jagged in imitation, but they lack the quavering lines of breakage found in the original fragments. On the seventeenth panel, where damage penetrates to its deepest point on the dish, the large area of new silver is broken by the meanderings of a deep and jagged false crack.[10]

The back of the dish is covered with a network of silver strips which back the seams and cracks of old and new silver. The false cracks lack this detail. At one time, the entire exterior was covered with a lacquer which is now discoloured. The lacquer covers the reinforcing strips and four chisel marks, three within the foot ring and one on the exterior surface of the eleventh panel.

Visconti: M–M, 13, pl. XVII; Dalton, *Catalogue*, no. 310, 69 (with plate).

*No. 5 Monogram Plate (figs. 13, 19, pl. 26)
Silver with gilding and niello inlay.
D 16.1 cm (6⅜ in).
BM M&LA 66, 12–29, 12.

Monogram (fig. 13): Centred on the surface of the dish, in gilded serif capitals outlined in niello:

Inscription (fig. 19): On the under surface, along the curve of the rim, in pointillé capitals: S̄CVT.IIII.P V (*Scut(ellae) IIII P(ondo) V*: Four small dishes (with a total weight of) five (Roman) pounds).

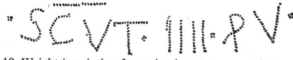

fig. 19 Weight inscription from circular monogram plate
(*no. 5). *Scale* 2:1

This dish is one of four almost identical pieces (*nos. 5–8), obviously understood to be a set as is indicated by the inscription cited above. The shallow circular dish has a flared foot ring and an eight-sided faceted rim. Decoration on the underside is limited to a centring point and an incised circle within the foot ring, and a single shallow groove running along the outer edge, echoing the rim. On the upper surface, the rim is similarly set off by an incised circle running approximately 0.3 cm (⅛ in) from its edge. Each of the facets of the rim carries a running groove, so that shallow grooves alternate with flat, sharp-edged bands.

A gilt and niello monogram, approximately 3.75 cm (1½ in) in diameter, is centred on the upper surface of the dish. The monogram, executed in gilded capitals outlined in niello, is enclosed within a circular wreath of gilt leaves edged in niello which alternate with niello berries on short stems. The leaves are almond-shaped and so abstractly depicted that an identification of the wreath with specific foliage such as myrtle, laurel, or olive is not possible. At the top centre of the wreath there is a four-petal rosette; at the bottom centre a highly stylised knot with twisted ribbon ends. These motifs are also gilded and outlined with niello. From the knot two stems curve symmetrically upwards towards the rosette. These stems, though outlined in niello, are not gilded; they are the silver of the dish surface, which surrounds the wreath and provides a contrasting background for both wreath and monogram.

The dish is well preserved with only small spots of surface discoloration.

Visconti: M–M, 9ff, pl. XIV; Dalton, *Catalogue*, no. 316, 71 (with figures).

*No. 6 Monogram Plate (fig. 20; see pl. 26)
Silver with gilding and niello inlay.
D 16.1 cm (6⅜ in).
BM M&LA 66, 12–29, 11.

Monogram: Identical with that of *no. 5.
Graffito (fig. 20): Within the foot ring, running along the incised circle, scratched in faint, irregular capitals:
VIVASINDEOMARCIANAVIVAS (*Vivas in Deo Marciana vivas*: Marciana, live in God).

This dish is part of the four-piece set. A broad chisel mark, like those found on other pieces in the treasure, has been made on the under-surface of the dish.

Visconti: M–M, 9ff, pl. XIV; Dalton, *Catalogue*, no. 318, 72.

*No. 7 Monogram Plate (see pl. 26)
Silver with gilding and niello inlay.
D 16.1 cm (6⅜ in).
BM M&LA 66, 12–29, 14.

Monogram: Identical with that of *no. 5.
The circle within the foot ring described in the entry for *no. 5 is missing from this dish which otherwise agrees with it in form and decoration. A broad chisel mark is found on the underside of this piece.

Visconti: M–M, 9ff, pl. XIV; Dalton, *Catalogue*, no. 317, 72.

*No. 8 Monogram Plate (see pl. 26)
Silver with gilding and niello inlay.
D 16.1 cm (6⅜ in).
BM M&LA 66, 12–29, 13.

Monogram: Identical with that of *no. 5.
Simplest of the four circular dishes, lacking inscriptions, graffiti and chisel marks, this piece nevertheless matches the description given for *no. 5.

Visconti: M–M, 9ff, pl. XIV; Dalton, *Catalogue*, no. 319, 72.

*No. 9 Monogram Plate (pl. 27)
Silver with gilding and niello inlay.
L 20.2 cm (7 15/16 in); W 14.6 cm (5¾ in).
BM M&LA 66, 12–29, 18.
Monogram: Identical with that of *no. 5.

This dish forms a set with three almost identical pieces (*nos. 9–12). The shallow rectangular dish has a straight-sided rectangular foot rim and a horizontal open-work border. From this border, the four sides of the dish slope inwards, diagonals at the corners gradually giving way to a seamless curving surface. There is no decoration on the underside of the dish. A gilt and niello monogram, like that on the round monogram plates (*nos. 5–8; see above) is

VIVASINDEOMARCIANAVIVASGII

fig. 20 Graffito from circular monogram plate (*no. 6). *Scale* 2:1

centred on the upper surface. Although the monogram *per se* is identical with that on the round plates, details of the wreath differ slightly. The main stems are single incised lines filled with niello rather than the double niello lines bordering a silver band seen on the circular dishes. The ribbon below the centre knot falls symmetrically in wavy outlines, where the ribbon on the round dishes extends horizontally to either side. An additional detail differs in the rectangular dishes: no attempt is made to indicate a twist or curve in the ribbon. The residual indication of three dimensions is eliminated, and the entire complex of wreath, monogram, and ribbon is treated two-dimensionally.

The horizontal rectangular border is a combination of pierce-work and surface decoration. The outline of the border is simple: a series of small scallops interrupted at the corners by oval projections. Pierced openings of a simplified pelta shape are placed below the scallops, grouping them in sets of two and replacing the small running series with larger, discrete units. The units are further elaborated with surface detail. The pierced openings are outlined with shallow grooves, and the lobes are stamped with small circular punches. The corner projections are engraved to resemble oval leaves with veins and serrated edges.

Of the four pieces of the set, this dish is the least worn with only small areas of surface discoloration. A broad chisel mark is found below the foot rim on the underside of the dish.

Visconti: M–M, 9ff, pl. XIII; Dalton, *Catalogue*, no. 315, 71 (with figures).

*No. 10   Monogram Plate (see pl. 27)
Silver with gilding and niello inlay.
L 20.2 cm (7 15/16 in); W 14.6 cm (5 3/4 in).
BM M&LA 66, 12–29, 15.

Monogram: Identical with that of *no. 5.
This dish agrees with the description of *no. 9, although it lacks the chisel mark on the underside. A considerable amount of the niello filling of both the monogram and the wreath is lost.

Visconti: M–M, 9ff, pl. XIII; Dalton, *Catalogue*, no. 314, 71.

*No. 11   Monogram Plate (see pl. 27)
Silver with gilding and niello inlay.
L 20.2 cm (7 15/16 in); W 14.6 cm (5 3/4 in).
BM M&LA 66, 12–29, 16.

Monogram: Identical with that of *no. 5.
Like the preceding piece, this rectangular dish has lost large amounts of the original niello.

Visconti: M–M, 9ff, pl. XIII; Dalton, *Catalogue*, no. 313, 71.

*No. 12   Monogram Plate (see pl. 27)
Silver with gilding and niello inlay.
L 20.2 cm (7 15/16 in); W 14.6 cm (5 3/4 in).
BM M&LA 66, 12–29, 17.

Monogram: Identical with that of *no. 5.
Like *nos. 10 and 11, this dish has lost much of the niello filling from the monogram and wreath.

Visconti: M–M, 9ff, pl. XIII; Dalton, *Catalogue*, no. 312, 71.

No. 13   Dish (see fig. 7, pl. 25)
Silver with gilding.
D 26 cm (10 1/4 in); H 2.7 cm (1 1/16 in).
BM M&LA 66, 12–29, 10.

The circular dish has a flat bottom and vertical fluted sides, concave on the interior face, convex on the exterior, with fillets between the flutes. The upper edge of the dish is scalloped with alternating large and small arcs which correspond respectively to the flutes and fillets.[11] There is little decoration on the exterior; three incised concentric circles are engraved on the bottom of the dish. The interior surface is covered with an overall geometric design which is set off from the fluted sides by a groove and an engraved line. The groove and line interrupt the overall design, cutting off segments of motifs. The design is also interrupted by a central raised medallion with a figural representation.

The medallion, framed by two concentric rings of punch-work, depicts a standing male figure in an outdoor setting. An uneven ground-line, a rock outcropping, a few scattered plants, and an altar are summarily indicated. The figure stands in a three-quarter pose, open to the left, with head in profile. The left hand holds an object, possibly a scroll, at waist level, while the right arm extends from the body at an angle holding a patera over the altar. The face is clean shaven, and the figure appears to wear an angle-length toga over a tunic.[12] The centring point of the plate can be seen in the folds of the drapery below the waist of the figure.

The medallion interrupts and partially obscures four smaller circles which are part of the overall geometric design. The pattern is one of circles placed at the intersections of a rectilinear grid. The visible grid is composed of two incised lines flanking a shallow groove, and the circles are framed with these three elements in concentric circles. When the outlines of a grid segment meet the frame of a circle, they diverge, continue around the circle in ninety-degree arcs, and rejoin the grid at right angles to their original orientation. The outlines are not broken; rather grid and circles are fused into a continuous decorative trellis. The resultant negative spaces are octagons with alternating straight and curving sides.

There are fifty-two circles on the surface of the plate, twenty of which are interrupted by the outer border. Each circle is decorated with one of eleven motifs. Nine of the eleven are radial designs based either on flowers or crosses; two shell motifs echo a vertical axis established in the central figural medallion. The octagonal spaces are each decorated with five punch marks, arranged in the shape of a cross. With the exception of the four circles at the centre of the dish, the background design is bilaterally symmetrical along two axes—a vertical axis suggested by the figure and a horizontal which passes through the centring point, crossing the figure at the waist. The obvious intention of arranging motifs to form identical quadrants suggests that the unexpected designs of the four central circles are simple variants.

All motifs on the surface of the dish are executed in incised line. Stippling is used within the circular fields as a background texture but also as a means of elaborating a given motif. The grooves were once gilded, but little gilding is now preserved. While no sign of gilding is present on the motifs within the smaller circles, traces of gilding are found on parts of the central medallion. The punch-work frame, the garments and hair of the standing figure, the patera, and the altar preserve traces. The surface of the dish is badly corroded. A series of cracks almost encircles the bottom surface, running in the groove which separates the bottom from the sides. A large, irregular fragment is missing from the bottom near the edge.[13] At present, the perimeter of the plate is reinforced on the exterior with a continuous right-angle moulding. In the area of the missing piece(s), the moulding expands to serve as a backing for both the sides and the broken edges of the dish surface.

Visconti: M–M, 21, pl. XXI; Dalton, *Catalogue*, no. 311, 70 (with figures).

No. 14   Dish (pl. 28)
Silver.
D 24.1 cm (9½ in); H 5.1 cm (2 in).
BM M&LA 66, 12–29, 9.

The circular dish has a flat bottom with curved sides, a flared foot ring, and a narrow faceted rim, semicircular in section.[14] The exterior is plain: within the foot ring there is a single incised circle and a deep mark corresponding to the centring point of the interior surface. Decoration inside the dish consists of concentric circles, both narrow incised lines and broad shallow grooves. One set of circles immediately surrounds the centring point; another marks the transition from the flat bottom to the curving sides. The simple motif of concentric circles is repeated in the grooves on the four facets of the rim of the dish.

Two fragments of different sizes are missing from the sides, and there is mild surface corrosion and some discoloration on the exterior. Except for this minor damage, the piece is well preserved. Two chisel marks, like those found on other pieces, have been made on the exterior of the dish: one within the foot ring, another on the inner face of the foot ring itself.[15]

Visconti: M–M, pl. XVIII; Dalton, *Catalogue*, no. 320, 72.

No. 15   Bowl (pl. 29)
Silver.
D 11.7 cm (4⅝ in); H 5.1 cm (2 in).
BM M&LA 66, 12–29, 8.

The small circular bowl rests on a low, flared foot ring; the overall shape of the vessel resembles a slightly flattened hemisphere.[16] Inside the single-shell bowl decoration is limited to four concentric incised circles at varying distances from a broad centring point. On the exterior, two rings mark the junction of the foot ring with the body of the bowl, and

three concentric circles decorate the area within the foot ring. The ribbing of the bowl's exterior is the most distinctive aspect of decoration. The ribs flare with the flare of the body, their surfaces are smooth, polished curves, and the divisions between the ribs are simple, soft-edged grooves. The bowl is in an excellent state of repair.

Visconti: M–M, pl. XV; Dalton, *Catalogue*, no. 321, 72 (with figure).

*No. 16   Flask (fig. 21, pl. 30)
Silver.
H 34.6 cm (13⅝ in).
BM M&LA 66, 12–29, 4.

fig. 21 Flask (*no. 16). *Scale* ¼:1

The vase has an ovoid body which tapers sharply to a narrow flaring foot with simple fillet and torus mouldings. The neck is more gradually tapered, and the mouth is capped with a quarter-round moulding elaborated with four concentric grooves. Decoration in low relief covers the body of the vase. The smooth surfaces of the foot and neck are visually distinct; the neck is further set off by a wreath moulding at the upper edge of the sculpted decoration of the body.

Two pairs of symmetrically opposed rinceaux rise from two acanthus calyxes depicted on the narrow foot. There are six spirals in each rinceau, and, since alignment among the four is exact, an effect of six horizontal registers is produced. The spirals grow and diminish in size as the body of the vessel swells and tapers. The spirals lie nearly tangent to one another, forming negative spaces of diamond shapes with four concave sides. The effect of horizontal zones is reinforced by the identity of size of the spirals within a given zone, by the tightness of their grouping, and by the secondary accent provided by the reserve spaces which form less emphatic horizontals of their own. In addition, there are representations of animals, birds, fruits, and Erotes which correspond in size and degree of elaboration to the six horizontal registers.

Above the last spiral and below the neck moulding are two pairs of birds, corresponding to the two pairs of rinceaux; in the intervals between the birds are two groups of three round objects, probably representing fruits. All other representations occur within the framework of the rinceaux. Each spiral completes two revolutions, ending in either fruit or foliage. The smallest spirals at the top and bottom contain no other representation: those at the top terminate in three round fruits; those at the bottom, in a three- or five-lobed leaf. The four larger spirals end in furled leaves.

The largest spirals, by virtue of relative size, placement on the most prominent area of the vase surface, inclusion of the largest number of objects, and representation of scenes with human figures, are the focal points of the piece. The spirals and reserve spaces of any one register have an internal consistency based in part on size but also on a repertory of motifs suited to that scale. The smallest contain fruits, leaves, grape clusters, birds, two crouched rabbits, and a grasshopper. The middle range contains recumbent sheep and goats, two grazing goats, and a leaping hare. These motifs are often accompanied by the formula of three balls of fruit. The symmetry established in the opposing rinceaux is not always followed in the orientation of the individual animals, but the overall effect is one of order.

The Erotes of the largest medallions are not symmetrically disposed: in three of the four medallions the Erotes move to the right, and the fourth moves to the left on a distinct diagonal. In the left medallion of a pair, an Erote is depicted as walking to the right, steadying a basket of fruit on his head. The furled leaf at the end of the framing spiral functions as a ground-line, and six motifs found elsewhere in the smaller spirals are reproduced in the area around the Erote. These motifs—a leaping hare, a flying bird, a grasshopper, a grape cluster, a five-lobed leaf, and three fruits—bear little relation to the space indicated by the walking Erote, whose nude body is turned in three-quarter view in opposition to the strictly frontal or profile views of the other objects.

In the other Erote medallions, the relationship between figures and surrounding objects is more naturalistically defined. In the pendant to the previous medallion, an Erote on the back of a donkey careens to the left down a slope. Scattered fruit lies before them, an over-turned basket of fruit lies below the donkey's body, and a grape leaf grows out of the spiral frame at the upper right. The last two medallions continue the harvest theme of the first. The left of a pair represents an Erote seated on a basket in profile to the right with a short cloak hanging down his back. A goat, standing on rear legs with forelegs on the Erote's knees, leans left towards a leaf and a cluster of grapes which the Erote pulls down from an overhead vine. The vine is simultaneously the framing spiral. A cluster of three fruits is found to the right of the goat. The fourth medallion depicts a standing nude Erote with lower torso and legs in three-quarter stance and upper body and head in profile to the right. The Erote plucks a grape cluster from the enframing

vine. To the right is an empty bowl, a flying bird, and three fruits; to the left three fruits and a large grape leaf.

The execution of the rinceaux gives the impression of careful planning and draftsmanship; centring points can be seen in several of the spirals. The relief work of the individual motifs shows swift, sure modelling. Most motifs are outlined and modelled with short, relatively broad strokes. Narrow incised lines are reserved for details such as hair, fur, and veining.

The vase is well preserved. The neck and foot are restored: the neck is original silver; the foot is a modern replacement.[17] There is one new piece of silver restored in a triangular patch between the medallions of the seated and the vintaging Erotes; the right edge of the vintaging medallion shows a small hole.

Visconti: M–M, 12, pl. xv; Dalton, *Catalogue*, no. 306, 66f (with figures).

*No. 17   Pelegrina Ewer (figs. 11, 22, pl. 31).
Silver with niello inlay.
H 27.9 cm (11 in); H (incl. handle) 34.3 cm (13½ in).
BM M&LA 66, 12–29, 5.
Inscription (fig. 11): On seven oval surfaces at the vessel shoulder in square serif capitals, filled with niello: PEL EGR INA VTE REF EL EX (hedera) (*Pelegrina utere felex* [*felix*]: Pelegrina, use (this vessel) to good fortune).

The ewer has a faceted body, an angular foot ring, an arching eight-sided handle with thumb plate, and a horizontal spout, triangular in section. A hinge for a lid is found at the junction of the handle and the rim of the ewer; the lid is now missing.[18] The foot and body of the ewer are divided into seventeen facets which continue to the first neck moulding. At the shoulder of the vessel, a concave oval surface interrupts each facet. On seven of these ovals, corresponding to the seven facets below and to either side of the spout, there is an inscription in niello-filled capitals which ends with a simple leaf form filled with niello.

The facets of the first convex neck moulding appear to continue those of the body, but the alignment of facets is not exact. A shallow groove separates this moulding from a second and more prominent hemispherical moulding with an angular rim or mouth. The second moulding and rim are also faceted. The spout is attached to the second moulding, and the horizontal incised line on each side of the spout is an extension of the division between moulding and rim. Two additional incised lines converge on the triangular upper surface of the spout.

Approximately half of the vessel is discoloured and pitted from surface corrosion. In this area the last two sections of the niello inscription are obscured and difficult to read. More serious damage is obvious on both the neck and shoulder of the ewer (fig. 22), and there is a major break below the shoulder surrounding the strut which attaches the handle to the body.[19] Both original fragments and four new pieces of silver have been restored to the vessel; the restorations are secured with solder and silver rivets. Three major pieces of new silver can be distinguished: two in the area of the neck and one at the rear of the vessel where the handle is

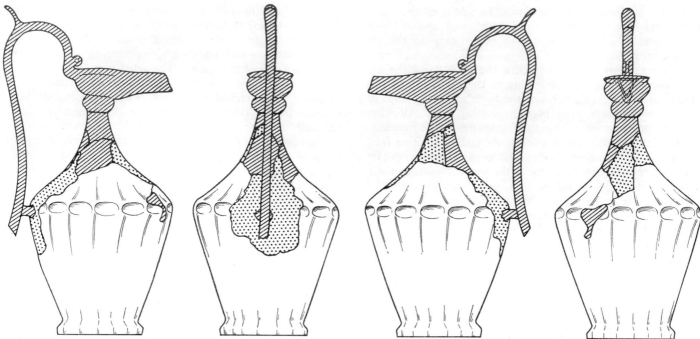

fig. 22 Pelegrina ewer (*no. 17). *Scale* ¼:1

attached. As mentioned previously, new pieces exhibit distinct characteristics, and the three large pieces of new silver on this vessel are elaborated with series of false cracks. In addition, solder is applied between sets of false cracks to simulate additional joints and thus to suggest multiple fragments within a single restored piece.

Visconti: M–M, 12, pl. xv, 1; Dalton, *Catalogue*, no. 307 68 (with figure).

*No. 18   Naples Ewer (pl. 32)
Bronze with silver inlay.
H 21.5 cm (8½ in).
Naples. Museo Nazionale.

The ewer takes the form of a human female head. Its concave foot corresponds to a human neck, its rounded body to a face, and its shoulder to an elaborate turban head-dress. The relatively long, narrow neck and trefoil mouth of the vessel are cast in one piece with the rest, but they are not translated into an aspect of female anatomy or costume. A curving, arched handle, which takes the form of a wreath of grape leaves, tendrils, and clusters, is attached to the ewer opposite the representation of the female face. The axis of the handle defines the back of the vessel and corresponds to the back of the human head. The surface of the ewer in the area of the handle attachment is quite plain: decoration is confined to leaves and tendrils raised in relief and a bead moulding on the curve of the foot.

The bead moulding translates into a necklace when the ewer is viewed from the front. Two additional bead mouldings define the edges of a band which crosses the forehead of the face near the shoulder of the ewer. The surfaces of the face are treated as smooth, rather abstract, curves; the features are executed in relatively low relief. The face is

symmetrical and characterised by large eyes, small, slender nose, small mouth, long full chin, and full, softly rounded cheeks and jaw.

Striated wavy locks of hair are depicted to either side of the face over the ears. Their incised surfaces are a distinct contrast to both the face and the turban which circles the head. A loose end of the turban, draped with elaborate folds, is represented above the forehead of the figure. The head-dress is detailed with a series of narrow, plastically rendered folds which cover the head, gradually giving way to the smooth surfaces of the neck and rear of the vessel.

Visconti: M–M, 21, pl. xxii.

No. 19   Amphora (pl. 33)
Silver.
H 20.2 cm (7¹⁵⁄₁₆ in).
BM M&LA 66, 12–29, 6.

The simple amphora forms a pair with no. 20. The profiles of the vessels are identical, and both have simple arching loop handles of thick solid wire soldered at neck and shoulder. The only applied decoration consists of four concentric circles engraved within a recess on the underside of the base. The amphora has had both handles broken at the shoulder, and the subsequent repairs are quite obvious. Directly below one handle, a roughly circular fragment of the vessel wall is missing. In addition, there are several minor dents and some corrosion of the surface. Despite this catalogue of damages, large areas of the vessel are well preserved, and the original effect of a highly polished, curving surface is only slightly diminished.

Visconti: M–M, pl. xv; Dalton, *Catalogue*, no. 308, 68 (with figure).

No. 20   Amphora (see pl. 33)
Silver.
H 20.3 cm (8 in).
BM M&LA 66, 12–29, 7.

In general, this amphora is less well preserved. While there is no breakage, the surface is heavily dented and rather badly corroded.

Visconti: M–M, pl. xv; Dalton, *Catalogue*, no. 309, 68 (with figure).

No. 21   Spoon (fig. 23, pl. 34)
Silver.
L 20.2 cm (7 15/16 in).
BM M&LA 66, 12–29, 35.

Inscription (fig. 23): On the upper surface of the handle, near the bowl, engraved in condensed, sans serif capitals: IVNONILANVMVINAESPSSVLPQVIRIN (*Iunoni Lanumvinae* [*Lanuvinae*] *s*(*ua*) *p*(*ecunia*) *S*(*ervius*) *Sulp*(*icius*) *Quirin*(*us*): Servius Sulpicius Quirinus (offers this spoon) at his own expense to Juno Lanuvina.[21]

IVNONILANVMVINAESPSSVLPQVIRIN

fig. 23 Inscription from spoon (no. 21). *Scale* 2:1

The narrow egg-shaped bowl has a smooth interior; the exterior surface of the bowl is marked with a faint ridge along its long axis.[22] A solid vertical disc attaches the bowl to the handle which is square in section at the point of attachment. As the handle tapers to a blunt point, the corners of the square are bevelled, resulting in an eight-sided stem.

Visconti: M–M, pl. xvi, 3; Dalton, *Catalogue*, no. 322, 72 (with figure).

No. 22   Spoon (fig. 24, pl. 34)
Silver (with niello inlay?).
L 19.1 cm (7½ in).
BM M&LA 66, 12–29, 33.

Inscription (fig. 24): On the lower curve of the vertical scroll, broadly engraved as if for inlay, square, serif capitals: M A. The initials appear on one side of the scroll, visible when the spoon is oriented with handle to the right.

fig. 24 Inscription from spoon (no. 22). *Scale* 2:1

The narrow egg-shaped bowl is joined to the handle by a simple vertical scroll. Wear, apparently from right-handed use, is evident near the tip of the bowl. The handle, which tapers to a blunt point, is so faintly faceted as to appear round.

Visconti: M–M, pl. xvi, 4; Dalton, *Catalogue*, no. 325, 73.

No. 23   Spoon (fig. 25, pl. 34)
Silver.
L 22.2 cm (8¾ in).
BM M&LA 66, 12–29, 34.

Monogram (fig. 25): Centred in the bowl, along the long axis, engraved in thin capitals with serifs, legible with the handle oriented to the right.

fig. 25 Monogram from spoon (no. 23). *Scale* 2:1

The egg-shaped bowl has a smooth interior and an exterior surface marked with faint relief ridges resembling the veins of a leaf. The handle is attached to the bowl with a simple vertical scroll. As the handle tapers to a blunt point, it changes from a square to an octagon in section. Each facet of the handle carries a shallow groove.

Visconti: M–M, pl. xvi, 1; Dalton, *Catalogue*, no. 323, 73 (with figure).

No. 24   Spoon (pl. 34)
Silver.
L 21 cm (8¼ in).
BM M&LA 66, 12–29, 31.

Although lacking the engraved monogram, this spoon agrees in detail with no. 23. Wear is evident on the bowl, apparently from right-handed use.

Dalton, *Catalogue*, no. 326, 73.

No. 25   Spoon (pl. 34)
Silver.
L 20.2 cm (7 15/16 in).
BM M&LA 66, 12–29, 32.

The narrow egg-shaped bowl is damaged along its long axis; fragments are missing. An open vertical scroll joins the bowl to the handle which is octagonal in section throughout.

Visconti: M–M, pl. xvi, 2; Dalton, *Catalogue*, no. 324, 73.

No. 26   Spoon (pl. 34)
Silver.
L 15.1 cm (5 15/16 in).
BM M&LA 66, 12–29, 36.

The asymmetrical pear-shaped bowl ends in a vertical scroll; pierce-work and simple mouldings near the bowl give way to a round, tapering stem.

Visconti: M–M, pl. xvi, 7; Dalton, *Catalogue*, no. 328, 73 (with figure).

No. 27 Spoon (pl. 34)
Silver.
L 14.4 cm (5 11/16 in).
BM M&LA 66, 12–29, 37.

The pear-shaped bowl attaches to the handle with a stout open curve. The handle, which is octagonal in section, ends in a faceted knob.

Visconti: M–M, pl. XVI, 8; Dalton, *Catalogue*, no. 329, 73.

No. 28 Spoon (pl. 34)
Silver.
L 15.2 cm (6 in).
BM M&LA 66, 12–29, 39.

The shallow oval bowl attaches directly to the handle without an intermediate scroll. An eight-sided handle rises from the bowl at an angle; it is bent midway, where it flattens to a spatulate end whose sides and long axis are marked with a simple incised line.

Visconti: M–M, pl. XVI, 6; Dalton, *Catalogue*, no. 327, 73.

No. 29 Spoon (fig. 26, pl. 34)
Silver.
L 9.8 cm (3 7/8 in).
BM M&LA 66, 12–29, 38.

Graffito (fig. 26): Scratched across the interior surface of the bowl, difficult to decipher, Dalton reads 'ЄYXЄ'.

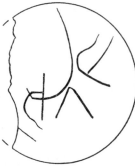

fig. 26 Graffito from spoon (no. 29). *Scale* 2:1

The thick, circular bowl attaches directly to a tapering handle which is round in section. An incised line runs around the interior of the bowl, just below the rim. Both the tip of the handle and approximately one-third of the bowl have been broken off.

Visconti: M–M, pl. XVI, 5; Dalton, *Catalogue*, no. 330, 73.

*No. 30 Furniture Ornament, Tyche of Constantinople (pls. 35–7)
Silver with gilding.
H approx. 14 cm (5½ in).
BM M&LA 66, 12–29, 23.

This piece is one of an apparent set of four ornaments (*nos. 30–3) which represent major cities of the late

Roman empire: Constantinople, Alexandria, Rome, and Antioch. The ornaments were probably intended to cap the ends of an elaborate piece of furniture; a *sedes gestatoria* is the most commonly accepted suggestion.[23] The ornament consists of a rectangular socket, approximately 5 cm (2 in) square in section, which terminates in a seated female figure. Although relative differences of size and surface texture cause the socket and the figure to be seen as distinct units, technical examination indicates that the entire object was cast in one piece. The square interior of the socket continues directly into an irregular hollow within the torso of the figure, with only limbs and attributes cast solid.

The mouth of the socket is framed with a simple rectilinear moulding, and, at the opposite end of the socket, below the seated figure, an ornament in the form of a leaf with a rounded knob finial is hinged to swing 180 degrees forward below the feet of the figure and back towards the socket opening. This ornament is pierced with four key-hole shaped openings and is heavily decorated with stippling and punch-work. The socket has two holes aligned for the reception of a pin which attached the ornament to its original fitting. Of the four ornaments, only *no. 31 preserves the tapered pin complete with safety chain mounted on the socket by means of an oval soldering plate. Two of the ornaments have fittings on the right socket wall; two have fittings on the left. This piece with the figure of Constantinople shows only the traces of a soldering plate on the right exterior wall of the socket near the rectilinear moulding at the opening.[24]

The four ornaments of the set form a visually coherent group; beyond the obvious identity of size and mounting, many other features are common to all four. In each, a female figure sits upon the flat upper surface of the socket as on a chair: the torso visually and physically supported by it, the lower limbs extending before it, and the feet, although depicted as though resting on a surface, hanging in space above the leaf ornament. There is a single facial type with long, straight nose, close-set eyes, sloping brows, and small mouth placed in a triangular face. The four figures are based on a canon of elongated proportions. All are plastically rendered, with draperies reflective of underlying postures, and all are detailed with decorative engraving and surface stippling. A consistent use of gilding on draperies, attributes, head-dresses, hair, and hinged ornaments, and the consistent identification of the ungilded silver with flesh and with small details such as footgear and the knob finials of the hinged ornaments show a unity of design. Iconographically, the four can be seen as variations on a theme: a seated female figure clothed in tunic, mantle, and soft cuffed boots, wearing a distinctive head-dress and carrying, or accompanied by, attributes signifying a specific city.

This general description is accurate for all four pieces, but while three of the four figures, Constantinople, Alexandria, and Rome (*nos. 30, 31, and 32), closely resemble one another in posture and costume, the fourth, Antioch (*no. 33), is modelled after a strikingly different type. The ornament of Constantinople is one of the group of three and, like its two companions, depicts a frontal figure with a seated *contrapposto* posture. An alternation of weight-bearing and relaxed limbs is seen in the opposition of the right leg, held close to the body forming a right angle, and the left leg, extended forward on a diagonal. The alternation is properly reversed in the upper body where, although both arms support attributes, the right arm is lowered and extended forward, while the left is held high with the elbow pulled back.

Costume, details of its decoration, and drapery patterns are similar for the three figures. All wear a simple tunic, girdled below the bust and decorated with two *clavi* in stippling and punch-work. In addition, there is a mantle which drapes over the left shoulder and forearm, falls diagonally across the back, and continues across the lap and lower legs of the figure. The mantle is edged with stippled bands and patterned with an all-over design of dots in groups of three. Almost identical systems of folds in both tunic and mantle are repeated on all three figures. Most obvious are the loops of drapery echoing the breasts, the smooth passages over the belly, revealing the navel, the horizontal ridges running between the knees, the doubled edge of the mantle crossing the lap, the diagonals across the back, and those from the hem of the mantle on the figure's receding right leg to the prominent left knee.

Within the group, each ornament is made visually and iconographically distinct through minor variations of posture and drape and relatively major changes of head-dress and attributes. The figure of **Constantinople** wears a crested helmet with elaborate cheek pieces of opposed volutes above a simple hair-style brushed back in sections and largely obscured by the helmet with its trailing crest. The tunic is sleeveless and its girdle is centred with a round brooch. The figure wears an armlet and a bracelet on the right arm and carries a patera in the right hand and a cornucopia of grapes, larger fruits, and sheaves of grain in the left. Each arm is braced: the right with a strut from hand to knee, the left from the tip of the cornucopia to the socket wall.

There is minor damage to the figure. Gilding has worn off the left knee and areas of the hair and the cornucopia. There are three small holes on the left side of the figure: two beneath the forearm, another behind the drapery covering the knee. There is a small hole in the right wall of the socket. One point has broken off the leaf ornament. In general the areas of ungilded silver show signs of mild surface corrosion.

Visconti: M–M, 14ff, pl. XIX, 2; Dalton, *Catalogue*, no. 333, 74 (with figure), pl. XX.

*No. 31   Furniture Ornament, Tyche of Alexandria

(pls. 35, 38–9)
Silver with gilding.
H approx. 14 cm (5½ in).
BM M&LA 66, 12–29, 24.

This ornament is a variant within the group of three outlined in the previous entry. As mentioned, it is the only piece in the set to preserve the mounting of the pin and safety chain, and, like *no. 30, the soldering plate is placed on the right wall of the socket. Minor variations within the group of three occur in posture and drapery. Although there is virtually no change in the general posture of this figure, it

should be noted that the face is less blandly characterised and more plastically modelled than that of any of the other Tyche ornaments. Changes can be seen in the representation of the tunic—the hem almost covers the boots, the sleeves reach to the elbow, fastened at intervals with small buttons, and the drapery over the belly lies in small folds—while the mantle is a duplicate of that described for the figure of Constantinople (*no. 30).

The major variations concern the head-dress and the choice of attributes. The figure of Alexandria wears an octagonal mural crown detailed with four turrets, two arched gates, and two masonry walls. The crown sits high on the head above a wreath of flowers, branches, and trailing ribbons. The hair-style, obscured in front by the wreath, consists of wavy sections brushed back into a loose knot worn low on the neck. It is possibly the same hair-style as that depicted for Constantinople where the opposite occurs and the back of the head is obscured.

The figure holds fruits and sheaves of grain in each hand, extending them forward horizontally over the legs; a supporting strut rises from each knee to the corresponding sheaf. There is an additional attribute indicative of a port city in the form of a ship's prow on which the figure rests its forward left foot.

There is little damage to the figure. Gilding is partially worn off the surfaces of the sheaves and the prow. There is a small hole in the right wall of the socket.

Visconti: M–M, 14ff, pl. XX, 2; Dalton, *Catalogue*, no. 335, 75 (with figure), pl. XX.

*No. 32   Furniture Ornament, Roma (pls. 35, 40–1)

Silver with gilding.
H approx. 14 cm (5½ in).
BM M&LA 66, 12–29, 21.

This ornament preserves the soldering plate and one attached link of the safety chain; the plate is mounted on the left wall of the socket in distinction to *nos. 30 and 31. It should be mentioned that there is an unattached pin with five links of chain in the treasure which is clearly part of this group. There is no reason, however, to suppose that it belongs to this ornament, as three of the four are missing a pin.[25]

The figure is the third of the group of three with costume, head-dress, and hair-style identical to those of *no. 30. The choice of attributes dictates some change in posture, as the figure of Roma grasps an upright staff with the right hand. The right arm extends outwards at an angle and bends at the elbow with the forearm raised. The hand holds the staff near its head with the back of the hand facing outwards, palm turned in. The left hand rests upon a second attribute, a shield decorated with stippling and a raised central boss. Only half the shield is represented. It is roughly divided on a vertical, and it thus appears whole when the figure is seen from the front. Its irregularity is noticed only in a left profile view. The staff and shield, because of their size and placement, act as braces linking both arms and hands to the socket wall.

The right forearm and both hands are relatively large and strangely devoid of modelling. This appears to be due to simple wear which is also evident on the face of the figure. The passage from the forehead down the nose to the upper lip is quite worn; the nose, in particular, is smooth and flat. A long chisel mark, like those found on other pieces in the treasure, is found on the back of the figure, discreetly echoing the diagonals of the mantle drapery.

Visconti: M–M, 14ff, pl. XIX, 1; Dalton, *Catalogue*, no. 332, 74, pl. XX.

*No. 33   Furniture Ornament, Tyche of Antioch
(pls. 35, 42–3)
Silver with gilding.
H approx. 14 cm ($5\frac{1}{2}$ in).
BM M&LA 66, 12-29, 22.

This ornament preserves only the traces of a soldering plate for the pin and chain, located, as in the previous example, on the left socket wall. Conforming to the general composition of the four ornaments, the socket terminates in a seated female figure, but, in this case, there is the addition of a stylised rock outcropping which gives the figure a defined setting best understood as a topographical attribute. The posture differs radically from that of the other three figures: seated with the right leg crossed over the left, the figure of Antioch leans to its right, placing the left hand a small distance from the body on the rock ledge. The right arm is bent at the elbow; the forearm rests on the raised right thigh. The emphasis placed on the right side is counteracted by the diagonal of the left arm and the distinct turn of the head towards the left.

The face and hair-style of the figure match those of the other three; the head-dress is a mural crown identical to that described for *no. 31. The garments, which consist of a tunic with *clavi* and a patterned mantle, are draped in a different manner. The mantle falls from the back edge of the mural crown, completely covering a knot of hair at the nape of the neck and the back of the figure. The mantle continues up and over the right arm, across the body, down into the hollow between the legs and the extended right arm, over the left arm to the back, where it hangs in folds from the left shoulder. The mantle covers the entire torso; the tunic shows only over the exposed right leg.

A half-figure of a nude youth, a personification of the river Orontes, emerges from below the figure in the hollow between the legs and the left arm of the Tyche. There is a further attribute of fruits and sheaves of grain held in the right hand of the female figure. The sheaves are braced with a strut from their tip to the right foot of the figure. The youth is attached to the main figure with struts at three points: from each hand of the youth to the bottom of the front socket wall and from the centre back of his head to a point corresponding to the main figure's veiled left thigh. The distinct posture, costume, and iconographic attributes of this figure have a clear source: the statuette is a reflection of the Tyche of Antioch, a famous large-scale work by the Greek sculptor Eutychides, commissioned in 296 BC.[26]

The surfaces of the ornament, especially the ungilded surfaces, are corroded; gilding has worn off the back in several areas. There are two small holes in the drapery

behind the left foot. There is another hole in the upper surface of the socket.

Visconti: M–M, 14ff, pl. XX, 1; Dalton, *Catalogue*, no. 334, 75, pl. XX.

*No. 34   Furniture Ornament, Right Hand (fig. 8, pl. 44)
Silver with gilding.
H approx. 33 cm (13 in).
BM M&LA 66, 12–29, 20.

The ornament, one of a symmetrical pair, represents a forearm and hand grasping a cylinder topped with a sphere which is, in turn, surmounted by a stylised floral finial. This ornament depicts a right arm and hand; its mate a left. The two agree in overall dimensions and detail, with differences arising primarily from misunderstandings in restoration. *No. 34 is well preserved and serves, in a sense, as a control for judging the alterations in *no. 35.

The ornament is hollow throughout with the exception of the floral finial. The diameters of both the cylinder and the forearm are the same, approximately 5 cm (2 in). The suggestion has been made that the ornament is 'from a chair'.[27] More specifically, the ornament appears to be a sleeve fitting for dowels meeting at right angles where a finial would be appropriate, such as the joints at the front of a chair arm or those at the top of a chair back.

Early engravings show the separation of the ornament into two sections: the finial and the hand grasping the cylinder. The engravings suggest that the separation is the result of breakage, which is not the case.[28] The ornament consists of two distinct pieces: the sphere is mounted on a short sleeve slightly narrower than the cylinder in which it nests. It is possible that the sphere of this ornament is not now matched with its original cylinder. An analysis of the restorations suggests, however, that the current mating is correct.

The floral finial is cast, and the grooved mouldings which cap the ends of the cylinder and the arm are applied. With these exceptions, the piece is worked entirely in repoussé. The forearm and cylinder are plain. At the wrist there is a torque bracelet centred with a bezel on its outer face. The hand is set off from the cylinder by its volume, its clearly defined contours, and its surface detail. The individual knuckles and cuticles are represented as ridges, and the nails as flat surfaces. The depiction of the grip is somewhat awkward: the heel of the hand as well as the ball of the thumb overlap the cylinder. The thumb is represented in a combination of profile and frontal views. The fingers are extremely long in relation to the size of the palm, and all four are uniform in length.

At the junction of the cylinder and the sleeve of the sphere there is another torque followed by a concave moulding marked with a single incised line. Above the sphere, there is another concave moulding which continues into the heavy stem of the floral finial. The surface of the sphere itself is composed of twenty concave surfaces separated by fillets. Both the width of the fillets, which remain quite narrow, and that of the flutes increase towards the middle of the sphere. Each flute ends in a semicircle, with the result that the top and bottom of the sphere are marked with scalloped ridges.

The floral finial surmounting the sphere consists of a prominent conical knob which rises above two layers of small pointed petals.[29] The entire finial is gilded as are the torque and the concave mouldings below the sphere. The remaining surfaces of the hand and cylinder are ungilded silver.

There is damage to the ornament at the upper end of the cylinder where four pieces of silver of varying sizes have been restored between the opening of the cylinder and the upper surface of the hand. As in other repairs, the new pieces of silver are distinguished by their smooth surfaces, regular outlines, and obvious colour contrast. There are major cracks running vertically on the cylinder, horizontally between the fingers, and along the upper and lower contours of the hand. The cracks, like the restored pieces, are backed with silver strips and occasionally secured with silver rivets.

The back of the hand and the corresponding section of the cylinder have suffered relatively little. The palm or grip side is pitted with surface corrosion. One half of the globe is in good condition. The other half is marked with two roughly horizontal series of cracks, one in the upper third, another in the lower third of the sphere. Several small pieces of silver are missing along these lines of deformation, and one piece contained within a single flute is restored, secured with solder. This general area is discoloured, and solder, used occasionally to patch inaccessible cracks, is found in several places on the surface of the sphere with no apparent function.

Visconti: M–M, 9, 13, pl. XII; Dalton, *Catalogue*, no. 336, 76 (with figure).

*No. 35   Furniture Ornament, Left Hand (fig. 9, pl. 45)
Silver with gilding.
H approx. 33 cm (13 in).
BM M&LA 66, 12–29, 19.

This ornament is the left-hand counterpart of *no. 34. As mentioned above, the differences between the two result from errors of restoration; judged as a whole, this piece is virtually identical with that described in the previous entry. Large areas of both the sphere and the cylinder of this piece are restored. Briefly stated, there are four contiguous areas of new silver on the cylinder. The first includes the three phalanges of the ring finger and the last two phalanges of the other three fingers. The second restored area consists of the thumb, parts of the ball of the thumb and the heel of the hand, and the surface of the cylinder between the ball and the tips of the fingers. The third area describes the surface of the cylinder to the right of a curving seam below the heel and to the left of a seam running downwards from the last knuckle of the little finger. The fourth area of restoration on the cylinder is the applied moulding which caps its lower end.

The restorations are discernible by their smooth surfaces, regular outlines, and colour contrast. Five false cracks can be seen on the restored pieces, one on the heel of the hand, and four on the surface of the cylinder. True cracks and seams between old and new silver are backed with silver strips; false cracks are only surface details. Solder is used to fill and to stabilise cracks, such as that across the back of the hand near the third and fourth fingers; it is also used on the

restored pieces as if to emphasise or to authenticate the age of the (new) silver.

The modelling of the restored areas can be distinguished from that of the original silver. The ridges marking the knuckles and cuticles are more angular, the nails are longer and more rounded, and the modelling of the entire hand is in higher relief. The sphere of this ornament is heavily restored, and, as in the case of the cylinder and the hand, misunderstandings of the original have led to errors. The sleeve is heavily damaged but preserved, and the torque moulding is original. The concave moulding, however, is a restoration: the surface is smooth; the gilt contrasts in tone with the original gilt preserved on the torque; its upper edge does not match the scalloped edge of the sphere; and the simple incised line found on *no. 34 is here translated into a step moulding. The concave moulding above the sphere is also a replacement whose surface and gilding contrast with original surfaces and whose lower edge does not match the scalloped edge of the flutes of the sphere. The restored concave moulding ends, topped with the original preserved finial which is mounted on a pin, free to rotate 360 degrees.

The surface of the sphere consists of eleven original and nine restored flutes in two distinct sections. As in *no. 34, there are two lines of breakage, one high and one low on the sphere. On the original half, small horizontal cracks form ragged networks. There are only two horizontal cracks on the restored surfaces. The two are false cracks, but they at least conform with the established patterns of breakage. Most of the false cracks in this area are long and angular, running along the vertical axes of the separate flutes.

Visconti: M–M, 9; Dalton, *Catalogue*, no. 337, 76.

*No. 36   Horse trapping (see pl. 46)
Silver with gilding.
L approx. 63.5 cm (25 in).
BM M&LA 66, 12–29, 29.

This ornament is one in a set of six similar pieces, two of which are in fragmentary condition. Although it is possible that there were once more than six ornaments,[30] those which remain can be evenly divided into two groups of three, according to the placement of the buckle, or three sets of opposing pairs, according to the placement of the buckle in combination with a key representation.

Each complete ornament consists of nine linked plates plus a buckle of faceted wire at one end and a decorative finial at the other. The nine plates are of two basic types which alternate to make up a chain. The more numerous, which both begin and end a given chain, have the appearance of opposed peltae centred with a quatrefoil. Two links or loops extend from the mid-point on either side of the pelta plate, pass through square openings in adjacent plates, and double back behind the pelta plate where they are secured by a knob-headed pin which also passes through and secures the decorative quatrefoil. The buckles are similarly attached; the finial plates, however, are cast in one piece with the last pelta plate on each trapping.

The second type of plate in the chain is circular and carries a representation in relief centred in a field surrounded by a moulded border. A highly stylised leaf shape with knob finial projects from the top of each circular plate on a roughly vertical axis; a pendant, attached in the manner of the pelta plates, hangs below. There are two types of circular plates which differ in regard to overall size, choice of subject matter, and size and shape of pendant. The smaller plates, of which there are three to a complete trapping, carry representations of lions' heads and simple tear-drop pendants. The larger plates, of which there is but one to a trapping, depict striding eagles with wings displayed. These plates carry as pendants large faceted crescents which terminate in knob finials.

An observation of the fourteen preserved small circular plates shows four variations in the depiction of the lions' heads. All roar—some more ferociously than others—but the four types are distinguished from one another by the relative prominence of brow ridge, teeth, and tongue, and the size and shape of the top knot, nose, and lower jaw. The variation in the large circular plates is less subtle. In three of the five preserved large plates, the eagle strides to the right, turning the head back in profile to the left. In the two remaining large plates, the posture is reversed. Because of the prominence of these plates and their crescent pendants, the two types of eagles, in combination with the placement of the buckles to either left or right, define one of the two groupings mentioned above: that which consists of three sets of opposing pairs of horse trappings.

The circular plates with their relief decorations and leaf finials, the pelta plates, the quatrefoils, the two types of pendants, the large finial plates, and the attachment plates for the buckles are all cast. Abstract and representational details are supplied by open-work, surface chasing, and engraving. There were two different moulds for the circular 'eagle' plates, four moulds for the four distinct representations of the lions, and three moulds for the pelta plates—one for the simple pelta plate, one for the pelta plate with terminal finial, and one for the pelta plate with buckle attachment which begins each trapping. In addition, there was a single mould for the tear-drop pendant and one for the crescent pendant as well.

Both the circular and the pelta plates are decorated with combinations of broad, shallow grooves and narrow, incised lines. The peltae, whose lobes are defined by crescents in pierce-work, are edged with broad, flat-ended grooves contained within continuous engraved lines. The circular plates of both sizes have borders composed of an outer broad groove and two closely spaced, incised lines in concentric circles. The loops which attach both the pelta plates and pendants to the circular plates are marked with grooves slightly narrower than those found on the face of the plates. The facets of the crescent pendants are outlined, as are the leaf finials of the circular plates. These finials are decorated, in addition, with crude engraved lines which resemble veining. The main finial, opposite the buckle on each trapping, is decorated with five petal motifs, each outlined and centred with a groove.[31] The relief areas of the lions' heads, the eagles, and the quatrefoils are embellished with engraved lines variously indicating fur, feathers, and veining.

The surfaces of each plate are enlivened by the juxtaposition of areas of silver and gilt. The pelta plates are gilded in the area of the outlined borders. The quatrefoils are also gilded, while the pin and the interior reserve field are silver. The lions and eagles of the circular plates are gilded as are the moulded, circular borders. The finials, the central reserve areas, and the tear-drop pendants of these plates are silver. The upper facet of each crescent pendant is gilded; the lower has a gilded edge and a silver interior. The buckle and the flange by which the buckle is attached are silver; opposite the buckle, the petal decorations of the silver finial alternate silver and gilded surfaces.

This particular horse trapping is organised with the buckle and its necessary attachment plate to the left, finial to the right. The most prominent plate, the eagle with its crescent pendant, is the fourth from the buckle as is the case with all six trappings. The eagle in this trapping strides to the right. No single trapping preserves all its movable parts: four pendants, five quatrefoils, and the tongue of the buckle.[32] The stationary parts of each plate and the crescent pendant are preserved on this trapping. The only tear-drop pendant completely preserved is that attached to the first circular plate to the right of the buckle. A second tear-drop pendant in fragmentary condition is attached to the sixth plate, and, apparently the result of a recent repair, a third is attached to the eighth plate with copper wire. Three quatrefoils remain intact on the third, fifth, and seventh plates, although that on the third plate is skewed forty-five degrees. A chisel mark is found on the back of the crescent pendant.

Visconti: M–M, 17, pl. XXIV; Dalton, *Catalogue*, no. 339, 77.

*No. 37 Horse trapping (pl. 46)
Silver with gilding.
L approx. 63.5 cm (25 in).
BM M&LA 66, 12–29, 28.

This ornament is oriented with the buckle to the left, finial to the right as in the preceding entry. The eagle strides to the left. The trapping is less well preserved; while two tear-drop pendants and four quatrefoils are intact, two pelta plates, the third and the fifth from the buckle, have lost fragments from their borders. Several plates have received surface damage. The first plate to the right of the buckle has lost three lobes of its quatrefoil, and the eighth, a lion plate, lacks its pendant.

Visconti: M–M, 17, pl. XXIV; Dalton, *Catalogue*, no. 338 76 (with figure).

*No. 38 Horse trapping (see pl. 46)
Silver with gilding.
L approx. 14.8 cm (5¹⁸⁄₁₆ in).
BM M&LA 66, 12–29, 30.

The third trapping with the buckle to the left preserves only two plates: the pelta plate with buckle attachment and the second, a lion plate, with its pendant missing. There is a chisel mark on the back of the pelta plate.

Visconti: M–M, 17, pl. XXIV; Dalton, *Catalogue*, no. 342, 77.

*No. 39   Horse trapping (see pl. 46)
Silver with gilding.
L approx. 63.5 cm (25 in).
BM M&LA 66, 12–29, 25.

This is the first of three trappings organised with the buckle to the right, finial to the left. The prominent eagle plate continues to be the fourth plate from the buckle, for this relationship is constant. In this trapping, the eagle strides to the left and looks to the right. The tongue of the buckle is missing, and the quatrefoil on the first plate to the left of the buckle is chipped. Most of the damage to the ornament occurs to the left of the eagle plate. The pendants of the sixth and eighth plates from the buckle are missing; the quatrefoil is missing from the ninth plate. In addition, the lower border of the ninth plate is broken, the gilding is worn, and the finial plate is damaged.

Visconti: M–M, 17, pl. xxiv; Dalton, *Catalogue*, no. 340, 77.

*No. 40   Horse trapping (pl. 46)
Silver with gilding.
L approx. 63.5 cm (25 in).
BM M&LA 66, 12–29, 26.

The second ornament with buckle mounted to the right carries the representation of an eagle striding to the right. One pendant, from the lion plate eighth from the buckle, is missing, and small pieces are broken off the upper borders of the fifth and ninth plates. The quatrefoil on the third plate has two lobes damaged; the quatrefoils of the fifth and seventh plates are each reduced to one lobe.

Visconti: M–M, 17, pl. xxiv; Dalton, *Catalogue*, no. 341, 77.

*No. 41   Horse trapping (see pl. 46)
Silver with gilding.
L approx. 29.5 cm (11⅝ in).
BM M&LA 66, 12–29, 27.

The third trapping with buckle attached to the right preserves only the buckle and four plates. The fourth plate shows an eagle striding to the right. While the crescent pendant is well preserved, all other movable parts are missing. These include the tongue of the buckle, the quatrefoils of the remaining pelta plates, and the tear-drop pendant from the one small circular plate, second from the buckle.

Visconti: M–M, 17, pl. xxiv; Dalton, *Catalogue*, no. 343, 77.

No. 42   Ring (pl. 47)
Silver with gold inlay.
D 2.2 cm (⅞ in).
BM M&LA 66, 12–29, 43.

The finger ring with flat circular hoop and oval bezel is formed from a single strip of silver.[33] The bezel area is set off by its distinct shape and by a small vandyke moulding around its edge. Centred in the oval, along its long axis, is a winged Victory standing in profile, facing left. The figure appears to carry a wreath in her right hand and perhaps another object, not easily identifiable, in her left. The moulding and the figure are engraved with short, quick strokes. To the right of the standing figure is a small gold oval, inlaid in the silver surface.

Visconti: M–M, pl. xxv, 9; Dalton, *Catalogue*, no. 238, 38 (with figure).

No. 43   Earring (pl. 47)
Silver.[34]
D 3.8 cm (1½ in).
BM M&LA 66, 12–29, 44.

This piece forms a pair with no. 44. The skeleton of this complex earring is a hollow sphere threaded on a large hollow-wire hoop.[35] Two triangular plates, with bases soldered to the sphere, rise symmetrically along the exterior curve of the hoop. The points of the triangles correspond to an opening in the hoop on one side and a triple torque moulding on the other, which effectively establish a horizontal division between an upper undecorated hoop and a lower, heavily decorated area.

To this base of sphere and triangles small ornaments are applied: torque mouldings, silver granules, pyramidal mounds of granules, small coils of tightly wound wire, and pyramids of such coils. The surfaces are covered with combinations involving all these ornaments, and the space between the sphere and the inner faces of the triangular plates is filled with wire coils. Although the earring is well preserved, some granules and coils have broken off.

Visconti: M–M, pl. xxv, 5; Dalton, *Catalogue*, no. 236, 37 (with figure).

No. 44   Earring (pl. 47)
Silver.
D 3.8 cm (1½ in).
BM M&LA 66, 12–29, 45.

This earring matches its mate in all but the smallest details of surface preservation.

Visconti: M–M, pl. xxv, 5; Dalton, *Catalogue*, no. 236, 37 (with figure).

No. 45   Earring (pl. 47)
Silver.
D 2.2 cm (⅞ in).
BM M&LA 66, 12–29, 46.

This piece, once undoubtedly one of a pair, is a smaller version of the earrings described above. It has suffered extensive surface damage.

Visconti: M–M, pl. xxv, 6; Dalton, *Catalogue*, no. 237, 38 (with figure).

No. 46   Pin (pl. 47)
Silver.
L 8.3 cm (3¼ in).
BM M&LA 66, 12–29, 42.

The round tapering shaft of the straight pin is topped at its wider end with an astragal moulding and a simple foliate capital. Atop the capital is a representation of a standing Venus at her toilet, nude to the waist with drapery knotted at the hips, blown back to reveal bare legs. With her left hand, the Venus holds a lock of her hair; with the right, she raises a mirror to her face. The mirror is also supported by a strut extending upwards from the right hip of the Venus. The pin is solid-cast silver; all motifs are plastically rendered with little surface engraving. The small scale and the corroded surface of the piece cause some blurring of detail.

Visconti: M–M, pl. xxv, 2; Dalton, *Catalogue*, no. 233, 37 (with figure).

No. 47   Pin (fig. 27)
Silver.
L 10.2 cm (4 in).
BM M&LA 66, 12–29, 41.

Similar to no. 46, this straight pin ends in a double-tiered foliate capital which serves as a base for a second representation of Venus.[36] It is the Venus Sandalbinder, supported on

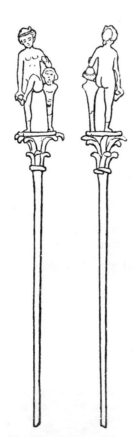

fig. 27   Dalton engraving of lost Venus pin (no. 47). *Catalogue.* no. 232.

her left by a herm. The scale, the workmanship, and even the surface preservation appear extremely close to that of the other Venus pin.

Visconti: M–M, pl. xxv, 1; Dalton, *Catalogue*, no. 232, 37 (with figure).

No. 48   Pin (pl. 47)
Silver.
L 7 cm (2¾ in).
BM M&LA 66, 12–29, 40.

The straight pin, topped with a simple cushion capital, is round in section, tapering to a blunt point.

Visconti: M–M, pl. xxv, 3; Dalton, *Catalogue*, no. 234, 37.

No. 49   Fibula (pl. 47)
Silver with niello inlay.[37]
L 6 cm (2⅜ in).
BM M&LA 66, 12–29, 52.

The piece is a fibula of the 'crossbow' type with a free-swinging pin, flat, elongated pin guard, six-sided bow and eight-sided crossbar. Two small scrolls extend horizontally from the head of the bow, marking the attachment of bow to bar. The head of the bow and both ends of the crossbar are capped with simple ring mouldings and finials, attached to the body of the fibula with silver pins. While the bow finial is an oval knob preceded by two simple convex mouldings, the finials of the crossbar neither match it nor agree with one another: one is an oval knob with a single moulding; the other is a round knob with two mouldings. These discrepancies suggest repairs.

Surface decoration is simple, limited to horizontal ridges on the flat upper surfaces of the pin guard and a running band of niello triangles on the uppermost facet of the bow.

Visconti: M–M, pl. xxv, 8; Dalton, *Catalogue*, no. 227, 36 (with figure).

No. 50   Fibula (pl. 47)
Silver with gilding.
L 7.1 cm (2 13/16 in).
BM M&LA 66, 12–29, 53.

The crossbow fibula has a free-swinging pin, now broken, a tapering pin guard, and a bow and crossbar both octagonal in section. The ends of the bar are capped with rounded knobs, while a knob at the head of the bow has been broken off. There are simple horizontal markings and gilding on the pin guard.

Dalton, *Catalogue*, no. 228, 36.

No. 51   Fibula (pl. 47)
Silver.
L 4.4 cm (1¾ in).
BM M&LA 66, 12–29, 55.

The bow fibula is made of a single piece of round, tapering wire: the spring is a two-coil mechanism, and the usual catch plate is replaced by a simple hook at the end of the bow. There are three identical mouldings of single rings flanking a bearded collar evenly spaced on the bow. The pin has broken off at the coil.[38]

Visconti: M–M, pl. xxv, 7; Dalton, *Catalogue*, no. 229, 36 (with figure).

No. 52 Fibula (pl. 47)
Silver.
L 4.9 cm (1 15/16 in).
BM M&LA 66, 12–29, 54.

The bow fibula has a two-coil spring and a large catch plate which terminates in a rounded knob. A ridge runs the length of the fusiform bow, and a smaller ridge intersects it at right angles at the top of the arch. A crude vandyke moulding outlines the upper edge of the catch plate on its outer face.

Dalton, *Catalogue*, no. 230, 36 (with figure).

No. 53 Fibula (pl. 47)
Silver.
L 4.4 cm (1 3/4 in).
BM M&LA 66, 12–29, 56.

The bow fibula has a two-coil spring and a flat pin guard. There is a ridge at the peak of the bow running at right angles to the long axis, and there are several short horizontal ridges on the bow where it joins the pin guard. Two curved discs, with concave surfaces facing, are threaded on a cylindrical extension of the guard. The fibula is badly damaged.

Dalton, *Catalogue*, no. 231, 36.

No. 54 Charm (pl. 47)
Silver with gilding.
L 2.2 cm (7/8 in).
BM M&LA 66, 12–29, 49.

The small charm takes the form of a crouching mouse eating a piece of fruit held between its forepaws. A long tail loops up and around, ending in a curl on the animal's back. The position and form of the tail suggest a handle or finger grip for the object. It is extremely stable for so small a piece: it is heavy in relation to its size, and it rests securely on flat surfaces below the hind and forequarters. For these reasons, the piece suggests a counter such as those employed in board games.[39] Indications of eyes, claws, and fur are rendered by surface gouging and striations. There are traces of gilding.

Visconti: M–M, pl. xxv, 4; Dalton, *Catalogue*, no. 239, 38.

No. 55 Charm (pl. 47)
Silver.
L 3.2 cm (1 1/4 in).
BM M&LA 66, 12–29, 47.

Unlike the mouse charm, this piece has no obvious stable orientation. It represents a left forearm and hand grasping a flaming torch. Despite the inherent suggestion of a figure fragment, the piece appears to be finished and complete unto itself; the forearm ends in a polished ovoid surface.[40] Summarily indicated drapery extends below the arm but breaks off quickly, leaving an oddly shaped scrap of silver. In general the surface of the piece is badly corroded.

Dalton, *Catalogue*, no. 241, 38 (with figure).

No. 56 Handle (pl. 48)
Silver.
L 19.7 cm (7 3/4 in).
BM M&LA 66, 12–29, 59.

Three discrete parts compose the handle. The handle *per se* is solid wire, octagonal in section, with a running groove on each of the eight facets. The handle forms a shallow s-curve, with mounts at both ends by which it was originally attached to a vessel—most probably to a tall jug or ewer.[41] The lower mount is a flat soldering plate in a simplified leaf shape with a surface crudely engraved to indicate a central stem and lateral veins.[42] The upper mount takes the form of a semi-circular horizontal collar which presumably fitted the neck or lip of a vessel. The collar is open-work, stippled on its upper surface. Stippling accents and distinguishes shapes in the open-work, defining swans' heads, dolphins, and scrolls in the absence of plastic divisions between the separate motifs. The ornaments are symmetrically disposed: from the centre large and small scrolls decorated with large points give way to dolphins and swans' heads in profile decorated with fine stippling. It should be remarked that the overall workmanship of the piece is rather crude.

Visconti: M–M, 12; Dalton, *Catalogue*, no. 344, 77.

No. 57 Handle (pl. 48)
Silver.
H 14.3 cm (5 5/8 in).
BM M&LA 66, 12–29, 57.

This swing handle forms a pair with no. 58. The handle consists of a semicircular arch of thick wire which curves back on itself to form a loop at each end. The wire is octagonal in section, and the loops terminate in swans' heads, stippled to indicate eyes and beak. The handle was originally attached to a vessel by means of two soldering plates which are also preserved.[43] The plates are simplified leaf shapes with octagonal wire loops terminating in swans' heads. While there is only mild surface corrosion on the piece, there are many patches of discoloration.

Visconti: M–M, 12; Dalton, *Catalogue*, no. 345, 77.

No. 58 Handle (pl. 48)
Silver.
H 14.3 cm (5 5/8 in).
BM M&LA 66, 12–29, 58.

This piece is almost identical with its mate. In addition to minor surface damage, however, there is a break in the arch of the handle. While the repair is simple, it is obvious.

Visconti: M–M, 12; Dalton, *Catalogue*, no. 345, 77.

No. 59 Handle (fig. 28, pl. 48)
Silver with gold and niello inlay.
L 6.9 cm (2⅝ in).
BM M&LA 66, 12–29, 50.

Inscription (fig. 28): In the centre panel of the middle register on each face in square serif capitals: on one side ΜΗΛΥΠΙ; on the other CΕΛΥΤΟΝ (μὴ λυπι [λῦπῃ] σελυτον [σεαυτόν]: Do not worry).

fig. 28 Inscription from knife handle (no. 59). *Scale 2:1*

The handle (originally belonging to a knife) is octagonal in section, flaring towards the butt end. The surfaces of six facets are covered with engraved ornament, while two, narrower, undecorated facets serve to divide the six into two distinct surfaces of three facets each. The decorative motifs of the two sides and their relative sizes and placement are the same. On each face the three horizontal registers are divided vertically into nine equal fields. The upper and lower registers are identical: a band of fretwork in niello, which incorporates small inlaid gold crosses with diagonals in niello, is flanked on either side by bands of guilloche in silver relief against niello backgrounds. An incised inscription occupies the centre panel of the middle register; to either side are vine scrolls with stems and tendrils in niello and leaves executed in gold inlay. The butt of the knife is outlined with vandyke moulding; the inner reserved area is filled with simple engraved designs in niello.

Dalton, *Catalogue*, no. 331, 74 (with figures).

No. 60 Finial (fig. 29, pl. 48)
Pewter.
L 2.5 cm (1 in).
BM M&LA 66, 12–29, 48.

Inscription (fig. 29): On the back of the hand, above the representation of a building, in engraved serif capitals: BYZAN. Also, on the flat circular end of the rod, serif capitals Λ (with back of hand facing) and Σ (with palm facing).[44]

fig. 29 Inscriptions from finial (no. 60). *Scale 2:1*

The piece, which is solid-cast pewter, takes the form of a miniature left hand grasping a short, circular-headed rod. The representation ends abruptly below the wrist where a short shaft of distinctly smaller diameter begins. Details of representation are summarily indicated; the decorative interest of the piece lies primarily in an incised design and inscriptions which have little or no obvious relevance to the representation of a hand *per se*.[45] On the back of the hand a schematic depiction of a building is engraved: the building

can be inferred to be longitudinal in plan with a pedimented façade and gable roof.

Visconti: M–M, pl. xxv, 10; Dalton, *Catalogue*, no. 235, 37 (with figure).

No. 61 Fragment (pl. 48)
Silver with gilding.
L 3.7 cm (1⁷⁄₁₆ in).
BM M&LA 66, 12–29, 51.

The head and forequarters of a grimacing panther terminate in a leafy scroll, while forepaws grasp the skull of a ram. The motifs are plastically rendered, with surface engraving restricted to details of fur and veining. There are traces of gilding throughout. At first glance, this small piece appears complete in itself.[46] It lacks a base as such, however, and has, in its place, an under-surface which slants at an acute angle to the vertical established by the body of the panther. In addition, there is a round hole directly below the body most easily interpreted as a means of attachment to another surface. The piece could well be a rim fragment from a lavishly decorated plate or bowl.

Dalton, *Catalogue*, no. 240, 38 (with figure).

The Missing Pieces

In addition to indefinite references to '*vasi*', '*anse*', and '*diversi cucchiari*' Visconti briefly described four objects which either no longer survive or, more probably, are no longer associated with the silver of the Esquiline Treasure. One of the four is a piece confused with the dish from the Mâcon treasure (no. 13), '*un piatto d'argento alquanto cupo ornato con degli arabeschi senza rilievo, ma soltanto battuti o grafiti*'.[47] Another is a rectangular monogram plate identical to the four in the treasure (*nos. 9–12). Visconti specifically indicated five in contrast to the group of four circular plates: '*cinque piattelli quadrilateri . . . e quattro scodelle leggermente concave. I quali tutti han nel centro due cifre o nessi di lettere . . . racchiuse entro una corona di lauro*'.[48] The third is a small lamp, '*una lucernina portatile di un sol lucignolo*',[49] and the fourth is an elaborate candelabrum. The candelabrum appeared in the second find of 1793 and was, by Visconti's testimony, one of the most striking pieces in the treasure:

> *un candelabro la cui base, e 'l cui padellino . . . sono d'argento, . . . son de' fogliami leggiadramente condotti che formano l'uno e l'altra: ma la base termina . . . in tre piedi ornati protome, e zampe di pantere. Lo scapo o asta è di ferro e vi sono inseriti per coprirlo ed ornarlo de' grossi pezzi di cristallo di monti traforati da un capo all' altro e di varie foggie, rotondi la maggior parte, eccetto uno o due che son poligoni; alcuni ancora intagliati con qualche modinatura o baccello, e fra questi uno dovea sottoporsi al padellino, lavorato con gran diligenza a modo di un capitello corintio . . . Il padellino . . . non era fatto per posarvi su la lucerna . . . ma è guernito della sua punto o cuneo per infiggervi la face o candela*'.[50]

NOTES

1. Both 1827 editions of Visconti comment that the author overlooked this inscription. Plates in the Montagnani-Mirabili edition show the inscription both *in situ* and as an isolated fragment. Visconti: M–M, 12, n.a., pls. I, V; Visconti: L, xi. The inscription was restored to the casket after 1793. Weight inscriptions are rarely found in so prominent a place. On the original casket, the inscription was undoubtedly located on either side or back.

2. Early representations of the casket show the Toilet of Venus aligned with what is now understood to be the back panel of the casket body (see the Seroux d'Agincourt engraving, fig. 4). The current arrangement is dictated by the obvious similarity of subject matter in the two front panels, by the repetition of a postural type for the central female figures of those two panels (pls. 2, 11), and by the striking evidence that the two back panels are ungilded while the four sides and two front panels are gilded. Visconti and Seroux d'Agincourt noted the omission of gilding from the lid panel which they identified as the back. The arrangement represented in the early engravings shows the Toilet of Venus above a procession of three female servants. A back view of the casket in this configuration would show the bath procession of the lid joined to the toilet of the Roman matron by three heavy hinges. No traces of hinges or of the solder necessary to attach them can be found on the toilet panel of the body which forms part of the 'façade' of the casket.

3. Dalton, *Catalogue*, 66; Wegner, *Musensarkophage*, 117.

4. For the association of attributes indicative of specific areas of influence with individual Muses see Wegner, *Musensarkophage*, *passim*, esp. 93ff, and K. M. Türr, *Eine Musengruppe hadrianischer Zeit*, Monumenta Artis Romanae, X, Berlin (1971), 9ff. Less informative is D. Pinkwart, '*Das Relief des Archelaos von Priene*', *Antike Plastik*, IV (1965), 55ff.

5. The association of Polyhymnia with mime is traditional; the 'mute' mask as an attribute is rare. Polyhymnia is most commonly depicted as a figure swathed in heavy drapery, without specific attribute but with a posture or facial expression indicative of quiet thought. See Wegner, *Musensarkophage*, 100f, 109f; Türr, *Musengruppe*, 14ff.

6. Türr assigns the scroll to Clio and the wax tablet or writing diptych to Calliope, while Wegner argues that writing instruments in general are the attributes of Clio and that the attributes of Calliope, first among the nine Muses, vary. Wegner's description of Calliope wrapped in a mantle with a scroll held before her accords with the representation on the Muse casket. Wegner, *Musensarkophage*, 99, 107f; Türr, *Musengruppe*, 26ff.

7. Visconti mentions the vestige of a lock and a hole for the reception of a bolt or key; Dalton identifies the present lock as a modern restoration. Visconti: M–M, 9; Dalton, *Catalogue*, 66.

8. The chisel mark found on the patera is identical to those found on eleven other objects in the treasure. These include *nos. 4, 6, 7, 9, 17, 32, 36, 38, the flask and canister within the Muse casket, *no. 2, and no. 14. There are sixteen chisel marks in all. Their purpose is obscure, but their presence allows certain simple observations concerning the treasure. The marks must have been made on all twelve pieces at a time before the patera was separated from the rest of the treasure and sold to the Gossellin family of Paris; Visconti indicates that this sale had taken place by 1807. All objects bearing the marks can be documented as part of the original find of 1793 except one, no. 14. The presence of the chisel marks on no. 14 may indicate that it was part of the original find or, at the very least, that it was held as part of the treasure before 1807. If these scrapings were part of the restoration effort, the repairs and restorations observed on various pieces of the original find might be given a terminus ante quem of 1807. Visconti on the Gossellin collection: Visconti: L, 233, n.1.

9. The fluted dish is the only piece which Visconti described as broken. The first illustration of the piece was that prepared for the 1827 Montagnani-Mirabili edition; it represents the dish perfectly preserved. Visconti: M–M, pl. XVII.

10. False cracks associated with large areas of restoration can also be found on *nos. 17 and 34.

11. This dish was discovered in 1764 in Mâcon (France) in a large hoard of metalwork and coins. By 1827, it was assumed to be part of the Esquiline Treasure. See above, pp. 21f, 23, n. 13.

12. Dalton identifies the figure as an emperor. Dalton, *Catalogue*, 70.

13. The engraving in the Montagnani-Mirabili edition of Visconti shows the breakage and subsequent reinforcement. The condition is noted in the British Museum register for 1866: 'portions of side wanting and repaired'. Visconti: M–M, pl. XXI; Antiquities Register, 66,12–29,10.

14. Visconti does not mention this dish in his text. The Montagnani-Mirabili edition contains an engraving of the plate labelled '*una scodella di buona forma sfuggita alle ricerche del Autore*'. Visconti: M–M, 13, n.a.

15. The rim is similar in form and technique to the rims of the monogram dishes (*nos. 5–8). The faceted and fluted wire of the rim links the dish with several of the pieces understood to be part of the original find. The chisel marks found on twelve objects in the treasure were apparently made before 1807; see above, n.8. The presence of chisel marks on this dish indicates that it was held with or considered part of the treasure by that date.

16. Visconti mentions '*cinque vasi di bella forma*' as part of the treasure. Montagnani-Mirabili illustrates this vague phrase with an engraving which represents the faceted ewer (*no. 17), the flask (*no. 16), one of the two amphorae (nos. 19–20), and this ribbed bowl. The engraving is captioned '*Vasi e Tazze diverse*'. The ewer and flask are specifically described by Visconti in his text of 1793; the amphorae and bowl are the interpretations of the editor.

17. The engravings of the vase in the Montagnani-Mirabili edition of Visconti show it in perfect condition. Seroux d'Agincourt, however, illustrates it with both neck and foot missing. Dalton notes that the foot was restored, while the neck was simply broken and mended. Visconti: M–M, pl. XV; Seroux d'Agincourt, *L'Histoire*, IV, pl. IX, 13; Dalton, *Catalogue*, 67.

18. Both Visconti and Dalton engravings restore a lid. Visconti: M–M, pl. XV; Dalton, *Catalogue*, 68.

19. Seroux d'Agincourt describes this vessel as fragmented, and his engraving illustrates the entire shoulder area of the ewer as missing. This could not have been the case, although the shoulder is heavily damaged. Seroux d'Agincourt, *L'Histoire*, III, 9; IV, pl. IX, 12.

20. The two amphorae are not discussed by Visconti.

21. Dalton states that the spoon must have been dedicated at the temple of Juno Sospita at Lanuvium. Dalton, *Catalogue*, 72.

22. The original 1793 Visconti essay mentions only '*diversi cucchiari*'. Montagnani-Mirabili notes that all the spoons are illustrated in his 1827 edition; he also suggests that not all the spoons were found at the same time. In fact, only eight of the nine spoons purchased by the British Museum in 1866 are illustrated in Montagnani-Mirabili's edition: no. 24 is omitted. Seroux d'Agincourt mentions spoons but only illustrates one. Visconti: M–M, 13, 27, n. 1; Seroux d'Agincourt, *L'Histoire*, II, 39; III, 9; IV, pl. IX, 14.

23. Visconti: M–M, 14f; Seroux d'Agincourt, *L'Histoire*, II, 39; III, 10; Dalton, *Catalogue*, 74.

24. Visconti writes as though all four fittings had preserved the attached chain and pin; the plates for both 1827 editions of his essay omit the complete apparatus. Visconti: M–M, 14, pls. XIX, XX; Visconti: L, pl. XVIII, 16–19.

25. The association of the loose pin and chain with this ornament is one made by Dalton, *Catalogue*, 74.

26. Dohrn, T., *Die Tyche von Antiochia*, Berlin (1960), nos. 12, 19, pl. 3.

27. Dalton, *Catalogue*, 76; also, G. Labus, '*Prefazione*', xi, and the Montagnani-Mirabili note to Visconti's text: Visconti: M–M, 13, n.b.

28. Visconti discussed the two parts of the ornament as two separate objects: the sphere was identified as a chair fitting; the hand and cylinder as a type of candle-holder. Visconti: M–M, 9, 13. Both 1827 editions of Visconti contain editorial notes to the effect that the two parts were understood, at that date, as forming a

single object which functioned as a chair ornament. See previous note for bibliographic references.

29. The entire finial has been identified as a 'conventional pomegranate': Dalton, *Catalogue*, 76; Newton, *Blacas Collection*, 26. For an alternative, if unnecessary, view see A. Seeberg, 'Poppies, not Pomegranates', *Acta ad archeologiam et artium historiam*, IV, 1969, 7–12. The finial cannot be identified so specifically; it is simply a stylised floral motif.

30. Visconti simply refers to '*falere equestri*', number unspecified. Visconti: M–M, 17.

31. The crude veining on the finials of the circular plates closely resembles that on the handle mounts of the ewer (*no. 17) and the two caskets (*nos. 1 and 2). The petal motifs on the finial plates match in specific detail those found in the decorations of the large fluted dish (*no. 4).

32. The Montagnani-Mirabili engraving of a horse trapping for the 1827 edition of the Visconti essay represents a hypothetical, perfectly preserved specimen. Dalton follows suit. Visconti: M–M, pl. XXIV; Dalton, *Catalogue*, 76.

33. Visconti mentions no charms or pieces of jewellery in his text of 1793. By 1827, however, the treasure was depicted as containing some eleven pieces (nos. 42–9, 51, 54, and 60). Visconti: M–M, pl. XXV. The Montagnani-Mirabili plate caption describes the ring incorrectly as being set with a cameo (pl. XXV, 9).

34. The caption of the Montagnani-Mirabili engraving describes the earrings (nos. 43–5) as gold earrings (pl. XXV, 5). They are silver.

35. The Dalton figure shows the sphere resting within the hoop; the rendering is incorrect. Dalton, *Catalogue*, 37.

36. Although the pin entered the British Museum with the other pieces of the treasure in 1866, it is now missing. Dalton's figure and a photograph taken before the loss record the object.

37. The caption of the Montagnani-Mirabili engraving identifies this fibula and no. 51 as gold; they are silver. Visconti: M–M, pl. XXV, 7, and 8.

38. The Dalton figure shows the fibula perfectly preserved. Dalton, *Catalogue*, 36.

39. The caption of the Montagnani-Mirabili engraving refers to the charm as the head of a pin, presumably on the model of nos. 46 and 47. Visconti: M–M, pl. XXV, 4. The charm, however, is not a fragment but a separate, whole object.

40. The British Museum accessions register refers to the charm as 'part of a figure'. Antiquities Register, no. 66,12–29,47.

41. See Strong, *Silver Plate*, 89, fig. 37a, for an example of the type of vessel.

42. Visconti refers to '*le anse d'altri vasi ed utensili perduti*' without specifying the number or the nature of the handles in question. The lower mount of the handle is reminiscent of the mounts on the Pelegrina ewer (*no. 17) and those on the Proiecta and Muse caskets (*nos. 1 and 2); it also resembles the engraved finials of the horse trappings (*nos. 36–41, pl. 46) in technique and crude decoration. The faceted and fluted octagonal wire also links the handle with several other pieces which can be documented as part of the original find. It might be appropriate to hypothesise that this handle was one of those to which Visconti made reference. Visconti: M–M, 12.

43. The British Museum accessions register identifies this piece as a 'handle with two plates to fix it to a vase possibly to [the fluted dish, *no. 4]'. The same is said for its mate, no. 58. Dalton suggested that they were attached to a casket. Antiquities Register, no. 66,12–29,57; Dalton, *Catalogue*, 77.

44. Dalton, apparently understanding the inscriptions to be Latin, turned the hand ninety degrees to read M and one hundred and eighty degrees to read v. Dalton, *Catalogue*, 37.

45. The caption of the Montagnani-Mirabili engraving identified the piece as the head of a pin. Dalton agreed. The British Museum's accessions register noted that the tooled fitting indicates that the object was once part of a larger whole but that it was now simply separated from its original setting, not necessarily broken off. Visconti: M–M, pl. XXV, 10; Dalton, *Catalogue*, 37; Antiquities Register, no. 66,12–29,48.

46. This undoubtedly led Dalton to group it with nos. 54 and 55 as a 'charm'. Dalton, *Catalogue*, 38.

47. Visconti: M–M, 21.

48. Visconti: M–M, 9f. Seroux d'Agincourt also specified five, *L'Histoire*, III, 9.

49. Visconti: M–M, 12.

50. Visconti: M–M, 20.

Concordance

Shelton Nos.	Dalton *Catalogue* Nos.	British Museum Antiquities Register Nos.	Shelton Nos.	Dalton *Catalogue* Nos.	British Museum Antiquities Register Nos.
*1	304	66,12–29,1	*32	332	66,12–29,21
*2	305	66,12–29,2	*33	334	66,12–29,22
*3	(in Musée du Petit Palais, Paris)		*34	336	66,12–29,20
*4	310	66,12–29,3	*35	337	66,12–29,19
*5	316	66,12–29,12	*36	339	66,12–29,29
*6	318	66,12–29,11	*37	338	66,12–29,28
*7	317	66,12–29,14	*38	342	66,12–29,30
*8	319	66,12–29,13	*39	340	66,12–29,25
*9	315	66,12–29,18	*40	341	66,12–29,26
*10	314	66,12–29,15	*41	343	66,12–29,27
*11	313	66,12–29,16	42	238	66,12–29,43
*12	312	66,12–29,17	43	236	66,12–29,44
13	311	66,12–29,10	44	236	66,12–29,45
14	320	66,12–29,9	45	237	66,12–29,46
15	321	66,12–29,8	46	233	66,12–29,42
*16	306	66,12–29,4	47	232	66,12–29,41
*17	307	66,12–29,5	48	234	66,12–29,40
*18	(in Museo Nazionale, Naples)		49	227	66,12–29,52
19	308	66,12–29,6	50	228	66,12–29,53
20	309	66,12–29,7	51	229	66,12–29,55
21	322	66,12–29,35	52	230	66,12–29,54
22	325	66,12–29,33	53	231	66,12–29,56
23	323	66,12–29,34	54	239	66,12–29,49
24	326	66,12–29,31	55	241	66,12–29,47
25	324	66,12–29,32	56	344	66,12–29,59
26	328	66,12–29,36	57	345	66,12–29,57
27	329	66,12–29,37	58	345	66,12–29,58
28	327	66,12–29,39	59	331	66,12–29,50
29	330	66,12–29,38	60	235	66,12–29,48
*30	333	66,12–29,23	61	240	66,12–29,51
*31	335	66,12–29,24			

Select Bibliography

ALFÖLDI, A. *A Conflict of Ideas in the Late Roman Empire*, trans. Mattingly, H., Oxford (1952).
The Conversion of Constantinople and Pagan Rome, trans. Mattingly, H., 2nd edn., Oxford (1969).
'On the Foundation of Constantinople: A Few Notes', *Journal of Roman Studies*, XXXVII (1947), 10–16.
Die Kontorniaten, Budapest (1943); rev. edn. with Alföldi, E., *Die Kontorniat-Medaillons*, Antike Münzen und geschnittene Steine, VI, Berlin (1976).
'*Die Spätantike*', *Atlantis: Länder, Völker, Reisen*, XXI (1949), 61–88.

ARNHEIM, M. T. W., *The Senatorial Aristocracy in the Later Roman Empire*, Oxford (1972).

ARRIAS, P., '*Il piatto argenteo di Cesena*', *Annuario della Scuola Archeologica di Atene*, N.S. VIII–X (1946–8), 309–45.
'*Il piatto argenteo di Cesena*', *Bolletino d'Arte*, XXXV (1950), 9–17.

BABELON, E., *Le trésor d'argenterie de Berthouville*, Paris (1916).

BALLINI, A. L., *Il valore giuridico della celebrazione nuziale cristiana dal primo secolo all'età giustinianea*, Pubblicazione dell'Università Cattolica del Sacro Cuore, ser. 2: Scienze giuridiche, LXIV, Milan (1939).

BALSDON, J. P. V. D., *Roman Women*, London (1962).

BARATTE, F., '*Les ateliers d'argenterie au bas-empire*', *Journal des savants* (1975), 193–212.
'*Le plat d'argent du Château d'Albâtre à Soissons*', *Revue du Louvre*, XXVII (1977), 125–30.

BARBIER, E., '*La signification du cortège représenté sur le couvercle du coffret de "Projecta"*', *Cahiers archéologiques*, XII (1962), 7–33.

BERGER, A., *Encyclopedic Dictionary of Roman Law*, Transactions of the American Philosophical Society, N.S. XLIII, pt 2, Philadelphia (1953).

BLANCKENHAGEN, P. H. von, '*Elemente der römischen Kunst am Beispiel des flavischen Stils*', *Das neue Bild der Antike*, Berve, H. (ed.), 2 vols., Leipzig (1942), II, 310–41.

BLOCH, H., 'A New Document of the Last Pagan Revival in the West', *Harvard Theological Review*, XXXVIII (1945), 199–244.
'The Pagan Revival in the West at the End of the Fourth Century', *The Conflict between Paganism and Christianity in the Fourth Century*, Momigliano, A. (ed.), Oxford (1963), 193–218.

BÖTTIGER, K. A., *Sabina oder Morgenscenen im Putzzimmer einer reichen Römerin*, Leipzig (1803).
Sabine, ou matinée d'une dame romaine, Paris (1813).

BOWERSOCK, G. W., *Julian, the Apostate*, Cambridge, Mass. (1978).

BRAILSFORD, J. W., *The Mildenhall Treasure*, 2nd ed., London (1955).

BRENDEL, O., 'The Corbridge Lanx', *Journal of Roman Studies*, XXXI (1941), 100–27.
'Prolegomena to a Book on Roman Art', *Memoirs of the American Academy in Rome*, XXI (1953), 9–73; rev. ed. *Prolegomena to the Study of Roman Art*, New Haven (1979).

BRETT, G. L., 'Formal Ornament on Late Roman and Early Byzantine Silver', *Papers of the British School at Rome*, XV (N.S. II) (1939), 33–41.

British Museum, The, Antiquities Register for 1866, London (1866).
A Guide to the Exhibition Galleries of the British Museum, rev. ed., London (1897).

BROWN, P. R. L., 'Aspects of the Christianization of the Roman Aristocracy', *Journal of Roman Studies*, LI (1961), 1–11.

BROWNING, R., *The Emperor Julian*, Berkeley (1976).

BUECHLER, F. (ed.), *Carmina latina epigraphica*, 2 vols., Leipzig (1895–7).

BURFORD, A., *Craftsmen in Greek and Roman Society*, London (1972).

BUSCHHAUSEN, H., *Die spätrömischen Metallscrinia und frühchristlichen Reliquiare*, Katalog, Wiener byzantinistische Studien, IX, Vienna (1971).

CAGNAT, R., *Cours d'épigraphie latine*, Paris (1914).

CALABI LIMENTANI, I., *Studi sulla società romana: Il lavoro artistico*, Biblioteca storica universitaria, ser. 2, IX, Milan (1958).

CALZA, R., *Iconografia romana imperiale da Carausio a Giuliano*, Rome (1972).

CAMERON, A., 'The Friends of Ammianus', *Journal of Roman Studies*, LIV (1964), 15–28.
'The Date and Identity of Macrobius', *Journal of Roman Studies*, LVI (1966), 25–38.

CARCOPINO, J., *Daily Life in Ancient Rome*, Rowell, H. T. (ed.), trans. Lorimer, E. O., New Haven (1940).

CAYLUS, le Comte de, *Recueil d'antiquités égyptiennes, étrusques, grecques, romaines et gauloises*, 7 vols., Paris (1752–67).

CHASTAGNOL, A., *Les fastes de la préfecture de Rome au bas-empire*, Etudes prosopographiques, II, Paris (1962).
La collection Dutuit, Paris [1903].

CORBETT, P. E., *The Roman Law of Marriage*, Oxford (1930).

CROKE, B. 'The Editing of Symmachus' Letters to Eugenius and Arbogast', *Latomus*, XXXI (1976), 533–49.

CURLE, A. O., *The Treasure of Traprain: A Scottish Hoard of Roman Silver Plate*, Glasgow (1923).

DAGRON, G., *Naissance d'une capitale: Constantinople et ses institutions de 330 à 451*, Paris (1974).

DALTON, O. M., *Catalogue of Early Christian Antiquities and Objects from the Christian East, British Museum*, London (1901).

DIEHL, E. (ed.), *Inscriptiones latinae christianae veteres*, 3 vols., Berlin (1924/25–28/31).

DODD, E. C., *Byzantine Silver Stamps*, Dumbarton Oaks Studies, VII, Washington, D.C. (1961).

DOHRN, T., 'Spätantikes Silber aus Britannien', *Mitteilungen des Deutschen Archäologischen Instituts*, II, (1949), 66–139.
Die Tyche von Antiochia, Berlin, 1960.

DREXEL, F., 'Der Silberschatz von Traprain', *Germania*, IX (1925), 122–8.

EMERY, W. B., *Nubian Treasure: An Account of the Discoveries at Ballana and Qustul*, London (1948).
The Royal Tombs of Ballana and Qustul, 2 vols., Cairo (1938).

FALDA, G. B., *Nuova pianta et alzata della città di Roma*, Rome (1676).

FERRETTO, G., *Note storico-bibliographiche di archeologia cristiana*, Vatican City (1942).

FERRUA, A. (ed.), *Epigrammata Damasiana*, Sussidi allo studio delle antichità cristiane, II, Vatican City (1942).

FINLEY, M. I., *The Ancient Economy*, Sather Classical Lectures, XLIII, Berkeley (1973).
'Technical Innovation and Economic Progress in the Ancient World',
Economic History Review, ser. 2, XVIII (1965), 29–45.

FRANCOVICH, G. de, *Il palatium di Teodorico a Ravenna e la cosidetta 'architettura di potenza'*, Rome (1970).

FRANK, T., *An Economic Survey of Ancient Rome*, 5 vols., Baltimore (1933–40).

FROEHNER, W., *Collection Auguste Dutuit*, Paris, 1897.

GALEANI NAPIONE, G. F., 'Lettera con alcune congetture intorno all'Asterio, possessore della suppellettile d'argento trovata in Roma', Lettera di Ennio Quirino Visconti intorno ad una antica supelletile d'argento scoperta in Roma nell'anno 1793, Montagnani-Mirabili, P. P. (ed.), Rome (1827), 31–44.

GARDNER, 'Countries and Cities in Ancient Art', *Journal of Hellenic Studies*, IX (1888), 47–81.

GARGER, E., 'Zur spätantiken Renaissance', *Jahrbuch der kunsthistorischen Sammlung in Wien*, N.S. VIII (1934), 1–28.

GERKE, F., *Der Sarkophag des Junius Bassus*, Berlin (1936).

GILLIARD, F. D., 'Notes on the Coinage of Julian the Apostate', *Journal of Roman Studies*, LIV (1964), 135–41.

GORDON, A. E., with GORDON, J. S., *Album of Dated Latin Inscriptions*, 4 vols., Berkeley (1958–65).

GRÜNHAGEN, W., *Der Schatzfund von Gross Bodungen*, Römisch-germanische Forschungen, XXI, Berlin (1954).

GUMMERUS, H., 'Die römische Industrie', *Klio*, XIV (1915), 129–89.
'Die römische Industrie', *Klio*, XV, 1918, 256–302.

HANFMANN, G. M. A., *The Season Sarcophagus in Dumbarton Oaks*, 2 vols., Cambridge, Mass. (1951).

HARRISON, E. B., 'The Constantinian Portrait', *Dumbarton Oaks Papers*, XXI (1967), 79–96.

HEINTZE, H. von, 'Ein spätantikes Mädchenporträt in Bonn: Zur stilistischen Entwicklung des Frauenbildnisses in 4. und 5. Jahrhundert', *Jahrbuch für Antike und Christentum*, XIV (1971), 61–91.

HIGGINS, R. A., *Greek and Roman Jewellery*, London (1961).

HOPKINS, M. K., 'The Age of Roman Girls at Marriage', *Population Studies*, XVIII (1965), 309–27.

HUGHES, M. J., and HALL, J. A., 'X-ray Fluorescence Analysis of Late Roman and Sassanian Silver Plate', *Journal of Archaeological Science*, 6 (1979), 321–44.

HUSKINSON, J., 'Some Pagan Mythological Figures and their Significance in Early Christian Art', *Papers of the British School at Rome*, N.S. XXIX (1974), 68–97.

IHM, M. (ed.), *Damasi epigrammata*, Leipzig, 1895.

INSTINSKY, H. U., *Der spätrömische Silberschatzfund von Kaiseraugst*, Akademie der Wissenschaften und der Literatur, Mainz, Abhandlungen der geistes- und sozialwissenschaftlichen Klasse, V, Wiesbaden (1971).

JONES, A. H. M., 'The Cloth Industry under the Roman Empire', *Economic History Review*, ser. 2, XIII (1960–1), 183–92.
The Later Roman Empire, 3 vols., Oxford (1964).
'The Social Background of the Struggle between Paganism and Christianity', *The Conflict between Paganism and Christianity in the Fourth Century*, Momigliano, A. (ed.), Oxford (1963), 17–37.

JONES, A. H. M. *et al.* (eds.), *The Prosopography of the Later Roman Empire*, A.D. 260–395, Cambridge, 1971.

JULIAN, *The Works of the Emperor Julian*, trans. Wright, W. C., The Loeb Classical Library, 3 vols., London (1913–30).

KENT, J. P. C. and PAINTER, K. S. (eds.), *Wealth of the Roman World*, A.D. 300–700, London (1977).

KITZINGER, E., *The Art of Byzantium and the Medieval West*, Kleinbauer, W. E. (ed.), Bloomington (1976).
Byzantine Art in the Making, Cambridge, Mass. (1977).
'Byzantine Art in the Period between Justinian and Iconoclasm', *Berichte zum XI. Internationalen Byzantinisten-Kongress*, Munich (1958), indep. numbered 1–50.
'On the Interpretation of Stylistic Change in Late Antique Art', *Bucknell Review*, XV (1967), 1–10.
'A Marble Relief of the Theodosian Period', *Dumbarton Oaks Papers*, XIV (1960), 17–42.
'The Sutton Hoo Ship Burial: The Silver', *Antiquity*, XIV (1940), 40–63.

KOCH, H., 'Zur Interpretation der "Corbridge Lanx"', *Archäologischer Anzeiger* (1955), 259–63.

KÖHLER, H. C. E., 'Uber die neue Ausgabe der Werke und Schriften des Visconti', *Amalthea*, I (1820), 292–308.

KRAUS, F. X., *Roma sotterranea: Die römische Katakomben*, Freiburg im Breisgau (1879).

KRAUTHEIMER, R., *et al.*, *Corpus Basilicarum Christianarum Romae*, 5 vols., Vatican City (1937–).

LAUR-BELART, R., *Der spätrömische Silberschatz von Kaiseraugst*, Katalog, Basle, (1967).

LAVIN, I., 'The Ceiling Frescoes in Trier and Illusionism in Constantinian Painting', *Dumbarton Oaks Papers*, XXI (1967), 97–113.

LEVI, A., *La patera d'argento di Parabiago*, Opere d'arte, V, Rome (1935–44).

LEVI, D., 'L'Arte romana: Schizzo della sua evoluzione e sua posizione nella storia dell'arte antica', *Annuario della Scuola Archeologica di Atene*, N.S. VIII–X (1946–8), 229–303.

LOANE, H. J., *Industry and Commerce of the City of Rome, 50 B.C.–200 A.D.*, The Johns Hopkins University Studies in Historical and Political Science, ser. 56, II, Baltimore (1938).

MARUCCHI, O., *Christian Epigraphy*, trans. Willis, J.A., Cambridge (1912).
Il pontificato del papa Damaso e la storia della sua famiglia, Rome (1905).

MATTHEWS, J., *Western Aristocracies and Imperial Court. 364–425*, Oxford (1975).

MATTINGLY, H., PEARCE, J. W. E., and KENDRICK, T. D., 'The Coleraine Hoard', *Antiquity*, XI (1937), 39–45.

MATZULEVITCH, L., *Byzantinische Antike*, Berlin (1929).

MAZZARINO, S., 'La propaganda senatoriale nel tardo impero, 1939–1951', *Doxa*, IV (1951), 121–48.

MÉLIDA Y ALINARI, J. R., *El disco de Teodosio*, Madrid (1930).

MUNKSGAARD, E., 'Late Antique Scrap Silver Found in Denmark: The Hardenberg, Høstentorp and Simmersted Hoards', *Acta archaeologica*, XXVI (1955), 31–67.

NEWTON, C. T., *Guide to the Blacas Collection of Antiquities, British Museum*, London (1867).

NOLLI, G. B., *La nuova topografia di Roma*, Rome (1748).

ODOBESCO, A., *Le trésor de Petrossa*, Paris (1889–1900).

OLIVER Jr., A., *Silver for the Gods: 800 Years of Greek and Roman Silver*, Toledo (1977).

OVERBECK, B., *Argentum Romanum: Ein Schatzfund von spätrömischem Prunkgeshirr*, Munich (1973).

PAINTER, K. S., 'A Fourth Century Christian Silver Treasure Found at Water Newton, England, in 1975', *Rivista di archeologia cristiana*, LI (1975), 333–45.
The Mildenhall Treasure, London (1977).
'The Mildenhall Treasure: A Reconsideration', *British Museum Quarterly*, XXXVII, London (1973), 154–80.

PANOFSKY, E., 'Renaissance and Renascences', *Kenyon Review*, VI (1944), 201–36.
Renaissance and Renascences, Stockholm (1960).

PELKA, O., *Ehedenkmäler*, Strasburg (1901).

PLUTARCH, *The Roman Questions of Plutarch*, Rose, H. J. (ed. and trans.), Oxford (1924); reprint ed., New York (1974).

POGLAYEN-NEUWALL, S., 'Uber die ursprünglichen Besitzer des spätantiken Silberfundes vom Esquilin und seine Datierung', *Mitteilungen des Deutschen Archäologischen Instituts, Römische Abteilung*, XLV (1930), 124–36.

POMEROY, S. B., 'The Relationship of the Married Woman to her Blood Relatives in Rome', *Ancient Society*, VII (1976), 215–27.

RAOUL-ROCHETTE, D., 'Oeuvres diverses italiennes et françaises d'Ennius Quirinus Visconti, recueillies et publiées par le docteur J. Labus', *Journal des savants* (1830), 611–29.

RIEGL, A., *Spätrömische Kunstindustrie*, 2nd ed., Vienna (1927); reprint ed., Darmstadt (1973).

ROBERTIS, F. M. de, *Lavoro e lavoratori nel mondo romano*, Bari (1967).

RODENWALDT, G., 'Das Problem der Renaissancen', *Archäologischer Anzeiger* (1931), 318–38.

ROSSI, G. B. de (ed.), *Inscriptiones christianae vrbis Romae septimo saeculo antiquiores*, 2 vols., Rome (1857–88).

RUMPF, A., *Stilphasen der spätantiken Kunst*, Arbeitsgemeinschaft für Forschung des Landes Nordheim-Westfalen, Geisteswissenschaften, Abhandlung, XLIV, Cologne (1957).

SANCLEMENTI, H., *Musei Sanclementiani: Numismata selecta*, 4 vols., Rome (1808–9).

SCHULTZE, V., *Archäologie der altchristlichen Kunst*, Munich (1895).

SEROUX d'AGINCOURT, J. B. L. G., *L'Histoire de l'art par les monuments depuis sa décadence au IVe siècle jusqu'à son renouvellement au XVIe*, 6 vols., Paris (1810–23).

SHELTON, K. J., 'Imperial Tyches', *Gesta*, XVIII (1979), 27–38.

SOMMERARD, A. du, *Les arts au moyen age*, 5 vols., Paris (1838–46).

STERN, H., *Le calendrier de 354: Etudes sur son texte et son illustration*, Paris (1953).

STRONG, D. E., *Greek and Roman Gold and Silver Plate*, London (1966).
Roman Art, Toynbee, J. M. C. (ed.), Baltimore (1976).

TOYNBEE, J. M. C., 'Roma and Constantinopolis in Late Antique Art from 312 to 365', *Journal of Roman Studies*, XXXVII (1947), 135–44.
'Rome and Constantinopolis in Late Antique Art from 365 to Justin II', *Studies Presented to D. M. Robertson*, 2 vols., St Louis (1953), II, 261–77.
A Silver Casket and Strainer from the Walbrook Mithraeum in the City of London, Leiden (1963).
Some Notes on Artists in the Roman World, Collection Latomus, VI, Brussels (1951).
'Some Notes on the Mildenhall Treasure', *Wandlungen christlicher Kunst im Mittelalter*, Forschungen zur Kunstgeschichte und christlichen Archäologie, II (1954), 41–57.

TOZZI, M. T., 'Il tesoro di Projecta', *Rivista di archeologia cristiana*, IX (1932), 279–314.

VISCONTI, E. Q., *Lettera di Ennio Quirino Visconti intorno ad una antica supelletile d'argento scoperta in Roma nell'anno 1793*, Montagnani-Mirabili, P. P. (ed.), Rome (1827).
'Lettera su di una antica argenteria nuovamente scoperta in Roma', *Opere varie italiane e francesi*, 4 vols., Labus, G. (ed.), Milan (1871–31), I, 210–35.

VOLBACH, W. F., 'Silber- und Elfenbeinarbeiten vom Ende des 4. zum Anfang des 7. Jahrhunderts', *Beiträge zur Kunstgeschichte und Archäologie des Frühmittelalters*, Akten zum VII Internationalen Kongress für Frühmittelalterforschung, 1958, Graz (1962), 21–36.
Elfenbeinarbeiten der Spätanike und des frühen Mittelalters, 3rd ed., Mainz am Rhein (1976).

WALTERS, H. B., *Catalogue of the Engraved Gems and Cameos, Greek, Etruscan and Roman in the British Museum*, London (1926).
Catalogue of the Silver Plate, Greek, Etruscan and Roman in the British Museum, London (1921).

WARD-PERKINS, J. B., 'Workshops and Clients: The Dionysiac Sarcophagi in Baltimore', *Rendiconti della Pontificia Accademia Romana di Archeologia*, XLVIII (1975–6), 191–238.

WAUGH, H., 'The Hoard of Roman Silver from Great Horwood, Buckinghamshire', *The Antiquaries Journal*, XLVI, (1966), 60–71.

WEGNER, M., *Die Musensarkophage*, Berlin (1966).

WESSEL, K., '*Römische Frauenfrisuren von der severischen bis zur konstantinischen Zeit*', *Archäologischer Anzeiger* (1946–7), 62–75.

Index

PLATE
1

Proiecta casket (*no. 1). Front, seen from left and right.

PLATE
2

Proiecta casket. *Above*: front. *Below*: right end.

PLATE
3

Above: back. *Below*: left end.

PLATE
4

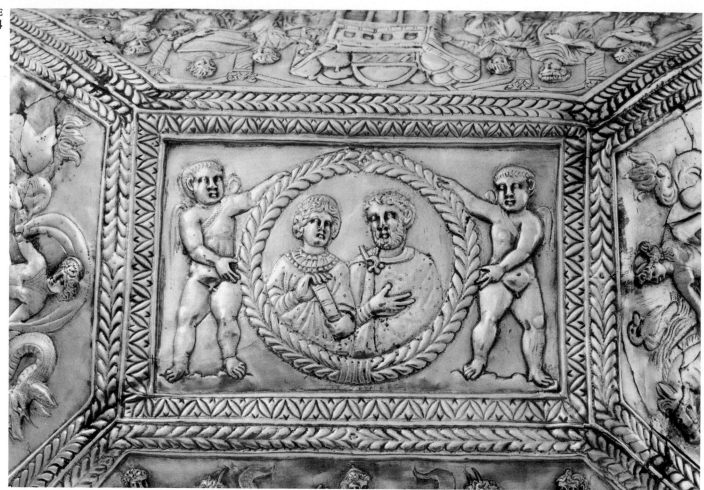

Proiecta casket lid. *Above*: top panel, portraits. *Below*: front panel, toilet of Venus.

PLATE
5

Above: right end, Nereid. *Below*: left end, Nereid.

PLATE
6

Proiecta casket lid. Back panel, bath procession.

PLATE
7

Bath procession mosaic from Piazza Armerina.

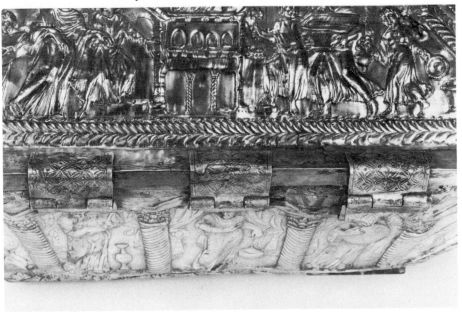

Proiecta casket. Hinges joining lid and body across back.

PLATE
8

Proiecta casket body. *Above*: front panel, toilet of Proiecta. *Below*: right end, servants in procession.

PLATE
9

Above: back panel, servants in procession. *Below*: left end, servants in procession.

PLATE
10

Proiecta casket, details. *Above* (left): Proiecta from portrait panel; (right): Proiecta from bath procession. *Below* (left and right): servants from toilet of Proiecta.

PLATE
11

Proiecta casket, details. *Left*: Proiecta from toilet scene. *Right*: Venus from toilet scene.

PLATE
12

Muse casket (*no. 2). *Above*: overall view from front. *Below* (left): Calliope; (right): Urania.

PLATE
13

Above: overall view from right. *Below* (left): Melpomene; (right): Clio.

PLATE
14

Muse casket. *Above*: overall view from back. *Below* (left): Polyhymnia; (right): Terpsichore.

PLATE
15

Above: overall view from left. *Below* (left): Euterpe; (right): Thalia.

PLATE
16

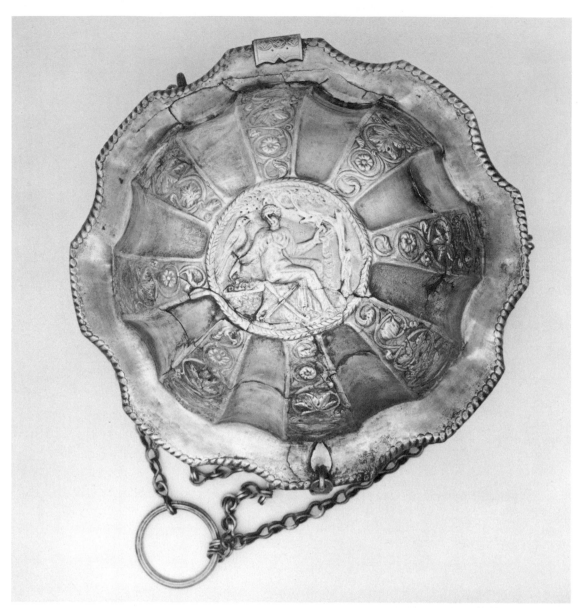

Muse casket. *Above*: lid. *Below* (left): top medallion; (right): hinge at centre back.

PLATE
17

Above: casket open, with five silver vessels. *Below* (left): canister; (right): flask.

PLATE
18

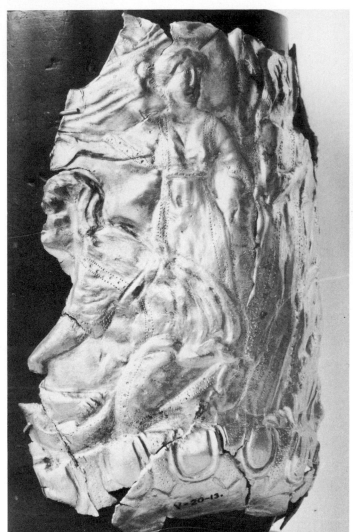

Traprain Law flagon.

Detail of standing figure.

Two fragments from flagon.

PLATE
19

Parabiago Patera.

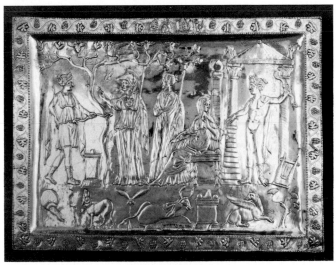

Corbridge lanx.

PLATE
20

Symmachorum ivory leaf.

PLATE
21

Petit Palais patera (*no. 3).

PLATE
22

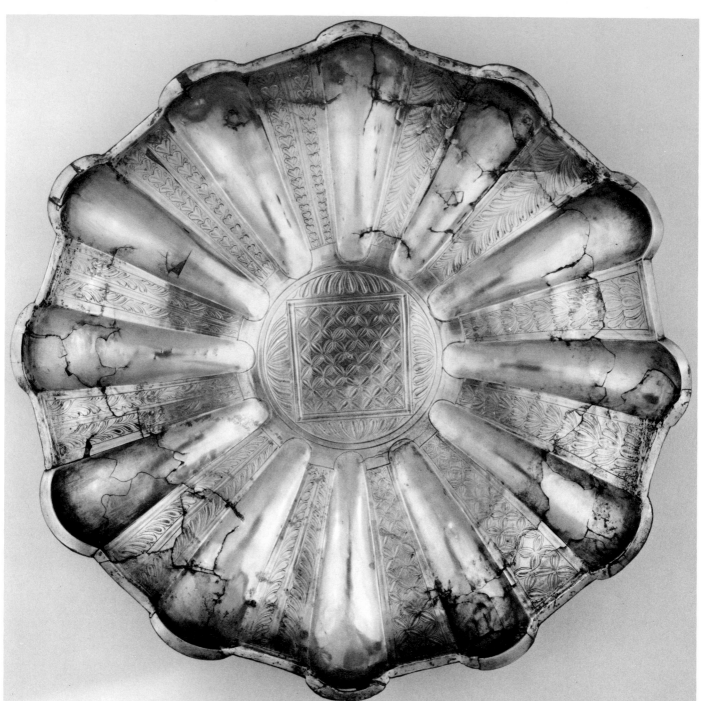

Fluted dish (*no. 4).

PLATE
23

Fluted dish, detail of central medallion.

Traprain Law, fragment of fluted bowl.

PLATE
24

Mildenhall Treasure fluted bowl.

PLATE
25

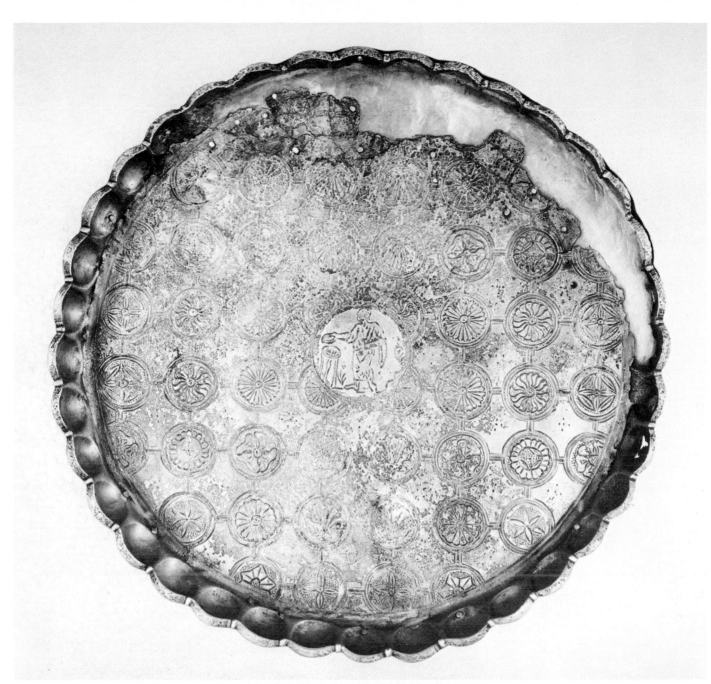

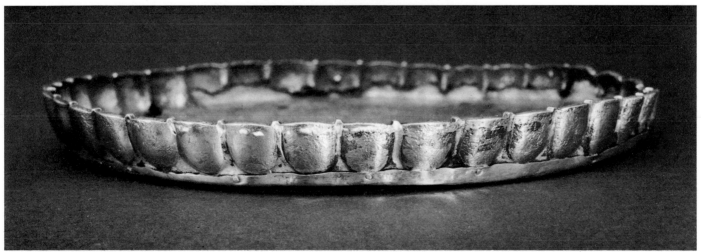

Dish (no. 13) from treasure of Mâcon.

PLATE
26

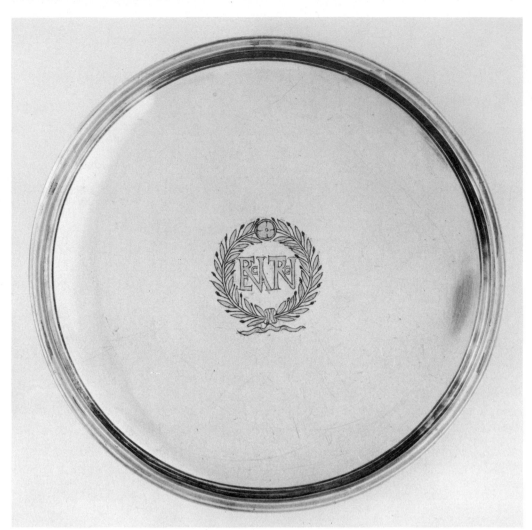

Circular monogram plate (*no. 5).

PLATE
27

Rectangular monogram plate (*no. 9).

PLATE
28

Dish (no. 14).

PLATE
29

Bowl (no. 15).

PLATE
30

Flask with vintaging Erotes (*no. 16).

PLATE
31

Pelegrina ewer (*no. 17).

PLATE
32

Naples ewer (*no. 18).

PLATE
33

Amphora (no. 19).

PLATE
34

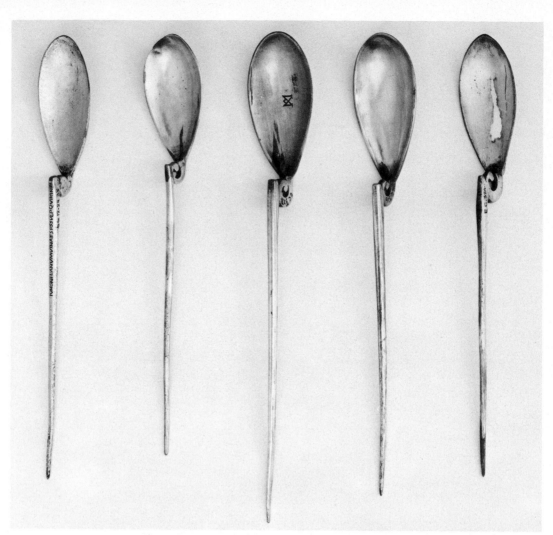

Spoons. *Left to right*: nos. 21, 22, 23, 24, 25.

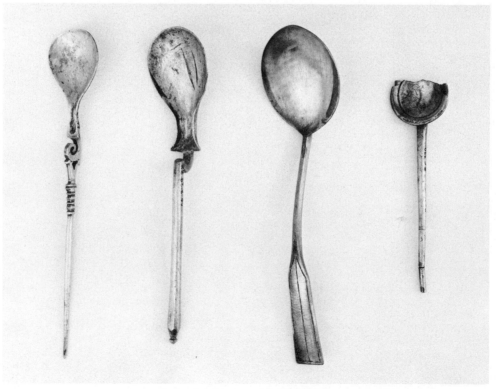

Left to right: nos. 26, 27, 28, 29.

PLATE
35

Tyche ornaments. *Left to right*: *nos. 32, 30, 33, 31—Roma, Constantinople, Antioch, Alexandria.

PLATE
36

Tyche of Constantinople (*no. 30).

PLATE
37

PLATE
38

Tyche of Alexandria (*no. 31).

PLATE
39

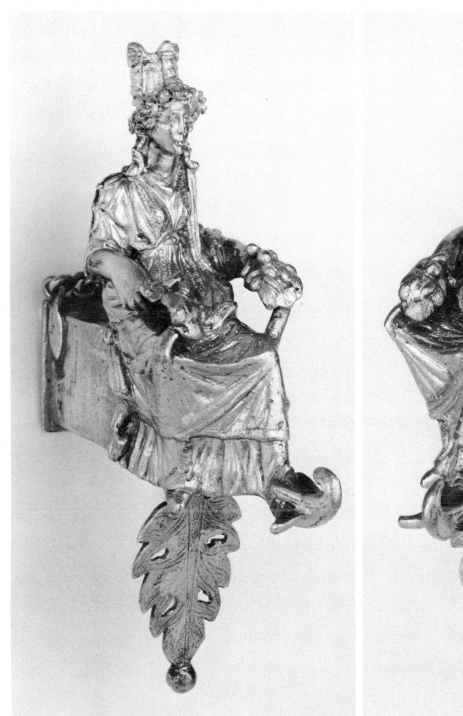

PLATE
40

Roma (*no. 32).

PLATE
41

PLATE
42

Tyche of Antioch (*no. 33).

PLATE
43

PLATE
44

Right arm ornament (*no. 34).

PLATE
45

Left arm ornament (*no. 35).

PLATE
46

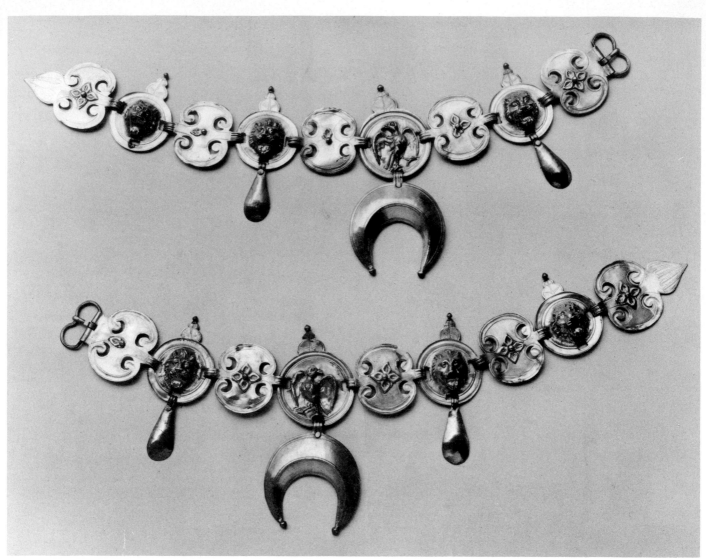

Horse trappings (*nos. 37, 40).

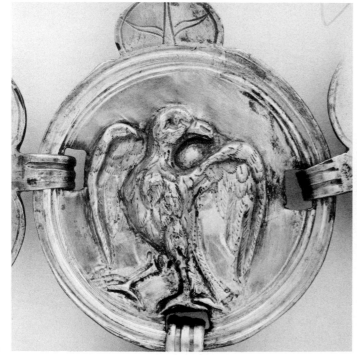

Eagle plate.

Lion, pelta plates and finial.

PLATE
47

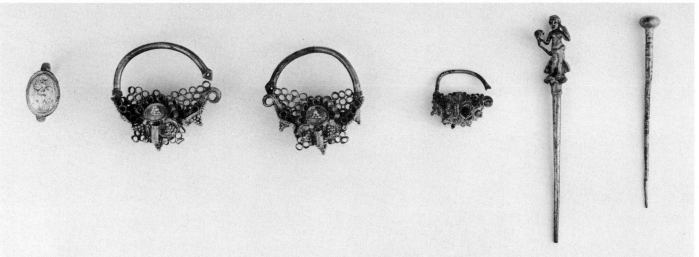

Jewellery: ring (no. 42), earrings (nos. 43–5), pins (nos. 46, 48).

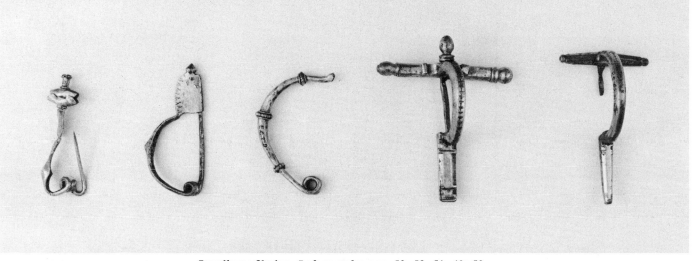

Jewellery: fibulae. *Left to right*: nos. 53, 52, 51, 49, 50.

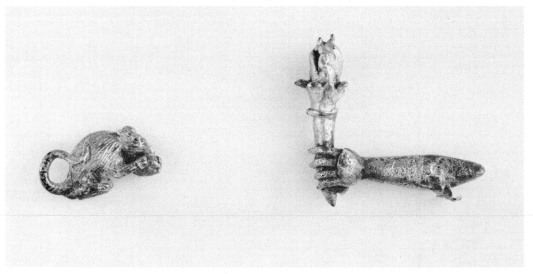

Charms (nos. 54, 55).

PLATE
48

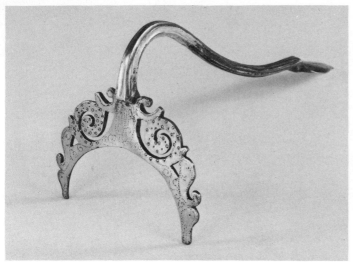

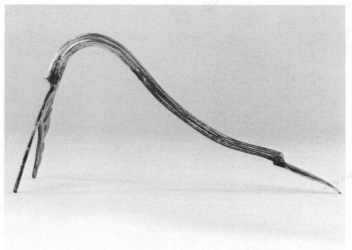

Handle (no. 56).

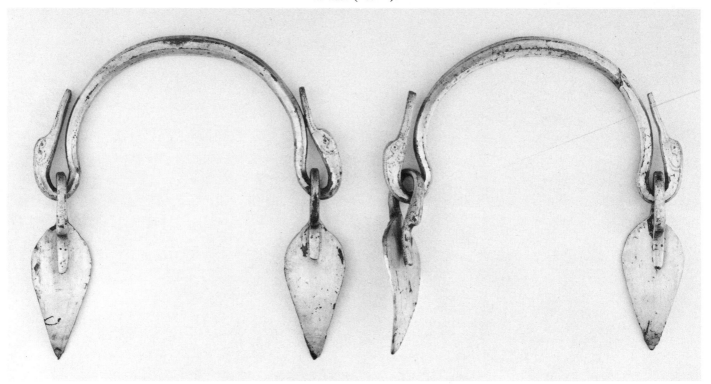

Handles (nos. 57–8).

Knife handle (no. 59), hand finial (no. 60), fragment (no. 61).